EXPLORING CONTENT 1

Reading
for
Academic
Success

LORRAINE C. SMITH

Adelphi University

Longman

Exploring Content 1: Reading for Academic Success

Pearson Education, 10 Bank Street, White Plains, NY 10606

Vice president of multimedia and skills: Sherry Preiss
Executive acquisitions editor: Laura Le Dréan
Development manager: Paula H. Van Ells
Marketing manager: Joe Chapple
Production editor: Andréa C. Basora
Production manager: Ray Keating
Senior manufacturing buyer: Dave Dickey
Photo research: Dana Klinek
Cover and text design: Pat Wosczyk
Cover art: Marjory Dressler Photo-Graphics
Production management and text composition: Elm Street Publishing Services, Inc.
Text font: 10/13 New Aster
Photo credits: see page xx
Text credits: see page xxi

Library of Congress Cataloging-in-Publication Data
Smith, Lorraine C.
    Exploring content : reading for academic success / Lorraine C. Smith
        p. cm.
    Includes bibliographical references.
    ISBN: 0-13-140198-X (alk. paper)
    1. College readers. 2. English language—Textbooks for foreign speakers. 3. Reading
(Higher education)—Problems, exercises, etc. I. Title.

PE1122.S535 2004
468.6'4—dc22

ISBN: 0-13-140198-X   2004058818

LONGMAN ON THE **WEB**

Longman.com offers online resources for teachers
and students. Access our Companion Websites, our
online catalog, and our local offices around the world.

Visit us at **longman.com**.

Printed in the United States of America
4 5 6 7 8 9 10—CRK—08

To Isabella

CONTENTS

UNIT 1   HOW DID IT ALL BEGIN?   1

CHAPTER 1   THE UNIVERSE AND THE EARTH   2

INTRODUCTORY READING The Beginning of the Universe and the Origin of the Earth   7

> *Scientific evidence supports the theory that the universe began billions of years ago as the result of a "big bang," and that our solar system, which includes the Earth and other planets, formed between 10 and 20 billion years ago as a large cloud of gases became concentrated through gravitational force.*

MAIN READING The Formation of Organic Molecules from Inorganic Molecules   19

> *Several theories have been proposed to explain how organic molecules formed from inorganic molecules. These theories differ in their details, but they are all based on the requirement that inorganic molecules must become concentrated, then interact, in order to form larger molecules.*

CHAPTER 2   DEVELOPMENTS ON EARLY EARTH   32

INTRODUCTORY READING The Formation of the First Living Cells   36

> *Fossil evidence indicates the existence of life on Earth at least 3.5 billion years ago. No one knows for sure how life on Earth originated, but two competing theories posit that life originated either on Earth or from an extraterrestrial source. Once life began, early life forms slowly created the Earth's oxygen atmosphere through the process of photosynthesis.*

MAIN READING The Changing Shape of Our World: The Theory of Continental Drift   44

> *In 1915, Alfred Wegener used biological, geological, and climatological evidence to support his theory that the Earth's continents do not remain in place. Wegener believed that the Earth's continents have always changed shape and moved across the surface of the Earth. Detailed mapping of the seafloor, which began in the 1950s, has provided further support for Wegener's theory of continental drift.*

Unit 2　Where Did We Come From?　58

Chapter 3　The Nature of Life　59

Introductory Reading The Classification of Life:
A Historical Overview　64

In the eighteenth century, Carolus Linnaeus established the modern system for the classification of all forms of life. Linnaeus's original system placed all life into two kingdoms, plant and animal, and divided each kingdom into smaller units, down to individual species. This system has been modified over time, and scientists now use five kingdoms. However, Linnaeus's basic system is still in use today.

Main Reading The Role of Natural Selection in Evolution　74

The roles of natural selection and survival of the fittest in the process of evolution are often misunderstood. Common misunderstandings include the idea that evolution took place in the past but does not occur today. In fact, evolution is a continuous occurrence, and several organisms have even evolved within fairly short time periods.

Chapter 4　Human Evolution　83

Introductory Reading Out of the Trees　87

Primates began to evolve over 65 million years ago. One of the first steps in the evolution of human beings was the shift from a primate that walked on four legs to a primate that stood upright and walked on two feet.

Main Reading The Evolution of *Homo sapiens*　95

The oldest fossils of apes date from about 23 million years ago. Early African apes are the ancestors of hominids, which walked upright on two feet. Over the next 20 million years, these hominids continued to evolve and developed larger brains. By 800,000 years ago, hominids were making and using tools. Although the fossil record of hominid evolution is unclear, new fossil discoveries are being made and may answer many current questions.

Unit 3　Where Did Civilization First Develop?　108

Chapter 5　First Steps Toward Civilization　109

Introductory Reading The Early Accomplishments of *Homo sapiens*　113

One of the first accomplishments of modern human beings was the creation of art. As early as 30,000 years ago, humans created wall paintings in caves of the many animals they hunted in their environment. Their other accomplishments included many tools for use in their daily lives, such as bows and arrows, fishhooks, and needles for sewing.

UNIT 5   HOW DOES OUR SOCIETY INFLUENCE HOW WE PERCEIVE THE WORLD?   214

CHAPTER 9   SOCIETY'S INFLUENCE ON OUR BEHAVIOR   215

CHAPTER 10   INTERPRETING HUMAN BEHAVIOR   245

SCOPE AND SEQUENCE

UNIT AND CHAPTERS	CONTENT	READING/STUDY SKILLS	CRITICAL THINKING SKILLS
UNIT 1			
HOW DID IT ALL BEGIN? CHAPTER 1: *The Universe and the Earth* CHAPTER 2: *Developments on Early Earth*	• beginning of the universe and formation of the solar system • the origin of the Earth • the origin of the Earth's oceans and oxygen atmosphere • formation of the first organic molecules • competing theories for the origin of life on Earth • formation of the first living cells • theory of continental drift	• preview key vocabulary • use titles and headings to predict content • highlight important information • monitor reading comprehension • use context to learn new vocabulary • use the dictionary to learn unfamiliar vocabulary • use illustrations and graphic organizers to aid in understanding text	• hypothesize • interpret • analyze • predict • identify • infer • organize • synthesize
UNIT 2			
WHERE DID WE COME FROM? CHAPTER 3: *The Nature of Life* CHAPTER 4: *Human Evolution*	• the Linnaean classification system • the concept of evolution • the theory of natural selection • relationships among primates • the evolution of *Homo sapiens* • early Hominid achievements	• review skills from Unit 1 • use font styles to identify and learn key vocabulary • create a time line to organize information in chronological order • use referents to aid in understanding text	• classify • organize • identify • infer • interpret • compare • predict • hypothesize

UNIT AND CHAPTERS	CONTENT	READING/STUDY SKILLS	CRITICAL THINKING SKILLS
UNIT 3			
WHERE DID CIVILIZATION FIRST DEVELOP? CHAPTER 5: *First Steps Toward Civilization* CHAPTER 6: *Early Civilization*	• factors leading to the development of the first civilization • development of agriculture • emergence of villages • the first civilization • the Sumerians' major achievements • Sumerian civilization and the Old Babylonian civilization • Hammurabi's Code of Law	• review skills from units 1 and 2 • learn and use word forms	• interpret • predict • organize • infer • compare • hypothesize • support answers
UNIT 4			
HOW HAVE PEOPLE REPRESENTED THE WORLD AROUND THEM? CHAPTER 7: *Definition and Context in Art* CHAPTER 8: *The Influence of History on Art*	• the nature of art • the role that imagination plays in art • the creative process • how to look at a work of art • purposes of ancient Egyptian art Egyptian art and its historical context	• review skills from units 1–3 • annotate text	• organize • predict • analyze • define • infer • argue • compare • evaluate advantages/ disadvantages • contextualize information
UNIT 5			
HOW DOES OUR SOCIETY AFFECT HOW WE PERCEIVE THE WORLD? CHAPTER 9: *Society's Influence on Our Behavior* CHAPTER 10: *Interpreting Human Behavior*	• concept of social psychology • how people are influenced by others • how people interpret the behavior of others • human motivation and human needs • human expectations of the social world	• review skills from units 1–4 • understand graphs	• predict • organize • make generalizations • infer • interpret • hypothesize • analyze • relate

ABOUT *EXPLORING* CONTENT

Exploring Content: Reading for Academic Success, Book One, is the first of two reading texts geared primarily toward incoming college English language learners who need to improve their reading proficiency, develop effective critical thinking and study skills, and build background knowledge and vocabulary essential to their understanding of specific content areas in required college courses.

Exploring Content embodies the concept of content-based instruction. This text has been designed to give students an introduction to a number of content areas, while at the same time fostering reading and study skills so essential to success in postsecondary education. The subject areas are represented by excerpts from college textbooks in that field. The readings are shorter than a complete textbook chapter, but they have not been simplified, in order to help students develop proficiency in reading unmodified material from a college text. Students are provided with illustrations, diagrams, and charts designed to facilitate understanding of text and non-text information (Hyerle, 1996). The questions and activities in each chapter help the students read, write, think about, organize, analyze, and understand the concepts and information in the chapters in a manner similar to what they will experience in college courses. While they are developing an understanding of concepts, vocabulary, and information, they are working on their reading, writing, and study skills and developing their speaking and listening skills as well.

Content-Based Instruction (CBI)

Content-based instruction is "the integration of content learning with language teaching aims. More specifically, it refers to the concurrent study of language and subject matter, with the form and sequence of language presentation dictated by content material" (Brinton, Snow, & Wesche, 1989, p. vii). Content-based instruction is multi-purpose. It involves helping students simultaneously develop their English proficiency and learn subject matter (Kasper, Babbitt, Mlynarczyk et al, 2000). Students use English to build background knowledge, and, through critical thinking, make connections and develop concepts. Students work together to construct knowledge and develop their ideas. Many activities involve purposeful listening and speaking. Writing is also an integral component in content-based instruction. The writing tasks in the books are "low stakes," or informal, ungraded assignments whose purpose is to help students reflect in writing on what they are learning and to make visible their emerging understanding of new content (Elbow, 1997).

Because content-based instruction is multi-faceted, assessment in CBI must be as well. Consequently, as students progress through a content-based curriculum, content knowledge and understanding, development and use of content-specific vocabulary, and improved English proficiency are assessed through formative and summative evaluations.

Critical Thinking Skills

The conceptual framework of the book incorporates Benjamin Bloom's taxonomy of educational objectives (1956). Bloom places cognitive skills into two general categories. The first involves learners in remembering and organizing; the second involves learners in analyzing and synthesizing. For students to develop critical thinking skills, they need to move beyond the first three cognitive levels, knowledge, comprehension, and application, in the first category and engage in the more active processes of analysis, synthesis, and evaluation. One of the goals of *Exploring Content* is to help students develop critical thinking skills, in part by incorporating analysis, synthesis, and evaluation in the second category throughout every chapter. Specific questions and activities at the prereading, reading, and postreading stages have been designed to take the students beyond Bloom's first category of cognitive skills. The development of all these essential skills takes place within the context of college-level academic reading.

TO THE TEACHER

How to Use This Book

Exploring Content contains five units of two chapters each, for a total of ten chapters. Each chapter in *Exploring Content* consists of the following:

A list of Chapter Goals and Key Vocabulary

An Introductory section which includes:

Activate Your Knowledge

Reading and Study Skill Strategies

Introductory Reading

Checking Comprehension

Learning Vocabulary

A Main Reading section which includes:

Activate Your Knowledge

Main Reading

Checking Comprehension

Learning Vocabulary

Follow-up assignments which include:

Writing Activities

Extension Activities

Internet Research

List of Chapter Goals and Key Vocabulary

The Chapter Goals section in each chapter lists reading and study skill strategies presented and practiced, as well as content-specific goals. This list and the list of content-specific vocabulary provide a focus for each chapter and serve as review guides once the class has completed the chapter.

The Preview Key Vocabulary section shows students what content-specific vocabulary will be presented in the chapter and gives them the opportunity to see which vocabulary they are already familiar with and which vocabulary they need to be aware of and learn as they progress through the readings and the activities. The purpose of the list is not to have students look up the words in a dictionary before they begin reading. Not only is doing so a laborious chore but it defeats the purpose of having students learn vocabulary from context, which is an essential reading strategy.

Introductory Section

ACTIVATE YOUR KNOWLEDGE

This section includes a range of activities designed to help the students become engaged in the topic and to evaluate what they may or may not already know about it. Students work alone, in pairs, or in small groups. Once individuals or groups have completed an activity, the whole class can be brought together to pool their knowledge through whole-class discussion and by recording groups' information and ideas on the blackboard. Throughout the process, students should be encouraged to think about the questions and to make reasonable guesses when they are unsure. They can return to their answers before beginning the main reading and check whether their answers were accurate and whether they now know the answers to questions they were unsure of initially. The process of thinking about, discussing, and making reasonable guesses is at the heart of this activity.

READING AND STUDY SKILL STRATEGIES

A range of reading and study skill strategies is presented in this section. Several strategies are introduced in the first chapter because they are so essential to understanding. From the first reading, students need to preview key vocabulary and to use titles and headings to gain an overview of a passage, and to predict content. While they are reading, students need to highlight important information, monitor their comprehension, and use illustrations and other graphics as aids to comprehension. Furthermore, they need to begin learning how to understand new vocabulary from context and to use a dictionary effectively.

Once a strategy is introduced, students use that strategy throughout the book. A new strategy is introduced in each subsequent unit. These strategies include those mentioned in the previous paragraph as well as using font styles to identify key vocabulary, learning word forms, identifying referents, creating time lines and flow charts, annotating text, outlining text, and analyzing graphs. By the end of the book, the students will be on their way to making these strategies an integral part of their reading, which is one of the main goals of the text.

INTRODUCTORY READING

Students should be encouraged to read the passage more than once, each time with a specific purpose. During the first reading, for example, students might highlight essential ideas and the vocabulary they consider important, including key vocabulary, and respond to the Before You Continue Reading questions as they read. The question always asks about the key point of the previous section and helps students monitor their comprehension before they have gone too far in the reading. If a student is unsure of the answer, rereading a few paragraphs will not take long and will help ensure understanding before moving on to the rest of the passage.

Students should be encouraged to highlight whenever they read and to use the wider right-hand margin to write questions and comments they may have as they read. This practice helps keep the students' attention focused on the reading. In addition, by writing questions in the margin as they read, they will not forget them, and they will be able to ask them in class, either of their classmates, or the teacher.

The readings are accompanied by illustrations which are designed to facilitate understanding of the text. Consequently, students should develop the habit of examining them carefully, relating them to the reading, and writing questions and comments about them as well.

CHECKING COMPREHENSION

This section includes the questions the students guessed about in the prereading activity and asks students to review those questions and check the accuracy of their knowledge prior to reading. This section also contains multiple choice and short answer questions designed to assess students' comprehension of the main ideas and details of the reading. Students may answer these questions individually first, then compare their answers with a classmate, in a small group, or together as a class. The questions may be multiple choice, true/false, or open-ended which ask for facts, conclusions, or opinions. This range of question types also helps prepare students for the various types of questions they will be asked on tests in college courses.

LEARNING VOCABULARY

The Learning Vocabulary section initially includes learning vocabulary from context and using the dictionary. In subsequent units, using fonts and learning and using word forms are added.

Students often have great difficulty figuring out the meaning of vocabulary from context. Even when they do so in an exercise such as this one, which provides them with multiple choice answers, they still have trouble transferring the skill to the reading in general. The purpose of this exercise is to provide a scaffold for students to learn how to figure out the meaning of unfamiliar words in a supportive activity. When students ask about other vocabulary that is not in this exercise or the Dictionary activity, they should be encouraged to try to figure out the meaning themselves, thus extending this exercise to more realistic circumstances.

Students all too often look up a word in their dictionary and select the first entry, without regard for the context in which the unknown word was read. What makes this activity more complex is that sometimes more than one entry is a reasonable choice. In such situations, both choices should be accepted. Here, too, once the students complete this activity, they can review the key vocabulary at the beginning of the chapter and check the words they have learned.

In college textbooks, new terms and vocabulary frequently appear in boldface or italics. Student do not always see these font changes as indicators of important vocabulary. Activities call out such conventions and help students learn vocabulary in this way.

Word forms are yet another means for learning new vocabulary, one which needs to be explicitly demonstrated to students. Word forms are incorporated into the book in later chapters.

Main Reading Section

ACTIVATE YOUR KNOWLEDGE

This section serves the same purpose as the Activate Your Knowledge section in the Introductory section. It also includes a range of activities designed to engage the students in the topic and to evaluate what they may or may not already know about it. Again, students will work in pairs or small groups, think about and discuss possible answers, and make reasonable guesses when they are unsure. They can return to their answers after completing the main reading and check whether their answers were accurate and whether they now know the answers to questions they were unsure of initially. It should be emphasized to the students that the process of thinking about, discussing, and making reasonable guesses is more important than "getting the right answer."

READING AND STUDY SKILL STRATEGIES

The reading and study skill strategies that were introduced in the Introductory section are presented for the main reading as well. In this manner, students are provided with ample opportunities for practice. A new strategy will be introduced and scaffolded in each unit and utilized for the remainder of the book.

MAIN READING

Because this passage is a longer reading than the Introductory Reading, students need to understand that they cannot expect to understand and to remember what they read after only one or two readings. Students should be encouraged to read the passage more than once, each time with a specific purpose. During the first reading, for example, students might highlight essential ideas and the vocabulary they consider important, including key vocabulary, and respond to the Before You Continue Reading questions. During a second reading, they might focus solely on key vocabulary. Later, as students become familiar with such practices as flow charts, time lines, and diagrams, they may read the passage a third time and create such a diagram as a study aid.

Students should also be encouraged to use the same strategies they used during the Introductory Reading, including highlighting, writing questions in the margins, responding to the Before You Continue Reading questions, and examining the illustrations accompanying the passage. These strategies need to be practiced in every chapter so they become an integral part of students' reading and study repertoire.

CHECKING COMPREHENSION

This section also includes multiple choice and short answer questions designed to assess students' comprehension of the main ideas and details of the reading. Students may answer these questions individually first, then compare their answers with a classmate, in a small group, or together as a class.

LEARNING VOCABULARY

These exercises provide students with further practice in developing their vocabulary-learning skills. As students become accustomed to doing these exercises, they might also explain their rationale for their choice of answer. Very often, an explanation of a wrong choice can be very helpful in understanding why a student continues to have difficulty learning meanings from context and determining the appropriateness of a definition in a dictionary entry.

Once the students complete this activity, they can review the key vocabulary at the beginning of the chapter and check the content-specific vocabulary they learned in both readings. At this point, the vocabulary items that a student has not checked off can be looked up in the relevant passage and discussed to ensure that all the key vocabulary items have been learned.

Follow-up Assignments

WRITING ACTIVITIES

One of the main goals of the writing section is to provide students with opportunities for meaningful use of the vocabulary they learn in the chapter. Content-specific vocabulary and general academic vocabulary are always listed at the beginning of the exercise and serve as a reference. Students should be encouraged to use the vocabulary as they respond in writing to the assignments. The writing section also gives the students practice in writing to clarify their understanding of the topics presented in the chapter and to develop their ideas in writing.

EXTENSION ACTIVITIES

This section incorporates a range of activities. Students may be instructed to complete or create a flowchart, a time line, or a chart, or to label or describe illustrations, and then to draw conclusions from these various formats. In activities involving writing, students should again be encouraged to use the vocabulary they have studied.

INTERNET RESEARCH

In this section, websites are provided so students can further investigate aspects of the chapter which especially interest them.

Assessment

Content-based assessments should not simply target isolated elements of language nor factual information, but should provide tasks that require students to integrate information and to form and articulate their own opinions about the subject matter.
Kasper, Babbitt, Mlynarczyk et al, 2000, p. 20

Assessment of student learning forms an integral component of this book and reflects the objectives of content-based instruction: (a) enhanced language proficiency, (b) improved study skills, and (c) knowledge of content and vocabulary. Assessment in *Exploring Content* is both formative and summative. Ongoing assessment of learning takes place while students are reading and at the end of each chapter as students answer questions about the content and the vocabulary in the reading. Tests are provided in the Teacher's Manual. For these tests, students utilize the strategies they learn in the text and then demonstrate their understanding of the material by answering questions, highlighting and annotating text, creating graphic organizers, and writing about figures found in the chapters.

Bibliography

Adamson, H. D. (1993). *Academic competence—Theory and classroom practice: Preparing ESL students for content courses.* New York: Longman.

Black, M. C., & Kiehnhoff, D. M. (1992). Content-based classes as a bridge from the EFL to the university classroom. *TESOL Journal, 1,* 27–28.

Bloom, B. S., Ed. (1956). *Taxonomy of educational objectives: The classification of educational goals, handbook 1: Cognitive domain.* New York: David McKay.

Brinton, D. M., Snow, M. A., & Wesche. M. B. (1989). *Content-based second language instruction.* New York: Newbury House.

Crandall, J. (1995). Content-based ESL: An introduction. In J. Crandall (Ed.), *ESL through content-area instruction.* (pp. 1–8). McHenry, IL: The Center for Applied Linguistics/Delta Systems.

Dubin, F., Eskey, D. E., & Grabe, W. (1986). *Teaching second language reading for academic purposes.* Reading, MA: Addison-Wesley.

Elbow, P. (1997). High stakes and low stakes in assigning and responding to writing. In M. D. Sorcinelli and P. Elbow (Eds.), *Writing to learn: Strategies for assigning and responding to writing across the disciplines, New Directions for Teaching and Learning,* Number 69, Spring, 1997. San Francisco, CA: Jossey-Bass.

Eskey, D. E. (1992). Syllabus design in content-based instruction. *The CATESOL Journal, 5*(1), 11–23.

Hyerle, D. (1996). *Visual tools for constructing knowledge.* Alexandria, VA: Association for Supervision and Curriculum Development.

Kasper, L. F. (1995). Theory and practice in content-based ESL reading instruction. *English for Specific Purposes, 14*(3), 223–230.

Kasper, L. F., Babbitt, M., Mlynarczyk, R. Brinton, D. M., Rosenthal, J. W., Master, P., Myers, S. A., Egbert, J. Tillyer, D. A., & Wood, L. S. (2000). *Content-based college ESL instruction.* Mahwah, NJ: Lawrence Erlbaum.

Manzo, A. V., Manzo U. C. & Estes, T. (2001). *Content area literacy: Interactive teaching for active learning* (3rd ed.). New York: Wiley.

Schleppegrell, M. J., & Colombi, M. C. (Eds.). (2002). *Developing advanced literacy in first and second languages: Meaning with power.* Mahwah, NJ: Lawrence Erlbaum.

Snow, M. A., & Brinton, D. M. (Eds.). (1997). *The content-based classroom: Perspectives on integrating language and content.* New York: Longman.

Valentine, J. F., & Repath-Martos, L. M. (1992). How relevant is relevance?: An examination of student needs, interests, and motivation in the content-based university classroom. *The CATESOL Journal, 5*(1), 25–42.

Zamel, V., & Spack, R. (Eds.). (1998). *Negotiating academic literacies: Teaching and learning across languages and cultures.* Mahwah, NJ: Lawrence Erlbaum.

TO THE STUDENT

Exploring Content is not a text about getting the right answers. Rather, the goal is to engage you in thinking, talking, reading, and writing about the subjects. In other words, the process is as important as— sometimes more important than—a product: a right answer. At times you will have more questions than the text, the teacher, or a fellow student may be able to answer. That is the nature of learning. Unanswered questions may challenge you to do some research in other books or online. Perhaps your curiosity will stimulate your interest in a semester-long course in a particular subject. Keep in mind that you are getting a brief introduction to each subject. What you learn in this book is like the tip of an iceberg—there is so much more beneath the surface!

At times the material—both the text and the illustrations—may be difficult to understand, and you may not grasp it on your first, or even your second, reading. Keep in mind that your goal is not to learn every new word, but to learn key content-related vocabulary and to gain an understanding of the concepts integral to that content area. Rereading, carefully examining illustrations, asking questions, making notes, and creating outlines, flowcharts, and time lines are all strategies that will help you develop your understanding of the content in these chapters. Be patient, be persistent. The skills you develop as you work with the book, your teacher, and your classmates will serve you well in your future college classes.

Each chapter in *Exploring Content* includes excerpts from chapters in current college textbooks. On average, the chapters in *Exploring Content* are 25 pages in length. In a class that meets four to six hours a week, a chapter will generally take about a week to work with. You need to understand that if you try to learn every word you will not be able to complete a typical class assignment within the time an instructor gives. Consequently, one of the goals of *Exploring Content* is to help you develop skills and strategies for reading fluently. Proficient readers do not stop and consider every unfamiliar word. They read for general knowledge, then review for the specifics they feel are essential. This proficiency is what *Exploring Content* is designed to help you achieve.

ABOUT THE AUTHOR

Lorraine C. Smith holds a doctorate in Curriculum and Teaching from Teachers College, Columbia University. She has taught ESL for 25 years on all levels, particularly the college level. She has co-authored six ESL reading skills texts and has presented at local, national, and international conferences. Professor Smith teaches in the M.A. TESOL/BE Program at Adelphi University in Garden City, New York.

Author's Acknowledgments

Although the idea for a content-based series had been in my mind for some time, the impetus for putting pen to paper (figuratively speaking!) came in a conversation with my editor, Laura Le Dréan, on the day we met. She has been enthusiastic about this series from Day One, and I am grateful for her unwavering support. I thank Paula Van Ells, my development editor, whose comments and suggestions helped me improve and polish the material, and who has always been a professional.

My special thanks go to Nancy Nici Mare of the English Language Institute at Queens College. She and her ESL students field tested the chapters and gave me valuable suggestions for revision. My thanks also go to Regina A. Rochford, who teaches ESL at Queensborough Community College, and who gave me useful insights and feedback. I am very grateful to my former ESL students at Queensborough, who willingly worked with early drafts of the chapters. Their questions and comments were invaluable to me as I developed the book. Finally, I acknowledge my husband, Joseph, who always said I could do it.

Lorraine C. Smith

CREDITS

Photo Credits

Pages 1, Jet Propulsion Labs/NASA. **Page 2,** left: Exploring the Planets by W. Kenneth Hamblin & Eric H. Christiansen. Macmillian Publishers. 1990. Modified after W.K. Hamblin, 1983. right: Jet Propulsion Labs/NASA. **Page 43,** From *Vertebrate Paleontology and Evolution* by Robert Carroll. © 1988 by W.H. Freeman and Company. Used with permission. **Page 57,** top: World Ocean Floor Panorama, Bruce C. Heezen and Marie Tharp, 1977. © Copyright by Marie Tharp 1977/2003. Reproduced by permission of Marie Tharp Oceanographic Cartographer, One Washington Ave., South Nyack, New York 10960. **Page 58,** Biology: *A Guide to the Natural World 2/e* by David Krogh. Prentice Hall. 2002. © Reprinted by permission of Pearson Education, Inc. **Page 59,** *Biological Science* by Freeman, © Reprinted by permission of Pearson Education, Inc., Upper Saddle River, NJ. **Page 65,** Hulton Archive/Getty Images. **Page 68,** left: James Sparshatt/Corbis. center: © Gallo Images/Corbis. right: © Stan Osolinski/Corbis. **Page 71,** *Vertebrate Paleontology and Evolution* by Robert Carroll. © 1988 by W.H. Freeman and Company. Used with permission. **Page 81,** *Biological Science* by Freeman, © Reprinted by permission of Pearson Education, Inc., Upper Saddle River, NJ. **Page 83,** *Biology: A Guide to the Natural World 2/e* by David Krogh. Prentice Hall. 2002. © Reprinted by permission of Pearson Education, Inc. **Page 84,** *Lower Palaeolithic Archaeology in Britain as represented by the Thames Valley* by John Wymer. 1968. Humanities Press Inc., New York. **Page 88,** top: © Archivo Iconografico, S.A./Corbis. **Page 94,** Reprinted by permission of Waveland Press, Inc. from *Human Origins: The Fossil Record, 3/e* by Larsen, et al. (Prospect Heights, IL: Waveland Press, Inc., 1998). All rights reserved. **Page 95,** Neg. no. 319565, courtesy the Library, American Museum of Natural. **Page 96,** © Yann Arthus-Bertrand/Corbis. **Page 97,** top: "Photo Copyright Boneclones® 2004, www.boneclones.com". bottom: Reprinted by permission of Waveland Press, Inc. from *Human Origins: The Fossil Record, 3/e* by Larsen, et al. (Prospect Heights, IL: Waveland Press, Inc., 1998). All rights reserved. **Page 98,** Reprinted by permission of Waveland Press, Inc. from *Human Origins: The Fossil Record, 3/e* by Larsen, et al. (Prospect Heights, IL: Waveland Press, Inc., 1998). All rights reserved. **Page 99,** © Gallo Images/Corbis. **Page 102,** Reprinted by permission of Waveland Press, Inc. from *Human Origins: The Fossil Record, 3/e* by Larsen, et al. (Prospect Heights, IL: Waveland Press, Inc., 1998). All rights reserved. **Page 108,** © Roger Wood/Corbis. **Page 109,** © Roger Wood/Corbis. **Page 113,** bottom left: © Pierre Vauthey/Corbis Sygma. bottom right: © Gianni Dagli Orti/Corbis. **Page 126,** © Archivo Iconografico, S.A./Corbis. **Page 127,** © Adam Woolfitt/Corbis. **Page 137,** © David Lees/Corbis. **Page 144,** © Peter Aprahamian/Corbis. **Page 150,** © Gianni Dagli Orti/Corbis. **Page 151,**

bottom: Ashmolean Museum, Oxford. **Page 153,** © Gianni Dagli Orti/Corbis. **Page 161,** bottom: Ashmolean Museum, Oxford. **Page 163,** top left: © Christie's Images/Corbis. top right: © Francis G. Mayer/Corbis. bottom left: © Gianni Dagli Orti/Corbis. bottom right: © Michael Freeman/Corbis. **Page 164,** © Peter Beck/Corbis. **Pages 174, 179,** © 2004 Estate of Pablo Picasso/Artists Rights Society (ARS), New York. **Pages 175, 180** © Arte & Immagini srl/Corbis. **Page 188,** © Gianni Dagli Orti/Corbis. **Pages 199,** top: Photograph © 2004 Museum of Fine Arts, Boston. *King Menkaure (Mycerinus) and Queen.* Egyptian, Old Kingdom, Dynasty 4, reign of Menkaure, about 2490-2472 B.C. Findspot: Egypt, Giza, Menkaure Valley Temple. Greywacke. Height x width x depth: 142.2 x 57.1 x 55.2 cm (56 x 22 1/2 x 21 3/4 in.). Museum of Fine Arts, Boston. Harvard University – Museum of Fine Arts Expedition. 11.1738. bottom: *Basic History of Art, 5/e* by Janson & Janson, © Reprinted by permission of Pearson Education, Inc., Upper Saddle River, NJ. **Page 205,** Photograph © 2004 Museum of Fine Arts, Boston. *King Menkaure (Mycerinus) and Queen.* Egyptian, Old Kingdom, Dynasty 4, reign of Menkaure, about 2490-2472 B.C. Findspot: Egypt, Giza, Menkaure Valley Temple. Greywacke. Height x width x depth: 142.2 x 57.1 x 55.2 cm (56 x 22 1/2 x 21 3/4 in.). Museum of Fine Arts, Boston. Harvard University – Museum of Fine Arts Expedition. 11.1738. **Pages 200, 204,** © Sandro Vannini/Corbis. **Page 203,** © Nigel Francis/Corbis. **Page 214,** AP/Wide World Photos. **Page 215,** ©Carlos Davila/SuperStock, Inc. **Page 226,** © Joel W. Sheagren/Corbis. **Page 232,** © Taxi/Getty Images. **Page 245,** © Ted Horowitz/Corbis. **Page 261,** © Gary D. Landsman/Corbis.

Text Credits

Pages 7, 19, 36, 64, 74, Enger, et al., Concepts in Biology. © 2002 McGraw-Hill. Reproduced with permission of the McGraw-Hill Companies. **Page 44,** Excerpt 55. 571-573 from *Conceptual Physical Science,* 2nd ed. by Paul G. Hewitt, John Suchocki, and Leslie A. Hewitt. Copyright © 1999 by Paul G. Hewitt, John Suchocki, and Leslie A. Hewitt. Reprinted by permission of Pearson Education, Inc. **Pages 87, 95,** Michael Alan Park, *Introducing Anthropology: An Integrated Approach.* © 2002 McGraw-Hill. Reproduced with permission of the McGraw-Hill Companies. **Pages 113, 123, 143, 150,** From *World Civilization,* Ninth Edition, Volume 1 by eds. Philip Ralph, Robert E. Lerner, et al.. Copyright © 1997, 1991, 1986, 1974, 1969, 1964, 1958, 1955 by W.W. Norton & Company, IncPL. Used by permission of W. W. Norton & Company, Inc. **Pages 169, 178, 192, 202,** *Basic History of Art* by Janson, © Reprinted by permission of Pearson Education, Inc., Upper Saddle River, NJ. **Page 202,** *Art Past, Art Present,* 4/E by Wilkins/Schultz/Linduff, © Reprinted by permission of Pearson Education, Inc., Upper Saddle River, NJ. **Pages 219, 231, 249, 258,** Social Psychology, 4/e by Aronson/Wilson/Akert, © Reprinted by permission of Pearson Education, Inc., Upper Saddle River, NJ.

Longman wishes to thank the following reviewers: **Lyn Buchheit,** Pennsylvania Community College of Philadelphia, Philadelphia, PA; **Susan Carkin,** Utah State University, Logan, UT; **Mary Di Stefano Díaz,** Broward Community College, Davie, FL; **Bernadette Garcia,** Suffolk County Community College, Brentwood, NY; **Virginia Guleff,** Miramar College, San Diego, CA; **Janet Harclerode,** Santa Monica College, Santa Monica, CA; **Alex Jones,** University of Washington, Seattle, WA; **Thomas Leverett,** Southern Illinois University, Carbondale, IL; **Christine Meloni,** George Washington University, Washington, D.C.; **Elizabeth Neblett,** Union County College, Elizabeth, NJ; **Marc Roberts,** Pine Manor College, Chestnut Hill, MA; **Esther Robbins,** Prince George's Community College, Largo, MD; **David Ross,** Houston Community College, Houston, TX; **Margaret Schieck,** Mission College, Santa Clara, CA; **Deborah Stone,** Bellevue Community College, Bellevue, WA; Cynthia Thornburgh, Portland Community College, Portland, OR; **Laura Walsh,** City College of San Francisco, San Francisco, CA.

HOW DID IT ALL BEGIN?

**Fig. 1.0 Spiral galaxy
(Galaxy NGC3310)**

CHAPTER 1

THE UNIVERSE AND THE EARTH

Skills Goals

- Preview key vocabulary.
- Use titles and headings to predict content.
- Highlight important information.
- Monitor reading comprehension.
- Use context to learn the meaning of new vocabulary.
- Use the dictionary to learn the meaning of new vocabulary.
- Use illustrations and graphic organizers to aid in understanding text.

Content-Specific Goals

- Study the formation of the universe and our solar system.
- Learn about the origin of the Earth.
- Learn about the origin of the Earth's oceans and oxygen atmosphere.
- Understand how organic molecules were first formed.
- Learn about competing theories of the origin of life on Earth.

Fig. 1.1a The Earth, about 4.6 billion years ago

Fig. 1.1b The Earth today

Chapter Readings

The Beginning of the Universe and the Origin of the Earth

The Formation of Organic Molecules from Inorganic Molecules

INTRODUCING THE READING

Activate Your Knowledge

The following activities will help you prepare for the Introductory Reading. They will help you focus on the topic—the beginning of the universe and the origin of the Earth—and discover what you already know about it. Do not worry if you do not know something. You will learn more as you work with the chapter.

A **Read the paragraph below, and then write some possible answers to the questions. Discuss your answers with a classmate, then with the class.**

> Ever since people first looked up at the sky and observed the sun, the moon, the stars and the planets, they wondered about them and tried to understand them. What are they made of? How far away are they? How old are they? How did it all begin? How did the universe begin?

_____

_____

_____

B **Below is an illustration showing the relative sizes of the Sun and the nine planets. Work with a partner. List the nine planets in order, beginning with the one closest to the Sun.**

Fig. 1.1c The Sun and the planets, in order of distance from the Sun (not to scale)

| Earth | Mars | Neptune | Saturn | Venus |
| Jupiter | Mercury | Pluto | Uranus | |

1. _____   4. _____   7. _____

2. _____   5. _____   8. _____

3. _____   6. _____   9. _____

Reading and Study Skill Strategies

Using strategies and skills when you work with a reading passage will help you understand and remember what you have read. This chapter introduces several strategies and skills that you will find effective in all your reading, regardless of the subject matter. Some of the strategies and skills may be unfamiliar or difficult to use at first. However, if you persevere, they will get easier. Eventually, they will become an automatic part of your reading and study habits. You will find that your comprehension improves and your vocabulary increases.

PREVIEW KEY VOCABULARY

Before you begin reading a passage, you will find it useful to examine the content-specific vocabulary that you will encounter. This practice helps you focus on the topic and judge the difficulty of the text you will read.

Read the list of content-specific vocabulary and check the ones you are familiar with. Leave the other spaces blank. Do not try to learn the unfamiliar items before you begin reading. You will learn them as you work with the chapter.

___ atmosphere	___ helium	___ nitrogen
___ atom	___ hydrogen	___ organic
___ the Big Bang	___ inorganic	___ oxygen
___ carbon dioxide	___ membrane	___ reducing atmosphere
___ crust	___ methane	
___ galaxy	___ molecule	___ theory
___ gravity	___ molten core	___ universe

USE TITLE AND HEADINGS TO PREDICT CONTENT

Reading the title and headings before reading an entire passage gives you an overview of the material because the title introduces the topic of a passage, and the headings introduce the topic of each section within a passage. The sections are presented in a logical order, too, so you get an idea of the sequence of events or ideas. In the Introductory Reading, the title and the headings are:

The Beginning of the Universe and the Origin of the Earth

The Big Bang Theory

The Formation of the Earth

The Formation of the Earth's Atmosphere and Oceans

A Read the following statements and check the ones that seem correct based on the title and headings. Then compare your answers with a classmate's. Keep in mind that you may not agree.

1. ___ The author will explain that no one knows how the universe began.

2. ___ The author will describe a "Big Bang" theory to explain how the universe began.

3. ___ The universe and the Earth were formed at the same time.

4. ___ The universe was formed before the Earth was formed.

5. ___ When the Earth was formed, it had an atmosphere and oceans.

6. ___ When the Earth was formed, it did not have an atmosphere or oceans.

B Go to page *iv* in the Table of Contents. Read the brief summary of the Introductory Reading. Then review the statements above, and decide whether to change any of your predictions.

HIGHLIGHT IMPORTANT INFORMATION

Highlighting the most important ideas of a passage as you read helps you maintain your focus. This practice also makes it easier for you to review the material. As you read, remember to highlight the most important ideas—the ones that give you information about the topic, help you understand the reading, explain the title and the headings, and include essential vocabulary.

A Read the following selection from the Introductory Reading and highlight the most important information.

THE FORMATION OF THE EARTH

[1]Many scientists believe that the Earth was formed at least 4.5 billion years ago. [2]A large amount of heat was generated as the particles became concentrated to form Earth. [3]Although not as hot as the Sun, the material of Earth formed a molten core (hot liquid rock center) that became encased by a thin outer crust as it cooled. [4]In its early stages of formation, about 4 billion years ago, there may have been a considerable amount of volcanic activity on Earth.

[5]Physically, Earth was probably much different from what it is today. [6]Because the surface was hot, there was no water on the surface or in the atmosphere. [7]In fact, the tremendous amount of heat probably prevented any atmosphere from forming. [8]The gases associated with our present atmosphere (nitrogen, oxygen, carbon dioxide, and water vapor) were contained in the planet's molten core. [9]These hostile conditions (high temperature, lack of water, lack of atmosphere) on early Earth could not have supported any form of life similar to what we see today.

---

1. Which sentences did you highlight? _____

2. Which sentences contain information that helped you understand

how the Earth was formed? _____

B **Read through the sentences that you highlighted. Make a list of the vocabulary that you think you need to know.**

_____   _____   _____

_____   _____   _____

C **Work with a classmate and compare your highlighting and your vocabulary lists. Then compare your highlighting with the highlighting in paragraph 3 on page 8.**

Highlighting has been done for you in the entire Introductory Reading, as an example.

MONITOR READING COMPREHENSION

Another useful strategy is to monitor (check) your comprehension by pausing after each section and asking yourself what that section was about. For example, what did it tell you about the heading? This strategy is effective because it helps ensure that you understand a reading passage while you are reading. This practice makes it easier for you to review parts of the text that may have been difficult to comprehend on first reading.

Read the following selection from the Introductory Reading. Monitor your comprehension by answering the Before You Continue Reading question that follows. Then compare your answer with a classmate's.

THE BIG BANG THEORY

As astronomers and others look at the current stars and galaxies, it can be observed that they are moving apart from one another. This and other evidence has led to the concept that our current universe began as a very dense mass of matter that had a great deal of energy. This dense mass of matter exploded in a "big bang" that resulted in the formation of atoms. According to the Big Bang theory, the original universe consisted primarily of atoms of hydrogen and helium. Our solar system is one small part of the universe. The *solar nebula theory* proposes that our solar system was formed from a large cloud of gases and developed some 10 to 20 billion years ago. The simplest and most abundant gases would have been hydrogen and helium. A gravitational force was created by the collection of particles within this cloud that caused other particles to be pulled from the outer edges to the center. As particles collected into larger bodies, gravity increased and more particles were attracted to the bodies. Ultimately a central body (the Sun) was formed and several other bodies (planets) formed that moved around it. The Sun consists primarily of hydrogen and helium atoms, which are being fused together to form larger atoms.

According to the "Big Bang" theory, the universe was created ____.

a. *from a large cloud of gases*

b. *when matter exploded and created atoms*

c. *when hydrogen and helium atoms formed larger atoms*

INTRODUCTORY READING

The following reading, "The Beginning of the Universe and the Origin of the Earth," is from the college textbook Concepts in Biology. *As you read, pay attention to the important ideas, which have been highlighted, and to the vocabulary in the highlighted sentences. Monitor your comprehension by answering the Before You Continue Reading questions that follow each section. If you have trouble answering a question, reread the section before you continue reading.*

Fig 1.1d The formation of our solar system

(a) As gravity pulled the gas particles into the center, the Sun developed.

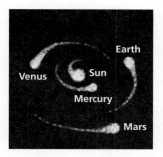

(b) In other regions, smaller gravitational forces caused the formation of the Sun's planets.

The Beginning of the Universe and the Origin of the Earth

1   Ever since people first looked up at the sky and observed the sun, the moon, the stars and the planets, they wondered about them and tried to understand them. What are they made of? How far away are they? How old are they? How did it all begin? Over thousands of years, in every culture in the world, people have tried to understand the nature of the universe. In the past several hundred years, with the advancement of science and the invention of telescopes, microscopes and other devices, we have come to understand the origin, age, and nature of the universe and of our own planet, Earth.

THE BIG BANG THEORY

2   As astronomers and others look at the current stars and galaxies, it can be observed that they are moving apart from one another. This and other evidence has led to the concept that our current universe began as a very dense mass of matter that had a great deal of energy. This dense mass of matter exploded in a "big bang" that resulted in the formation of atoms. According to the Big Bang theory, the original universe consisted primarily of atoms of hydrogen and helium. Our solar system is one small part of the universe. The *solar nebula theory* proposes that our solar system was formed from a large cloud of gases and developed some 10 to 20 billion years ago. The simplest and most abundant gases would have been hydrogen and helium. A gravitational force was created by the collection of particles within this cloud that caused other particles to be pulled from the outer edges to the center. As particles collected into larger bodies, gravity increased and more particles were attracted to the bodies. Ultimately a central body (the Sun) was formed and several other bodies (planets) formed that moved around it. The Sun consists primarily of hydrogen and helium atoms, which are being fused together to form larger atoms.

BEFORE YOU
CONTINUE
READING

1. **According to the "Big Bang" theory, the universe ___.**

   a. *has always existed in time and space*

   b. *was created after an explosion that formed atoms*

   c. *was created by the force of gravity*

THE FORMATION OF THE EARTH

3   Many scientists believe that the Earth was formed at least 4.5 billion years ago. A large amount of heat was generated as the particles became concentrated to form Earth. Although not as hot as the Sun, the material of Earth formed a molten core (hot liquid rock center) that became encased by a thin outer crust as it cooled. In its early stages of formation, about 4 billion years ago, there may have been a considerable amount of volcanic activity on Earth.

4   Physically, Earth was probably much different from what it is today. Because the surface was hot, there was no water on the surface or in the atmosphere. In fact, the tremendous amount of heat probably prevented any atmosphere from forming. The gases associated with our present atmosphere (nitrogen, oxygen, carbon dioxide, and water vapor) were contained in the planet's molten core. These hostile conditions (high temperature, lack of water, lack of atmosphere) on early Earth could not have supported any form of life similar to what we see today.

BEFORE YOU
CONTINUE
READING

2. **When the Earth was formed, it ___.**

   a. *was very hot and had a gas atmosphere*

   b. *was just as hot as the Sun, with gases on the surface*

   c. *began to cool and to form an outer crust*

THE FORMATION OF THE EARTH'S ATMOSPHERE AND OCEANS

5   Over hundreds of millions of years, Earth is thought to have slowly changed. As it cooled, volcanic activity probably caused the release of water vapor (H_2O), carbon dioxide (CO_2), methane (CH_4), ammonia (NH_3), and hydrogen (H_2), and the early atmosphere was formed. These gases formed a *reducing atmosphere*—an atmosphere that did not contain molecules of oxygen (O_2). Any oxygen atoms (O_2) would have quickly combined with other atoms to form compounds, so a significant quantity of molecular oxygen (O_2) would have been highly unlikely. Further cooling enabled the water vapor in the atmosphere to condense into droplets of rain. The water ran over the land and collected to form the oceans we see today.

Checking Comprehension

A **Read the following statements. Check the correct ones. Then compare these responses with your responses on page 5. Discuss your answers as a class.**

1. ___ The author explained that no one knows how the universe began.

2. ___ The author described a "Big Bang" theory to explain how the universe began.

3. ___ The universe and the Earth were formed at the same time.

4. ___ The universe was formed before the Earth was formed.

5. ___ When the Earth was formed, it had an atmosphere and oceans.

6. ___ When the Earth was formed, it did not have an atmosphere or oceans.

How many of your predictions on page 5 were correct? ___

B **Circle the correct answers.**

1. What force helped to form the Sun and the planets?
   a. volcanoes
   b. gravity
   c. magnetism

2. How did the Sun and the planets form and become large bodies?
   a. They each collected particles through gravitation.
   b. They were already large when they formed.
   c. They collided with other large bodies.

C **Answer the following questions in complete sentences.**

1. Reread the questions about the origins of the universe on page 3. What questions do you still have? Discuss them now in class.

   _____

   _____

2. Briefly describe how the universe was formed.

   _____

   _____

   _____

3. Astronomers have observed that the stars and galaxies are moving apart. What can we infer about their positions in the past?

_____

_____

_____

4. In what ways was the early Earth different from the Earth today? Refer to the illustrations on page 2 to help you.

_____

_____

_____

Learning Vocabulary

Two effective strategies for learning new vocabulary involve using context to figure out the meaning and using a dictionary to learn the definition.

VOCABULARY FROM CONTEXT

When you encounter new vocabulary that you need to know, you can often figure out the meaning from context. In the following three examples, the meaning of the word in italics can be determined from context.

A **Read the examples. Then read the explanations.**

1. The Sun consists primarily of hydrogen and helium atoms, which are being _fused_ together to form larger atoms.

    (The sentence tells us that two different types of atoms, hydrogen and helium, are _fused together_ and that, as a result, they form _larger atoms_. The sentence tells us that two different types of atoms come _together_ and that they _form_ something _larger_. From this information, we can understand that _fused_ means combined in some way.)

     Fused probably means ___.
     a. observed
     b. closed
     c. joined

    (_Joined_ is the answer because _joined_ means connected or combined. _Observed_ and _closed_ do not convey the meanings of _connected_ or _combined_, so they do not convey the same meaning as _fused_.)

2. As the Earth cooled, volcanic activity probably caused the release of water vapor (H_2O), carbon dioxide (CO_2), methane (CH_4), ammonia (NH_3), and hydrogen (H_2), and the early atmosphere was formed. These gases formed a *reducing atmosphere*—an atmosphere that did not contain molecules of oxygen (O_2).

   (The term *reducing atmosphere* is followed by a dash (—). A dash usually indicates that additional information will be given. In this sentence, additional information about *reducing atmosphere* has been given.)

   A reducing atmosphere is a special term which means ___.
   (a.) an atmosphere with no free oxygen
   b. an atmosphere with oxygen

   (After the dash, we read that, of all the molecules listed, none are molecules of oxygen by itself [O_2]. Oxygen is always joined with other molecules such as carbon or hydrogen. Therefore, a *reducing atmosphere* is *an atmosphere with no free oxygen*.)

3. As the Earth cooled, volcanic activity probably caused the release of *water vapor* (H_2O), *carbon dioxide* (CO_2), *methane* (CH_4), *ammonia* (NH_3), and *hydrogen* (H_2), and the early atmosphere was formed. These gases formed a reducing atmosphere—an atmosphere that did not contain molecules of oxygen (O_2).

   (The context mentions *water vapor, carbon dioxide, methane, ammonia,* and *hydrogen,* then states that *these gases* formed a reducing atmosphere.)

   Water vapor, carbon dioxide, methane, ammonia, hydrogen, and *oxygen* are all kinds of ___.
   a. liquids
   (b.) gases
   c. atoms

   (The second sentence refers to *water vapor, carbon dioxide, methane, ammonia,* and *hydrogen* as *these gases,* so they are all *gases.*)

B **Read the following sentences. Circle the best choice to complete the sentences. Then circle the reason for your choice.**

1. The *hostile conditions* (high temperature, lack of water, lack of atmosphere) on early Earth could not have supported any form of life similar to what we see today.

   (1) From this context, we can understand that *hostile conditions* are ___.
   a. angry and unfriendly conditions
   b. conditions that prevent plans or ideas
   c. conditions that make it difficult for life to exist

   (2) How were you able to guess the meaning of *hostile conditions* from the context?
   a. The term was defined in the sentence.
   b. The sentence included examples in parentheses.
   c. The early Earth did not have similar life.

2. According to the Big Bang theory, the original universe *consisted primarily* of atoms of hydrogen and helium. Our solar system is one small part of the universe. The solar nebula theory proposes that our solar system was formed from a large cloud of gases and developed some 10 to 20 billion years ago. The simplest and most abundant gases would have been hydrogen and helium.

   (1) From this context, we can understand that *consisted of* means ____.

      a. was made of
      b. exploded into
      c. pulled away from

   (2) How did you figure out what *consisted of* means?
      a. The verb was defined in the sentence.
      b. The Big Bang created the universe.
      c. The original universe had to be made of something.

   (3) From the context, we can guess that *primarily* means ____.
      a. densely
      b. mostly
      c. accordingly

   (4) How did you figure out what *primarily* means?
      a. The paragraph explains that the solar system was formed mainly from hydrogen and helium.
      b. The paragraph explains that hydrogen and helium are gases.
      c. I know that hydrogen and helium still exist.

3. Although not as hot as the Sun, the material of Earth formed a *molten core* (hot liquid rock center) that became encased by a thin outer *crust* as it cooled.

   (1) What is the Earth's *molten core*?
      a. the same material as the Sun
      b. a hot liquid rock center
      c. the Earth's outer crust

   (2) How did you figure out what a *molten core* is?
      a. The Earth originally formed from the Sun.
      b. The Earth cooled, but the Sun did not.
      c. The sentence gives an explanation in parentheses.

   (3) What is a *crust*?
      a. an outer case
      b. outer gases
      c. an outer liquid

   (4) How did you guess the meaning of *crust*?
      a. The sentence explains that the Earth's core was encased in a crust.
      b. The sentence describes the Earth as cooler than the Sun.
      c. The sentence states that the core was liquid.

USING THE DICTIONARY

You can also use a dictionary to learn new words. Dictionary entries often have several definitions for a word, so you need to consider the context in order to figure out the appropriate definition.

A Read the following example. Then read the explanations.

The original universe consisted primarily of atoms of hydrogen and helium. The solar nebula theory proposes that our solar system was formed from a large cloud of gases. The simplest and most abundant gases would have been hydrogen and helium. A gravitational force was created by the collection of *particles* within this cloud that caused other particles to be pulled from the outer edges to the center. As *particles* collected into larger bodies, gravity increased and more *particles* were attracted to the bodies.

> **par·ti·cle** /ˈpɑrṭɪkəl/ *n.* [C] **1** a very small piece of something: [+ **of**] *tiny particles of dust in the air* **2** one very small piece of matter that an atom consists of: *subatomic particles such as protons* **3** TECHNICAL a type of word in grammar, such as a CONJUNCTION (3) or PREPOSITION, that is usually short and does not belong to one of the main word classes. Some particles such as "in" and "up" can combine with verbs to form PHRASAL VERBS

(The first entry is too general because it refers to a very small piece of something. The second entry refers to a very small piece of matter that an atom consists of. The text is discussing atoms; therefore, this entry is specific to our context. The third entry does not fit our context because it relates to grammar.)

(1) The definition of *particle* in the context of the example is number _2_.

(If entry 2 is used to complete the sentence below, it will have the same meaning it has in the original text.)

(2) The gravitational force which caused the collection of _b_ within the cloud of gases caused others to be pulled to the center of the cloud too.
  a. small pieces
  b. small pieces of matter
  c. words in grammar

B **Read the following sentences and dictionary entries. Select the best entry for the context, and circle the correct choice to complete the sentences that follow.**

1. The solar nebula theory *proposes* that our solar system was formed from a large cloud of gases. A gravitational force was created by the collection of particles within this cloud that caused other particles to be pulled from the outer edges to the center. As particles collected into larger bodies, gravity increased and more particles were attracted to the bodies.

> **pro·pose** /prəˈpoʊz/ *v.* **1** [T] to formally suggest a plan, time, or way of doing something: *We proposed several dates for the next meeting, but they were all rejected.* | [**propose sth to sb**] *We'll have to wait and see what kind of solutions they propose to us.* | [**propose that**] *What do you propose that Michael do?* | [**propose doing sth**] *The new administration has proposed scrapping more than 400 obsolete government programs.* | [**propose to do sth**] *One council member proposed to close three of the schools to save money.* | [**propose sb**] *I didn't feel comfortable proposing him for the award* (=suggesting he receive the award). **2** [T] FORMAL to intend to do something: [**propose to do sth**] *What do you propose to do about it?* **3 a)** [I] to ask someone to marry you, especially in a formal way: [+ **to**] *Did he propose to her, or did she propose to him?* **b) propose marriage** FORMAL to ask someone to marry you **4** [T] FORMAL to suggest an idea, method etc. as an answer to a scientific question: [**propose that**] *It has been proposed that Japanese and Korean are descendants of a common language.*

(1) The best definition of *propose* in this entry is number ___.

(2) The solar nebula theory ___.
   a. formally suggests a plan to explain the way our solar system was formed
   b. intends to tell us how to form our solar system
   c. suggests an idea to answer the question of how our solar system was formed

2. The solar nebula theory proposes that our solar system was formed from a large cloud of gases. A *gravitational* force was created by the collection of particles within this cloud that caused other particles to be pulled from the outer edges to the center. As particles collected into larger bodies, *gravity* increased and more particles were attracted to the bodies. Ultimately the Sun was formed and the planets formed and moved around it.

> **grav·i·ty** /ˈɡrævəti/ *n.* [U] **1** TECHNICAL the force that causes something to fall to the ground or one planet to be attracted to another one: *Mars' gravity is only about 38% of Earth's.* **2** FORMAL the seriousness or importance of an event, situation etc.: *I don't think you quite understand the gravity of the situation.* **3** an extremely serious way of behaving, speaking etc.: *They speak with passion and gravity.* –see also CENTER OF GRAVITY

(1) The best definition of *gravity* in this entry is number ___.

(2) As particles collected into larger bodies, ___ increased and more particles were attracted to the bodies, gradually forming the Sun and the planets.

    a. the force that causes one planet to be attracted to another
    b. the seriousness of the situation
    c. the extremely serious way the bodies behaved

INTRODUCING THE MAIN READING

Activate Your Knowledge

The following activities will help you prepare for the Main Reading. They will help you focus on the topic, the formation of organic molecules, and discover what you already know about it. Do not worry if you do not know something. You will learn more as you work with the chapter.

A **The Introductory Reading on pages 7–8 discussed atoms, molecules, and compounds. The Main Reading on pages 19–22 discusses them in more detail, so it is important to know what they are before beginning the reading. Read the following paragraphs about atoms, molecules, and compounds.**

Put simply, an *atom* is the smallest particle of an element that keeps the properties of that element. Helium (He), oxygen (O), hydrogen (H), carbon (C), and nitrogen (N) are some of the most abundant elements in the universe. All atoms consist of different numbers of protons (p), neutrons (n), and electrons (e). Scientists usually illustrate atoms as follows:

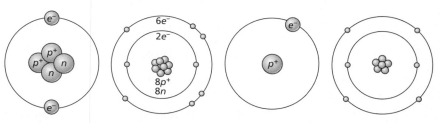

Fig. 1.1e   **Helium (He)**   **Oxygen (O)**   **Hydrogen (H)**   **Carbon (C)**

Fig. 1.1f

Methane (CH$_4$)

H — N — H
   |
   H

Ammonia (NH$_3$)

O — H
|
H

Water (H$_2$O)

When atoms combine, they form something new. For example, when two atoms of hydrogen (H) combine with one atom of oxygen (O), they form water. Therefore, water is represented as H$_2$O. Even when atoms of the same element combine, they form something new. For example, when three atoms of oxygen combine, they form ozone (O$_3$). When two atoms of oxygen (O$_2$) combine, they are called *molecular oxygen* to distinguish them from a single atom of oxygen (O). Scientists write NH$_3$, CH$_4$, and H$_2$O, for example, to represent *molecules,* instead of writing out the names: methane, ammonia, or water. They also sometimes make a simple diagram, like those in Figure 1.1f, to show how the atoms are connected.

B Work with a partner or in a small group. Write the vocabulary words on the correct lines. Use the singular or plural form. You may use words more than once.

atom(s)　　element(s)　　molecule(s)　　proton(s)

1. _____ : the smallest particle of an element that keeps the properties of that element

2. _____ : a combination of two or more atoms

3. _____ : a component of an atom

4. _____ : O, He, H, N

5. _____ : H_2O, NH_3, CH_4, CO_2, H_2

Reading and Study Skill Strategies

USE TITLE AND HEADINGS TO PREDICT CONTENT

Remember that reading the title and headings before reading the entire passage gives you an overview of the material because the title introduces the topic of a passage and the headings introduce the topic of each section within a passage. The sections are presented in a logical order, too, so you get an idea of the sequence of events or ideas. In the Main Reading, the title and the headings are:

The Formation of Organic Molecules from Inorganic Molecules

Steps in the Formation of Organic Molecules

A Theory of the Formation of the First Organic Molecules

Testing the Theory

Explanations for the Concentration of Simple Organic Molecules

A Read the following statements and check the ones that seem correct based on the title and headings. Then compare your answers with a classmate's. Keep in mind that you may not agree.

1. ___ Organic molecules were formed, then inorganic molecules were formed.

2. ___ Inorganic molecules were formed, then organic molecules were formed.

3. ___ Organic molecules were formed in a number of stages.

4. ___ Organic molecules were formed in one big step.

5. ___ Organic molecules are still being formed today.

6. ___ Organic molecules are no longer being formed today.

7. ___ H_2O, O_3, CO_2, CH_4, NH_3, H_2, and O_2 are all inorganic molecules.

8. ___ H_2O, O_3, CO_2, CH_4, NH_3, H_2, and O_2 are all organic molecules.

B Go to page *iv* in the Table of Contents. Read the brief summary of the Main Reading. Then review the statements above, and decide whether to make any changes to your predictions.

HIGHLIGHT IMPORTANT INFORMATION

As you read, remember to highlight the most important ideas—the ones that give you information about the topic, help you understand the reading, explain the title and the headings, and include essential vocabulary.

A Read the following selection from the Main Reading, and highlight the most important information.

EXPLANATIONS FOR THE CONCENTRATION OF SIMPLE ORGANIC MOLECULES

[1]Several ideas have been proposed for the concentration of simple organic molecules and their combination into macromolecules (large molecules). [2]A portion of the early ocean could have been separated from the main ocean by geologic changes. [3]The evaporation of water from this pool could have concentrated the molecules, which might have led to the manufacture of macromolecules by dehydration synthesis. [4]It has also been proposed that freezing may have been the means of concentration. [5]When a mixture of alcohol and water is placed in a freezer, the water freezes solid and the alcohol becomes concentrated into a small portion of liquid. [6]A similar process could have occurred on Earth's early surface, resulting in the concentration of simple organic molecules. [7]In this concentrated solution, dehydration synthesis in a reducing atmosphere could have occurred, resulting in the formation of macromolecules. [8]A third theory proposes that clay particles may have been a factor in concentrating simple organic molecules. [9]Small particles of clay have electrical charges that can attract and concentrate organic molecules. [10]Once the molecules became concentrated, it would have been easier for them to interact to form larger macromolecules.

---

1. Which sentences did you highlight? _____

2. Which sentences contain information that explains how simple

   organic molecules became concentrated? _____

B Read through the sentences that you highlighted. Make a list of the vocabulary that you think you need to know.

_____ _____ _____

_____ _____ _____

C Work with a classmate and compare your highlighting and your vocabulary lists. Then compare your highlighting with the highlighting in paragraph 6 on page 22.

Highlighting has been done for you in the entire Main Reading, as an example.

MONITOR READING COMPREHENSION

Remember that you can monitor your comprehension by pausing after each section and asking yourself what it was about. For example, what did it tell you about the heading?

Read the following section from the Main Reading. Monitor your comprehension by answering the Before You Continue Reading question that follows. Then compare your answer with a classmate's.

EXPLANATIONS FOR THE CONCENTRATION OF SIMPLE ORGANIC MOLECULES

[1]Several ideas have been proposed for the concentration of simple organic molecules and their combination into macromolecules (large molecules). [2]A portion of the early ocean could have been separated from the main ocean by geologic changes. [3]The evaporation of water from this pool could have concentrated the molecules, which might have led to the manufacture of macromolecules by dehydration synthesis. [4]It has also been proposed that freezing may have been the means of concentration. [5]When a mixture of alcohol and water is placed in a freezer, the water freezes solid and the alcohol becomes concentrated into a small portion of liquid. [6]A similar process could have occurred on Earth's early surface, resulting in the concentration of simple organic molecules. [7]In this concentrated solution, dehydration synthesis in a reducing atmosphere could have occurred, resulting in the formation of macromolecules. [8]A third theory proposes that clay particles may have been a factor in concentrating simple organic molecules. [9]Small particles of clay have electrical charges that can attract and concentrate organic molecules. [10]Once the molecules became concentrated, it would have been easier for them to interact to form larger macromolecules.

BEFORE YOU
CONTINUE
READING

1. **Several ideas have been proposed to explain how simple organic molecules combined into macromolecules (larger molecules). All three theories maintain that ____.**

   a. *water had to come from the oceans and either freeze or evaporate*

   b. *simple organic molecules had to become concentrated and then combine*

   c. *geologic changes had to take place and then macromolecules could form*

MAIN READING

The Main Reading, "The Formation of Organic Molecules from Inorganic Molecules," is also from Concepts in Biology. *As you read, pay attention to the important ideas, which have been highlighted, and to the vocabulary used to express these ideas. Monitor your comprehension by answering the Before You Continue Reading questions that follow each section. If you have trouble answering a question, reread the section before you continue.*

The Formation of Organic Molecules from Inorganic Molecules

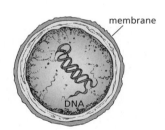

membrane

DNA

Fig. 1.1g A simple cell, showing the outer membrane and the DNA, which enables the cell to reproduce itself

1   When we consider the nature of the simplest forms of life today, we find that living things consist of an outer membrane that separates the cell from its surroundings, genetic material in the form of nucleic acids (DNA or RNA), and many kinds of enzymes that control the activities of the cell. Therefore, when we speculate about the origin of life from inorganic material, it seems logical that several events or steps were necessary.

STEPS IN THE FORMATION OF ORGANIC MOLECULES

1. Organic molecules must be formed from inorganic molecules.
2. The organic molecules must be collected together and segregated from other molecules by a membrane.
3. Collections of organic molecules must become self-sustaining by making new molecules as older ones are randomly destroyed.
4. Ultimately this first cellular unit must be able to reproduce more of itself.

BEFORE YOU
CONTINUE
READING

1. **According to the introduction, for life to form, organic molecules ____.**

   a. *must combine and be protected by an outer casing, must be able to make new molecules, and must be able to reproduce*

   b. *must be segregated from each other, must destroy each other, and must be able to produce something*

A THEORY OF THE FORMATION OF THE FIRST ORGANIC MOLECULES

2   In the 1920s, a Russian biochemist, Alexander I. Oparin, and a British biologist, J. B. S. Haldane, working independently, proposed that the first organic molecules were formed spontaneously in the reducing atmosphere thought to be present on the early Earth. The molecules of water vapor (H_2O), ammonia (NH_3), methane (CH_4), carbon dioxide (CO_2), and hydrogen (H_2) supplied the atoms of carbon, hydrogen, oxygen, and nitrogen, and lightning, heat from volcanoes, and ultraviolet radiation furnished the energy needed for the synthesis of simple organic molecules.

3   It is important to understand the significance of a reducing atmosphere to this theory. The absence of oxygen in the atmosphere would have allowed these organic molecules to remain and combine with one another. This does not happen today because organic molecules are either consumed by organisms or oxidized to simpler inorganic compounds in the atmosphere.

4   After these simple organic molecules were formed in the atmosphere, they probably would have been washed from the air and carried into the newly formed oceans by the rain. Here, the molecules could have reacted with one another to form the more complex molecules of simple sugars, amino acids, and nucleic acids. This accumulation is thought to have occurred over half a billion years, resulting in oceans that were a dilute organic soup. These simple organic molecules in the ocean served as the building materials for more complex organic macromolecules, such as complex carbohydrates, proteins, lipids, and nucleic acids. Recognize that all the ideas presented so far cannot be confirmed by direct observation because we cannot go back in time. However, we can test several of the assumptions that are central to this theory of the origin of life.

- ● Carbon
- ● Nitrogen
- ○ Oxygen
- ○ Hydrogen

Fig. 1.1h The formation of the first organic molecules

BEFORE YOU
CONTINUE
READING

2. The first, simple, organic molecules ___ .

a. *formed in an atmosphere that did not contain oxygen, then fell into the oceans, combined, and became more complex*

b. *formed in an oxygen atmosphere, combined and became more complex, then fell into the oceans*

TESTING THE THEORY

5   In 1953 Stanley L. Miller conducted an experiment to test the idea that organic molecules could be synthesized in a reducing environment. Miller constructed a simple model of the Earth's atmosphere. In a glass apparatus he placed distilled water to represent the early oceans. The reducing atmosphere was simulated by adding hydrogen, methane, and ammonia to the water. Electrical sparks provided the energy needed to produce organic compounds. By heating parts of the apparatus and cooling others, he simulated the rains that are thought to have fallen into the early oceans. After a week of operation, he removed some of the water from the apparatus. When this water was analyzed, it was found to contain many simple organic compounds. Although Miller demonstrated nonbiological synthesis of simple organic molecules like amino acids and simple sugars, his results did not account for complex organic molecules like proteins and DNA. However, other researchers produced some of the components of DNA under similar primitive conditions.

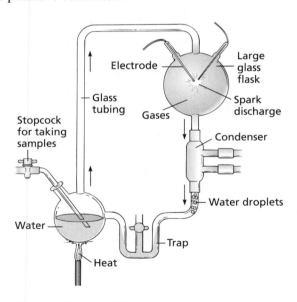

Fig. 1.1i Stanley Miller's experiment

3. **Stanley Miller tested whether organic molecules could be synthesized in a reducing environment. His experiment was only partly successful because it produced ____.**

   a. *both simple and complex organic molecules*

   b. *simple organic molecules but did not produce complex organic molecules*

EXPLANATIONS FOR THE CONCENTRATION OF SIMPLE ORGANIC MOLECULES

6   Several ideas have been proposed for the concentration of simple organic molecules and their combination into macromolecules (large molecules). A portion of the early ocean could have been separated from the main ocean by geologic changes. The evaporation of water from this pool could have concentrated the molecules, which might have led to the manufacture of macromolecules by dehydration synthesis. It has also been proposed that freezing may have been the means of concentration. When a mixture of alcohol and water is placed in a freezer, the water freezes solid and the alcohol becomes concentrated into a small portion of liquid. A similar process could have occurred on Earth's early surface, resulting in the concentration of simple organic molecules. In this concentrated solution, dehydration synthesis in a reducing atmosphere could have occurred, resulting in the formation of macromolecules. A third theory proposes that clay particles may have been a factor in concentrating simple organic molecules. Small particles of clay have electrical charges that can attract and concentrate organic molecules. Once the molecules became concentrated, it would have been easier for them to interact to form larger macromolecules.

Checking Comprehension

A **Read the following statements. Check the correct ones. Then compare these responses with your responses on pages 16–17. Discuss your answers as a class.**

1. ___ Organic molecules were formed, then inorganic molecules were formed.

2. ___ Inorganic molecules were formed, then organic molecules were formed.

3. ___ Inorganic molecules were formed in a number of stages.

4. ___ Organic molecules were formed in one big step.

5. ___ Organic molecules are still being formed today.

6. ___ Organic molecules are no longer being formed today.

7. ___ H_2O, O_3, CO_2, CH_4, NH_3, H_2, and O_2 are all inorganic molecules.

8. ___ H_2O, O_3, CO_2, CH_4, NH_3, H_2, and O_2 are all organic molecules.

How many of your predictions on pages 16–17 were correct? ___

B **Circle the correct answers.**

1. Why did Stanley L. Miller have to simulate (i.e., replicate) a reducing atmosphere in a glass apparatus in his laboratory?
   a. because a reducing atmosphere no longer exists on Earth
   b. because it would be difficult to conduct this experiment outside
   c. because he could create different molecules in the glass apparatus

2. What is the most important idea in paragraph 6 on page 22?
   a. Water in the ocean had to either freeze or evaporate to change the molecules.
   b. It was easy for simple organic molecules to combine and become larger.
   c. The simple organic molecules had to be concentrated so they could interact.

3. Examine the illustration below, and reread pages 15 and 19–22. Then answer the questions.

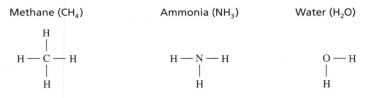

Methane (CH_4)   Ammonia (NH_3)   Water (H_2O)

1. How many atoms are in each of the following molecules?
   a. methane ___
   b. ammonia ___
   c. water ___

2. Can the atoms in these molecules recombine to form different materials? ___

C **Answer the following questions in complete sentences.**

1. What conditions made it possible for organic molecules to combine with each other?

_____

_____

_____

2. Organic molecules no longer combine with each other. Why?

_____

_____

_____

D Examine the flowchart below. Then answer the questions that follow.

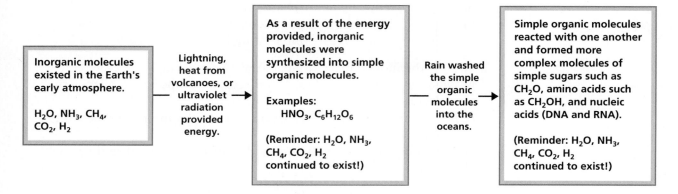

1. The best title for this flowchart is ____.
   a. The Beginning of Life in the Rain and the Oceans
   b. The Formation of Organic Molecules from Inorganic Molecules
   c. The Effects of Energy and Rain on Several Kinds of Atoms

2. Through all the stages of the process illustrated here, were any new atoms formed? ____

3. How many different **atoms** (_not_ molecules) are represented in the first box? ____

4. How many different atoms are represented in the center box? ____

5. How many different atoms are represented in the right-hand box? ____

6. From the time of the Earth's early atmosphere to the time that complex organic molecules first formed, were any atoms lost? ____

7. What happened to the atoms?
   a. All the atoms changed.
   b. Some of the atoms were destroyed.
   c. Some of the atoms recombined.

Learning Vocabulary

VOCABULARY FROM CONTEXT

Read the following paragraphs. Then circle the correct choice to complete the sentences after each paragraph.

1. When we study the simplest forms of life today, we find that they consist of an outer *membrane* that separates (seals off) the cell from its *surroundings*, genetic material in the form of nucleic acids (DNA or RNA), and many kinds of enzymes that control the activities of the cell. Therefore, when we *speculate* about the origin of life from inorganic material, it seems logical that several events or steps were necessary.

    (1) From this context, we can understand that an example of an outer *membrane* is ____.
    a. an outer cover, like skin
    b. an outer coating of hair, like an animal's fur
    c. an outside shell, like a clam shell

    (2) A living thing's *surroundings* are its ____.
    a. genetic material
    b. inner organs
    c. environment

    (3) When people *speculate*, they ____.
    a. are active
    b. make a guess
    c. try to control

2. After the simple organic molecules were formed in the atmosphere, they probably would have been washed from the air and carried into the newly formed oceans by the rain. Here, the molecules could have reacted with one another to form the more complex molecules of simple sugars, amino acids, and nucleic acids. This *accumulation* is thought to have occurred over half a billion years, resulting in oceans that were a dilute organic soup.

    From this context, and from the illustration on page 20, we can understand that *accumulate* means ____.
    a. build up together
    b. float in the water
    c. stay in one place

3. Organic molecules must be collected together and *segregated* from other molecules by a membrane.

    From this context, we can understand that *segregated* means ____.
    a. studied
    b. separated
    c. understood

4. Stanley Miller conducted an experiment to test the idea that organic molecules could be *synthesized* in a reducing environment. Miller constructed a simple model of the Earth's atmosphere (see the illustration on page 21). In a glass apparatus he placed distilled water to represent the early oceans. The reducing atmosphere was *simulated* by adding hydrogen, methane, and ammonia to the water. Electrical sparks provided the energy needed to produce organic compounds.

   (1) Miller tested the idea that organic molecules could be *synthesized* in a reducing environment. In other words, they could be ___.
   a. manufactured
   b. seen
   c. photographed

   (2) Miller *simulated* the reducing atmosphere by adding hydrogen, methane, and ammonia to the water in his glass apparatus. In other words, he ___ the process.
   a. showed
   b. analyzed
   c. imitated

5. A portion of the early ocean could have been separated from the main ocean by geologic changes. The *evaporation* of water from this pool could have concentrated the molecules, which might have led to the manufacture of macromolecules by *dehydration synthesis*.

   (1) From this context, we can understand that when a part of the ocean is separated into a pool of water, the *evaporation* of the water in the pool means that ___.
   a. the water froze
   b. the water dried up
   c. the water boiled

   (2) *Dehydration* refers to the process of ___.
   a. separation
   b. concentration
   c. evaporation

   (3) In this paragraph, a synonym for *synthesis* is ___.
   a. separation
   b. manufacture
   c. change

USING THE DICTIONARY

Remember that you can also use a dictionary to learn new words. Dictionary entries often have several definitions for a word, so you need to consider the context in order to figure out the appropriate definition.

Read the sentences and dictionary entries on the following page. Select the best entry for the context, and circle the correct choice to complete the sentences that follow.

1. After the simple organic molecules were formed in the atmosphere, they probably would have been washed from the air and carried into the newly formed oceans by the rain. Here, the molecules could have *reacted* with one another to form the more complex molecules of simple sugars, amino acids, and nucleic acids. This accumulation is thought to have occurred over half a billion years, resulting in oceans that were a dilute organic soup.

> **re•act** /ri'ækt/ *v.* [I] **1** to behave in a particular way because of something that has happened or something that has been said to you: *How did Dad react when he found out Vicky was pregnant?* | [**+ to**] *Residents reacted angrily to the city council's decision.* | [**react by doing sth**] *Parents reacted by setting up their own neighborhood watch.* —see also OVERREACT **2** to become sick when you take a particular drug, eat a particular kind of food etc.: [**+ to**] *The patient reacted badly to penicillin.* **3** TECHNICAL if a chemical substance reacts, it changes when it is mixed with another chemical substance: [**+ with/on**] *An acid reacts with a base to form a salt.* —compare RESPOND

   (1) In this context, the best definition of *react* is number ___.

   (2) The molecules ___ and formed more complex molecules.
   a. behaved in a particular way because something happened to them
   b. became sick when they ate a particular kind of food
   c. changed when they were mixed with other chemical substances

2. In the 1920s, a Russian biochemist, Alexander I. Oparin, and a British biologist, J. B. S. Haldane, working independently, proposed that the first organic molecules were formed *spontaneously* in the reducing atmosphere thought to be present on the early Earth.

> **spon•ta•ne•ous** /spɑn'teɪniəs/ *adj.* APPROVING **1** happening or done without being planned or organized: *The group was greeted by spontaneous applause.* **2** doing things when you want to, without planning or organizing them: *I'm trying to be more spontaneous.* —**spontaneously** *adv.* —**spontaneousness** *n.* [U]

   (1) In this context, the best definition of *spontaneous* is number ___.

   (2) Oparin and Haldane each proposed that the first organic molecules were formed ___.
   a. without being planned or organized
   b. because they wanted to be organized

3. Miller constructed a simple model of the Earth's atmosphere in a glass *apparatus*. After a week of operation, he removed some water from his *apparatus*. The water was found to contain many simple organic compounds.

> **ap•pa•rat•us** /ˌæpə'rætəs, -'reɪtəs/ *n.* plural **apparatus** or **apparatuses** [C,U] **1** a tool, machine, or set of equipment used especially for scientific, medical, or technical purposes: *The astronauts have special breathing apparatus.* | *This wooden apparatus was used for weaving.* **2** a system or process for doing something: *The East German security apparatus used these kinds of devices to overhear conversations.*

(1) In this context, the best definition of *apparatus* is number ___.

(2) Which of the following are examples of an apparatus? Make a check (✔).

a. ___ a microscope   **d.** ___ a calculator

b. ___ an eraser   **e.** ___ an electric pencil sharpener

c. ___ a dictionary   **f.** ___ a measuring cup

FOLLOW-UP ASSIGNMENTS

Before you begin any of the follow-up assignments, review the content-specific vocabulary and the academic vocabulary below. If you are still unsure what any words or terms mean, go back through the chapter and review. As you complete the assignments, be sure to incorporate the appropriate vocabulary in your writing.

Content-Specific Vocabulary

atmosphere	gravity	methane	oxygen
atom	helium	molecule	reducing atmosphere
the Big Bang	hydrogen	molten core	theory
carbon dioxide	inorganic	nitrogen	universe
crust	membrane	organic	
galaxy			

Academic Vocabulary

accumulate	formation	particle	simulate
analyze	fuse	primarily	speculate
combine	gas	propose	spontaneous
concentrate	hostile	react	surroundings
consist of	join	segregate	synthesize
evaporation	origin		

Writing Activities

1. Write a paragraph explaining how the first organic molecules were formed. Write in your own words, but use the vocabulary you have studied in this chapter.
2. Write a paragraph explaining the importance of the work of Alexander I. Oparin and J. B. S. Haldane.
3. Based on what you have read so far and on what you already know about the universe, write a paragraph in which you speculate on the possibility of life originating on other planets.

Extension Activities

1. Reread "The Beginning of the Universe and the Origin of the Earth" on pages 7–8. Complete the flowchart below.

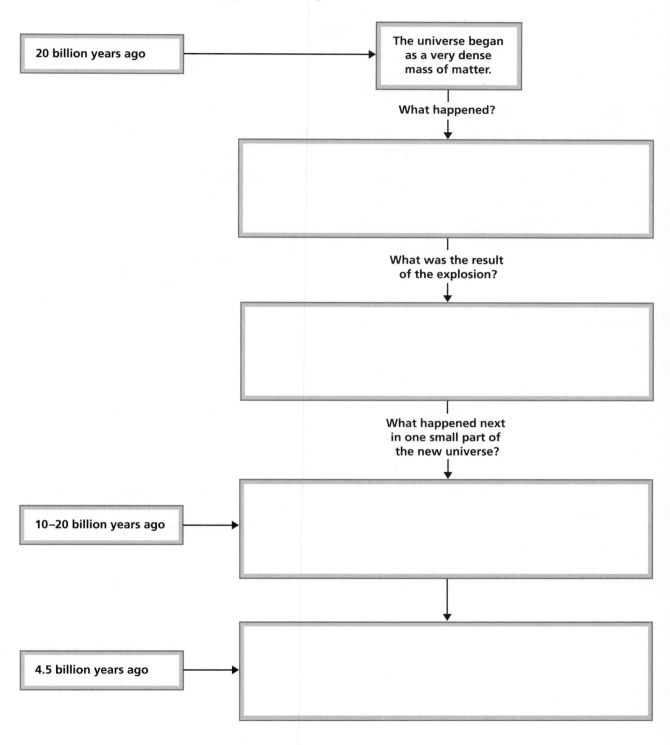

20 billion years ago

The universe began as a very dense mass of matter.

What happened?

What was the result of the explosion?

What happened next in one small part of the new universe?

10–20 billion years ago

4.5 billion years ago

2. Reread paragraphs 2, 3, and 4 on page 20, which describe how organic molecules were first formed. Label the illustration below to show the steps in the process.

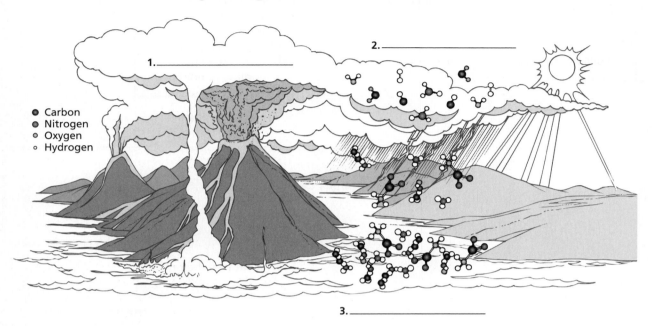

1. _____

2. _____

3. _____

● Carbon
● Nitrogen
○ Oxygen
○ Hydrogen

Fig. 1.1h The formation of the first organic molecules

Now describe the three main steps in the process by which organic molecules were formed.

1. _____

2. _____

3. _____

3. Reread page 21, then examine the illustration of Stanley Miller's experiment on the following page. The illustration shows how his apparatus simulated the conditions for the formation of organic molecules.

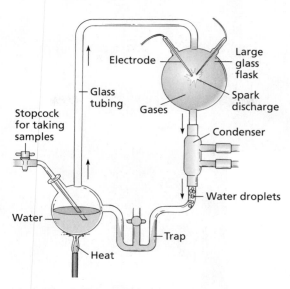

Fig 1.1i Stanley Miller's experiment

Now match the labels in the illustration above with the conditions that Miller was attempting to simulate.

a. _____: the Earth's early atmosphere

b. _____: the Earth's oceans

c. _____: energy from lightning or ultraviolet radiation

d. _____: rain

Internet Research

Go online, and go to one of the websites listed below. Investigate a topic related to the information you read about in Chapter 1. Choose a topic that especially interests you. Use some of the website's search features. Search by keywords such as *origins, Earth's origins, origin of life*.

National Aeronautics and Space Administration (NASA):
    http://www.nasa.gov
NASA's Jet Propulsion Laboratory:
    http://www.jpl.nasa.gov
NASA's Origins Program seeks to answer two questions: Where do we come from? Are we alone?
    http://origins.jpl.nasa.gov/science/science.html
Life in the Universe:
    http://www.lifeinuniverse.org/
American Museum of Natural History:
    http://www.amnh.org
Origins Education Forum:
    http://origins.stsci.edu/
New York Center for Studies on the Origins of Life:
    http://www.origins.rpi.edu/

CHAPTER 2

DEVELOPMENTS ON EARLY EARTH

Skills Goal

- *Review skills from Chapter 1.*

Content-Specific Goals

- *Learn about the origins of the Earth.*
- *Understand the origin of the Earth's oxygen atmosphere.*
- *Understand how the first living cells may have formed.*
- *Learn Alfred Wegener's theory of continental drift.*

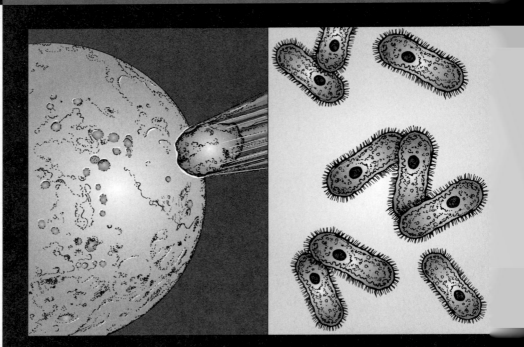

Fig. 1.2a An asteroid approaching ancient Earth; microbial life in water

Chapter Readings

The Formation of the First Living Cells

The Changing Shape of Our World: The Theory of Continental Drift

INTRODUCING THE READING

Activate Your Knowledge

A Work alone or in a small group. Answer the following questions. Do not worry if you do not know something. You will learn more as you work with the chapter.

1. How old is the Earth?
   a. 20 billion years old
   b. 10 billion years old
   c. 4.5 billion years old
   d. 3.8 billion years old

2. When did life begin?
   a. about 10 billion years ago
   b. about 4.5 billion years ago
   c. about 3.5 billion years ago
   d. about 2 billion years ago

B Discuss the following questions in a small group. Take notes on your ideas.

1. In a few sentences, describe how you think life probably began.

   _____

   _____

   _____

2. What are all living things made of?

   _____

   _____

3. What were the first life forms (organisms) like?

   _____

   _____

C Examine the illustrations below, and label the ones you know.

atom   cell   inorganic molecule   organic molecule

1. _____

Hydrogen (H)

2. _____

H_2O

Water

3. _____

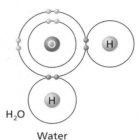

Glucose

4. _____

DNA

Reading and Study Skill Strategies

PREVIEW KEY VOCABULARY

Before you begin reading a passage, remember to examine the content-specific vocabulary that you will encounter. This practice helps you focus on the topic and judge the difficulty of the text you will read.

Read the list of content-specific vocabulary on the following page and check the ones you are familiar with. Leave the other spaces blank. Do not try to learn the unfamiliar items before you begin reading. You will learn them as you work with the chapter.

___ aerobic	___ fossil	___ Pangaea
___ atom	___ hypothesis	___ photosynthesis
___ cell	___ macromolecule	___ reducing atmosphere
___ continental drift	___ molecule	___ seafloor spreading
___ diversify	___ mutation	___ trench
___ evolution	___ organic	___ upwelling
___ extraterrestrial	___ oxidizing atmosphere	

USE TITLE AND HEADINGS TO PREDICT CONTENT

Remember that reading the title and headings before reading an entire passage gives you an overview of the material because the title introduces the topic of a passage, and the headings introduce the topic of each section within a passage.

A Before you work with the Introductory Reading on pages 36–37, go through it and write down the headings on the lines below.

The Formation of the First Living Cells

_____

_____

_____

B Read the following statements and check the ones that seem correct based on the title and headings. Then compare your answers with a classmate's. Keep in mind that you may not agree.

1. ___ The first life on Earth was probably a simple cell.

2. ___ The first life on Earth was probably a simple animal.

3. ___ We are sure how life on Earth originated.

4. ___ We may never know for sure how life on Earth originated.

5. ___ Once life began to exist, it did not change very much.

6. ___ Once life began to exist, it changed considerably.

7. ___ Life began, and then an atmosphere with oxygen developed.

8. ___ An atmosphere with oxygen developed, and then life began.

C Go to page *iv* in the Table of Contents. Read the brief summary of the Introductory Reading. Then review the statements above, and decide whether to change any of your predictions.

INTRODUCTORY READING

The following reading, "The Formation of the First Living Cells," is also from Concepts in Biology. *As you read, highlight the important ideas and vocabulary used to express those ideas. Monitor your comprehension by answering the Before You Continue Reading questions that follow each section. If you have trouble answering a question, reread the section before you continue reading.*

The Formation of the First Living Cells

1   Geologists and biologists typically measure the history of life by looking back from the present. Therefore, time scales are given in "years ago." It has been estimated that the formation of simple organic molecules in the atmosphere began about 4 billion years ago and lasted approximately 1.5 billion years. The oldest known fossils of living cells are thought to have formed 3.5 billion years ago.

Fig. 1.2b A primitive cell

HOW LIFE ON EARTH ORIGINATED

2   Fossil evidence indicates that there were primitive forms of life on Earth about 3.5 billion years ago. Several theories have been proposed for the formation of nonliving structures that led to the formation of the first living cells. However, you should understand that we do not know how life on Earth originated. Scientists look at many kinds of evidence and continue to explore new avenues of research. We currently have two competing theories for the origin of life on Earth:

> **1.** Life arrived from some extraterrestrial source.
> **2.** Life originated on Earth.

No matter how life originated on Earth, simple life forms evolved and changed, not only themselves, but even the nature of the Earth itself.

> **BEFORE YOU CONTINUE READING**
>
> **1. No one knows how life originated on Earth, but it is clear that ____.**
>
> **a.** *life originated from nonliving materials*
>
> **b.** *life required oxygen for breathing*
>
> **c.** *life took 3.5 billion years*

MAJOR EVOLUTIONARY CHANGES IN THE NATURE OF LIVING THINGS

3   Once living things existed and had a genetic material that stored information but was changeable (mutational), living things could have proliferated into a variety of kinds that were adapted to specific environmental conditions. Remember that the Earth has not been static but has been changing as a result of its cooling, volcanic activity, and encounters with asteroids. In addition, the organisms have had an impact on the way in which the Earth has

developed. Regardless of the way in which life originated on Earth, there have been several major events in the subsequent evolution of living things.

BEFORE YOU CONTINUE READING

2. **Living things** ____.

   a. *caused the Earth to cool*

   b. *changed due to volcanic activity*

   c. *affected the way the Earth has developed*

THE DEVELOPMENT OF AN OXIDIZING ATMOSPHERE

4   Ever since its formation, Earth has undergone constant (continuous) change. In the beginning, it was too hot to support an atmosphere. Later, as it cooled and as gases escaped from volcanoes, a reducing atmosphere (an atmosphere lacking oxygen) was likely to have been formed. The early life forms would have lived in this reducing atmosphere. However, today we have an oxidizing atmosphere and most organisms use this oxygen as a way to extract energy from organic molecules through a process of aerobic respiration, that is, breathing air. But what caused the atmosphere to change?

5   Today it is clear that the oxygen in our atmosphere is the result of the process of photosynthesis. *Prokaryotic Cyanobacteria* are the simplest organisms that are able to photosynthesize, so it seems logical that the first organisms could have accumulated many mutations (changes) over time that could have resulted in photosynthetic organisms. One of the waste products of the process of photosynthesis is molecular oxygen (O_2). This would have been a significant change because it would have led to the development of an *oxidizing atmosphere,* which contains molecular oxygen. The development of an oxidizing atmosphere created an environment unsuitable for the formation of organic molecules. Organic molecules tend to break down (oxidize) when oxygen is present. The presence of oxygen in the atmosphere would make it impossible for life to spontaneously originate in the manner described on pages 20–22 in Chapter 1 because an oxidizing atmosphere would not allow the accumulation of organic molecules in the seas. However, new life is generated through reproduction, and new kinds of life are generated through mutation and evolution. The presence of oxygen in the atmosphere had one other important outcome: it opened the door for the evolution of aerobic (air breathing) organisms.

6   It appears that an oxidizing atmosphere began to develop about 2 billion years ago. Although various chemical reactions released small amounts of molecular oxygen into the atmosphere, it was photosynthesis that generated most of the oxygen. The oxygen molecules also reacted with one another to form ozone (O_3). Ozone collected in the upper atmosphere and acted as a screen to prevent most of the ultraviolet light from reaching Earth's surface. The reduction of ultraviolet light diminished the spontaneous formation of complex organic molecules. It also reduced the number of mutations in cells. In an oxidizing atmosphere, it was no longer possible for organic molecules to accumulate over millions of years to be later incorporated into living material. The appearance of oxygen in the atmosphere also allowed for the evolution of aerobic respiration. Because of this development, life on Earth was able to spread to the land, and to diversify into many thousands of different species.

Checking Comprehension

A Review your labels for the four illustrations on page 34. Revise them if necessary.

B Read the following statements and check the correct ones. Then compare these responses with your responses on page 35. Discuss your answers as a class.

1. ___ The first life on Earth was probably a simple cell.

2. ___ The first life on Earth was probably a simple animal.

3. ___ We are sure how life on Earth originated.

4. ___ We may never know for sure how life on Earth originated.

5. ___ Once life began to exist, it did not change very much.

6. ___ Once life began to exist, it changed considerably.

7. ___ Life began, and then an atmosphere with oxygen developed.

8. ___ An atmosphere with oxygen developed, and then life began.

How many of your predictions on page 35 were correct? ___

C Circle the correct answers.

1. When the Earth formed and began to cool, did it have an atmosphere containing molecular oxygen? Yes/No

2. Were the first living organisms air breathing (aerobic)? ___

3. What created the Earth's oxygen atmosphere?
   a. living organisms
   b. volcanic activity
   c. lightning

4. The first organisms needed a source of energy in order to live. They acquired this energy through the process of photosynthesis. Photosynthesis is the ability to convert sunlight into chemical energy in the form of sugar (carbohydrates). You will recall that a simple sugar is CH_2O. When photosynthesis takes place, it produces both a simple sugar and free oxygen (O_2).

   (1) Examine the following formulas. Which one is the process of photosynthesis?
   a. CO_2 + H_2O + light energy $\longrightarrow$ CH_2O + O_2
   b. NH_3 + O_3 + light energy $\longrightarrow$ NH + HO_3
   c. CH_4 + CO_2 + light energy $\longrightarrow$ C_2H_2 + H_2 + O_2

   (2) What do you observe about the process of photosynthesis?
   a. When the atoms react with light energy, some of the atoms are lost.
   b. When the atoms react with light energy, new atoms are created.
   c. When the atoms react with light energy, none of the atoms are lost.

D **Answer the following questions in complete sentences.**

1. How did the Earth's oxygen atmosphere develop?

   _____

   _____

   _____

2. Once an oxygen atmosphere had developed, what process was no longer possible? Why?

   _____

   _____

Learning Vocabulary

VOCABULARY FROM CONTEXT

Read the sentences below. Use the context to figure out the meaning of the italicized words. Then circle the correct choice to complete the sentences. Then circle the reason for your choice.

1. The reduction of ultraviolet light *diminished* the spontaneous formation of complex organic molecules. It also reduced the number of mutations in cells.

   (1) In this context, the synonym for *diminish* is the word ___.
   a. form
   b. mutate
   c. reduce

   (2) How did you figure out what *diminish* means?
   a. The sentence discusses ultraviolet light.
   b. The sentence discusses spontaneous formation.
   c. The sentence discusses reduction.

2. The Earth has not been *static* but has been changing as a result of its cooling, volcanic activity, and encounters with asteroids. In addition, organisms have had an *impact* on the way in which the Earth has developed.

   (1) From this context, we can understand that *static* means ___.
   a. changing
   b. unchanging

   (2) From this context, we can understand that *impact* means ___.
   a. collision
   b. influence
   c. encounter

3. As the Earth cooled and as gases escaped from volcanoes, a reducing atmosphere (an atmosphere *lacking* oxygen) was likely to have been formed. The early life forms would have lived in this reducing atmosphere. However, today we have an oxidizing atmosphere and most organisms use this oxygen as a way to extract energy from organic molecules through a process of aerobic respiration.

An atmosphere which *lacks* oxygen ___.
a. has oxygen
b. does not have oxygen
c. is forming today

4. The appearance of oxygen in the atmosphere also allowed for the evolution of *aerobic* respiration, that is, breathing air. Because of this development, life on Earth was able to spread to the land, and to *diversify* into many thousands of different species.

(1) From this context, we can understand that *aerobic* refers to ___.
a. exercise
b. evolution
c. air

(2) How did you figure out what *aerobic* means?
a. *Aerobic* is followed by *that is,* which explains the preceding word.
b. Aerobic respiration was a new development for life on Earth.
c. Life on Earth diversified into many different species.

(3) From this context, we can understand that *diversify* means ___.
a. travel
b. spread
c. change

5. Once living things existed and had a genetic material that stored information but was changeable (*mutational*), living things could have proliferated into a variety of kinds that were adapted to specific environmental conditions. Prokaryotic Cyanobacteria are the simplest organisms that are able to photosynthesize, so it seems logical that the first organisms could have accumulated many *mutations* (changes) over time that could have resulted in photosynthetic organisms.

From these contexts, we can understand that a *mutation* is a type of ___.
a. simple organism
b. environmental condition
c. change

USING THE DICTIONARY

Remember that using a dictionary can help you learn new words. Sometimes an entry has only one definition. In such cases, read the definition for that specific meaning. When an entry has more than one definition, consider the context to figure out the appropriate definition.

Read the following sentences and dictionary entries. Select the best entry for the context, and circle the correct choice to complete the sentences that follow.

1. We currently have two competing theories for the origin of life on Earth:

   (1) Life arrived from some *extraterrestrial* source.

   (2) Life originated on Earth.

   No matter how life originated on Earth, simple life forms *evolved* and changed, not only themselves, but even the nature of the Earth itself.

   > **ex·tra·ter·res·tri·al**[1] /ˌɛkstrətə'rɛstriəl/ *n.* [C] a living creature that people think may live on another planet
   >
   > **extraterrestrial**[2] *adj.* relating to things that do not come from Earth or do not exist or happen on Earth: *extraterrestrial exploration*

   > **e·volve** /ɪ'vɑlv/ *v.* [I,T] to develop by gradually changing, or to make something do this: [**+ from/into**] *SuperMart was a small family store that evolved into a national supermarket chain.*

   (1) *Extraterrestrial* has two dictionary entries, one for use as a noun and one for use as an adjective. The best definition for this context is (entry) number ___.

   (2) According to the first theory, ___.
   a. living creatures from another planet were the first life on Earth
   b. things such as organic molecules came to Earth from somewhere else

   (3) Once life originated, simple life forms *evolved*. This means that they ___.
   a. changed gradually
   b. changed because someone made them

2. Once living things existed and had a genetic material that stored information but was changeable (mutational), living things could have *proliferated* into a variety of kinds that were adapted to specific environmental conditions.

   > **pro·lif·er·ate** /prə'lɪfəˌreɪt/ *v.* [I] if something proliferates, it increases rapidly and spreads to many different places: *Fast-food restaurants have proliferated in the area.*

   After reading the dictionary, it is clear that living things ___.
   a. increased rapidly, but stayed in the same environment
   b. increased rapidly, and moved to a variety of environments

INTRODUCING THE MAIN READING

Activate Your Knowledge

Work alone or in a small group. Answer the following questions.

1. Examine the map of the world. What do you notice about the shapes of South America and Africa? Why do you think they are shaped this way?

_____

_____

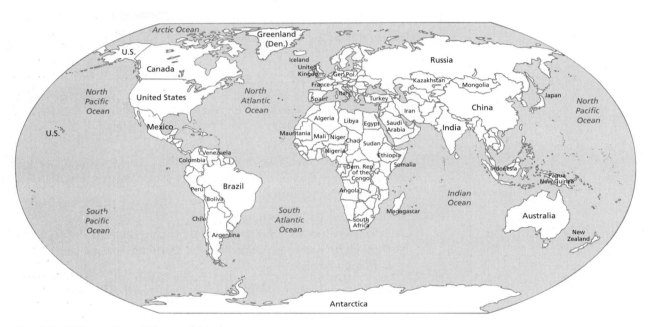

Fig. 1.2c Illustration of the world today

2. Antarctica is the coldest place on Earth and is covered by very thick ice. However, scientists have found fossils of extinct animals and tropical plants on Antarctica. Why do you think the fossils are there?

_____

_____

3. Cynognathus and mesosaurus are reptiles that lived between 285 million and 250 million years ago. Scientists have found the fossils of these animals in both South America and Africa. Why do you think these fossils are in both places?

_____

_____

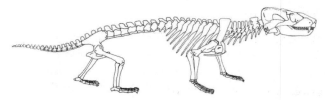

Fig. 1.2d Skeleton of Cynognathus

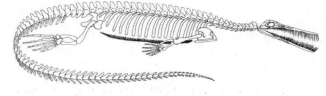

Fig. 1.2e Skeleton of Mesosaurus

Reading and Study Skill Strategies

USE TITLE AND HEADINGS TO PREDICT CONTENT

A Before you work with the Main Reading on pages 44–47, go through it and write down the headings on the lines below.

<u>**The Changing Shape of Our World: The Theory of**</u>

<u>**Continental Drift**</u>

_____

_____

_____

_____

B Read the following statements and check the ones that seem correct based on the title and headings. Then compare your answers with a classmate's. Keep in mind that you may not agree.

1. ___ The Earth has been changing and continues to change.

2. ___ The Earth changed in the past but does not change anymore.

3. ___ Someone named Wegener proposed the theory of continental drift.

4. ___ Someone proposed the theory of continental drift; we do not know who.

5. ___ Wegener had some support for his theory.

6. ___ Wegener had little or no support for his theory.

7. ___ Wegener's theory was accepted with little opposition.

8. ___ Wegener's theory was met with opposition.

9. ___ The concept of seafloor spreading is a theory that Wegener did not accept.

10. ___ The concept of seafloor spreading is a theory that Wegener did not propose.

C Go to page *iv* in the Table of Contents. Read the brief summary of the Main Reading. Then review the statements above, and decide whether to change any of your predictions.

MAIN READING

The Main Reading, "The Changing Shape of Our World: The Theory of Continental Drift," is from Conceptual Physical Science. *As you read, highlight the important ideas and the vocabulary used to express those ideas. Monitor your comprehension by answering the Before You Continue Reading questions that follow each section. If you have trouble answering a question, reread the section before you continue.*

The Changing Shape of Our World: The Theory of Continental Drift

1   Scientists of the early 20th century believed that oceans and continents were geographically fixed. They regarded the surface of the planet as a static skin spread over a molten, gradually cooling interior. They believed that the cooling of the planet resulted in its contraction, which caused the outer skin to contort and wrinkle into mountains and valleys. Many people noticed, however, that the eastern shorelines of South America and the western shoreline of Africa seemed to fit together like a jigsaw puzzle.

WEGENER'S THEORY

2   One scientist who took this observation seriously was Alfred Wegener, who saw the Earth as a dynamic planet with the continents in constant motion. He believed that all the continents had once been joined together in one great supercontinent he called **Pangaea**, meaning "all land." His hypothesis was that Pangaea had fractured into a number of pieces, and that South America and Africa had indeed once been joined together as part of a larger landmass.

Fig. 1.2f When Gondwanaland and Laurasia collided in the late Paleozoic Era (about 200 million years ago), the supercontinent Pangaea was formed.

BEFORE YOU
CONTINUE
READING

1. **The main idea of the first two paragraphs is ____.**

   a. *Wegener noticed what other scientists noticed and developed a theory to explain these observations*

   b. *early twentieth-century scientists agreed with Wegener's theory that the continents moved*

   c. *Wegener observed the continents and developed a theory to explain how mountains were formed*

SUPPORT FOR WEGENER'S THEORY

3   Wegener supported his hypothesis with impressive geological, biological, and climatological evidence. He proposed that the geological boundary of each continent lay not at its shoreline but at the edge of its *continental shelf* (the gently sloping platform between the shoreline and the steep slope that leads to the deep ocean floor). When Wegener fit Africa and South America together along their continental shelves, the fit was even better than it was at the shorelines. Furthermore, rocks on different continents that are brought into juxtaposition when the continental shelves are matched up are virtually identical. In addition, many of the mountain systems in Africa and South America show strong evidence of a previous connection. Similarly, fossils of identical land-dwelling animals are found in South America and Africa but nowhere else. And fossils of identical trees are found in South America, India, Australia, and Antarctica.

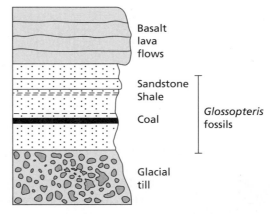

Basalt
lava
flows

Sandstone
Shale

Glossopteris
fossils

Coal

Glacial
till

Fig. 1.2g Similar layers of rock

BEFORE YOU
CONTINUE
READING

2. **Name the three types of evidence Wegener gave in support of his theory of continental drift.**

   a. _____

   b. _____

   c. _____

CRITICISM OF WEGENER'S THEORY

4   Wegener described continental drift in *The Origin of Continents and Oceans,* published in 1915. Although he used evidence from different scientific disciplines, his well-founded hypothesis was ridiculed by the community of Earth scientists. Antagonists complained that Wegener failed to provide a suitable driving force to account for the continental movements. (Wegener wrongly proposed that the tidal influence of the Moon could produce the needed force. He also proposed that the continents broke through the Earth's crust like ice breakers cutting through ice.) Without a convincing explanation for his theory, the scientific community of the early part of the 20th century was not ready to believe that the continents had drifted to their present position. It is only recently, with new-found discoveries, that Wegener's concept has become accepted.

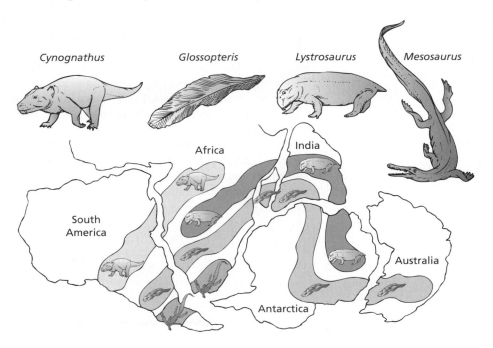

Fig. 1.2h Distribution of fossils across the southern continents of Pangaea

BEFORE YOU CONTINUE READING

3. **The community of Earth scientists rejected Wegener's hypothesis of continental drift because ____.**

   a. *he could not explain what could make the continents move*

   b. *he used evidence from different scientific disciplines*

   c. *he said the Earth had been covered in ice*

THE CONCEPT OF SEAFLOOR SPREADING

5   The 1950s were a time of extensive and detailed mapping of ocean floors. Topographic features revealed huge mountain ranges running down the middle of the Atlantic, Pacific, and Indian Oceans; a major rift valley along each crest; and deep ocean trenches near some of the continental landmasses, particularly around the edges of the Pacific. So, some of the deepest parts of the ocean are actually near some of the continents, and out in the middle of the oceans the water is relatively shallow because of the underwater mountains. Volcanism and high thermal energies were found to be generated at the ridge systems. With this new information, H. H. Hess, an American geologist, presented the hypothesis of **seafloor spreading**. Hess proposed that the seafloor is not permanent but is constantly being renewed. He theorized that the ocean ridges are located above upwelling convection cells in the mantle. As rising material from the mantle oozes upward, new lithosphere is formed. The old lithosphere is simultaneously destroyed in the deep ocean trenches near the edges of continents. Thus in a conveyor belt fashion new lithosphere forms at a spreading center, and older lithosphere is pushed from the ridge crest to be eventually recycled back into the mantle at a deep ocean trench.

6   The theory of seafloor spreading provided a mechanism for continental drift. The time was right for the revolutionary concepts to follow. The tide of scientific opinion had indeed switched in favor of a mobile Earth.

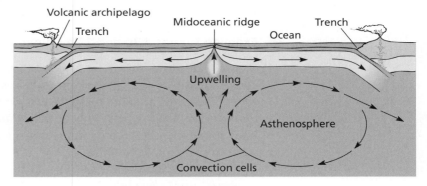

Fig. 1.2i The mechanics of seafloor spreading

Checking Comprehension

A Read the following statements. Check the correct ones. Then compare these responses with your responses on page 43.

1. ___ The Earth has been changing and continues to change.

2. ___ The Earth changed in the past but does not change anymore.

3. ___ Someone named Wegener proposed the theory of continental drift.

4. ___ Someone proposed the theory of continental drift; we do not know who.

5. ___ Wegener had some support for his theory.

6. ___ Wegener had little or no support for his theory.

7. ___ Wegener's theory was accepted with little opposition.

8. ___ Wegener's theory was met with opposition.

9. ___ The concept of seafloor spreading is a theory that Wegener did not accept.

10. ___ The concept of seafloor spreading is a theory that Wegener did not propose.

How many of your predictions on page 43 were correct? ___

B **Circle the correct answers.**

1. When Wegener published his theory, other scientists rejected it. What discovery would have persuaded scientists to accept Wegener's theory of continental drift?
   a. The discovery of more of the same plants and animals on different continents.
   b. The discovery that the Earth's crust was breakable.
   c. The discovery of a force powerful enough to move continents.

2. How does the concept of seafloor spreading support Wegener's theory?
   a. Seafloor spreading answered the question of how the continents were able to move.
   b. Seafloor spreading happened in the past but does not occur today.
   c. Seafloor spreading pushed animal fossils onto different continents.

C **Examine Figures 1.2g and 1.2h on pages 45–46.**

1. Figure 1.2g shows several layers of different types of rock, and some layers contain fossils of the same plant, *Glossopteris*. Similar layers in the same order, and with the same fossils, were found on continents that today are thousands of miles apart. This evidence indicates that ___.
   a. at some time in the past, these continents were connected, like pieces from the same layer cake
   b. there are many similarities in nature, both with rocks and plants, that occur simply by chance
   c. all continents are always made up of the same rocks layered in the same order

2. Figure 1.2h shows five continents drawn together. Today these continents are thousands of miles apart. Who probably first made a drawing of these five continents showing them connected?
   a. a critic of Alfred Wegener
   b. H. H. Hess
   c. Alfred Wegener

3. Today Antarctica is the coldest place on Earth. Fossils of *Lystrosaurus* and of *Glossopteris* have been found on Antarctica. What conclusion can we draw from these findings?
   a. *Lystrosaurus* and *Glossopteris* were able to survive in an extremely cold environment.
   b. The climate of Antarctica must have been much warmer in the past.
   c. Some of these fossils fell into the sea and washed onto the coastline of Antarctica.

4. The fossils of *Lystrosaurus* and of *Glossopteris* are examples of ___.
   a. biological evidence
   b. climatological evidence
   c. geological evidence
   d. biological and climatological evidence
   e. biological and geological evidence

D Read paragraph 3 on page 45 carefully. Wegener used three types of evidence to support his theory of continental drift. What examples did he give for each type of evidence? Keep in mind that his examples may support more than one kind of evidence. Use the diagram below to help you organize the information.

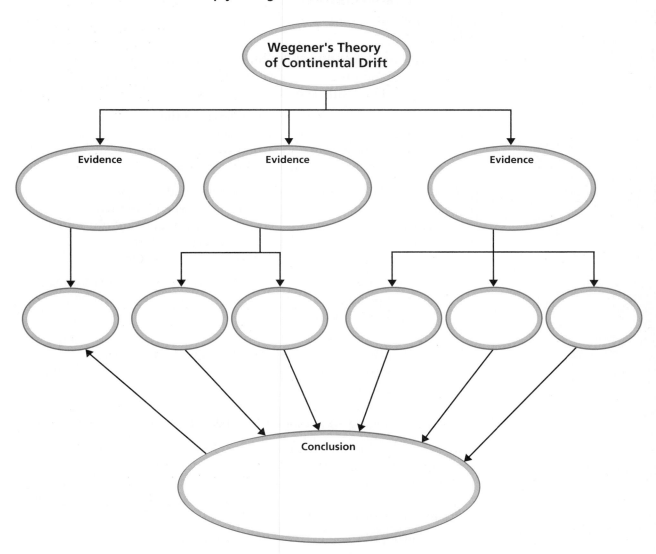

E **Answer the following question in complete sentences.**

Do you think that Wegener's supporting evidence was convincing? Explain your reasons for your answer.

_____

_____

_____

Learning Vocabulary

VOCABULARY FROM CONTEXT

Read the following sentences. Then circle the correct choice to complete them.

1. *Fossils* of identical land-dwelling animals are found in South America and Africa but nowhere else. And *fossils* of identical trees are found in South America, India, Australia, and Antarctica.

   From this context we can understand that a *fossil* is ___.
   a. a picture of an ancient plant or animal
   b. the place where an ancient plant or animal lived
   c. the remains of an ancient plant or animal

2. Wegener believed that all the continents had once been joined together in one great supercontinent he called **Pangaea**, meaning "all land." His hypothesis was that Pangaea had *fractured* into a number of pieces, and that South America and Africa had indeed once been joined together as part of a larger landmass.

   (1) From this context, we can understand that *fractured* means ___.
   a. broken up
   b. pulled together
   c. looked like

   (2) How did you figure out the meaning of *fractured*?
   a. Pangaea was made up of all the continents joined together.
   b. Pangaea was one supercontinent that became a number of different pieces.
   c. Pangaea started out as a single continent.

3. When Wegener fit Africa and South America together along their continental shelves, the fit was even better than it was at the shorelines. Furthermore, rocks on different continents that are *brought into juxtaposition* when the continental shelves are matched up are virtually identical.

   From this context, we can understand that *brought into juxtaposition* means ___.
   a. put next to each other
   b. carefully examined
   c. forced to fit

4. Hess proposed that the seafloor is not permanent but is constantly being renewed. He theorized that the ocean ridges are located above *upwelling* convection cells in the mantle. As rising material from the mantle oozes upward, new lithosphere is formed.

   (1) From these sentences, we can understand that *upwelling* means
   ____.
   a. being located
   b. moving up
   c. slowly forming

   (2) In these sentences, a synonym for *upwelling* is the word ____.
   a. rising
   b. renewing
   c. oozing

USING THE DICTIONARY

Read the following sentences and dictionary entries. Select the most appropriate entry for the context, and circle the correct choice to complete the sentences that follow.

1. Alfred Wegener saw the Earth as a *dynamic* planet with the continents in constant motion. He believed that all the continents had once been joined together in one great supercontinent he called **Pangaea**, meaning "all land." His hypothesis was that Pangaea had fractured into a number of pieces.

   > **dy·nam·ic** /daɪˈnæmɪk/ *adj.* **1** full of energy and new ideas, and determined to succeed: *a dynamic young businesswoman* **2** continuously moving or changing: *Markets are dynamic and a company must learn to adapt.* **3** TECHNICAL relating to a force or power that causes movement **–dynamically** /-kli/ *adv.*

   (1) In this context, the best definition of *dynamic* is number ____.

   (2) Wegener believed that the Earth was a planet ____.
   a. full of energy and new ideas
   b. that was continuously changing
   c. that caused movement

2. Hess theorized that the ocean ridges are located above upwelling convection cells in the mantle. As rising material from the mantle oozes upward, new lithosphere is formed. The old lithosphere is simultaneously destroyed in the deep ocean *trenches* near the edges of continents. Thus new lithosphere forms at a spreading center, and older lithosphere is pushed down, to be eventually recycled back into the mantle at a deep ocean *trench*.

> **trench** /trɛntʃ/ *n.* [C] **1** a long narrow hole dug into the surface of the ground: *Workers dug a trench for gas lines.* **2** TECHNICAL a long narrow valley in the ground beneath the ocean: *the Puerto Rico Trench* **3** [C usually plural] a deep trench dug in the ground as a protection for soldiers: *the fighting men in the trenches of France* **4 the trenches** the place or situation where most of the work or action in an activity takes place: *Tobias spent 35 years **in the trenches** of the feminist movement.*

(1) In this context, the best definition of *trench* is number ___.

(2) The *trench* in the illustration below is ___.
    a. a long narrow hole dug into the surface of the ground
    b. a trench dug to protect soldiers
    c. a long narrow valley in the ground beneath the ocean

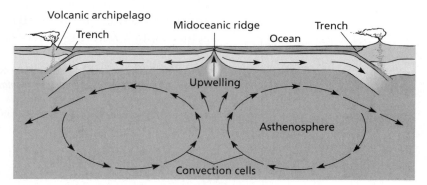

Fig. 1.2i The mechanics of seafloor spreading

FOLLOW-UP ASSIGNMENTS

Before you begin any of the follow-up assignments, review the content-specific vocabulary and the academic vocabulary below. If you are still unsure what any words or terms mean, go back through the chapter and review. As you complete the assignments, be sure to incorporate the appropriate vocabulary in your writing.

Content-Specific Vocabulary

aerobic	extraterrestrial	organic	reducing
atom	fossil	oxidizing	atmosphere
cell	hypothesis	atmosphere	seafloor
continental drift	macromolecule	Pangaea	spreading
diversify	molecule	photosynthesis	trench
evolution	mutation		upwelling

Academic Vocabulary

concept	dynamic	fractured	originate
constant	evidence	impact	proliferate
develop	fixed	influence	static
diminish	formation	lack	theorize

Writing Activities

1. Review the description of seafloor spreading on page 47 and examine the accompanying illustration. Write a paragraph describing seafloor spreading.
2. The Earth has always been a changing planet. Write two paragraphs. In the first paragraph, describe how you think the Earth may change over the next several hundred million years. In the second paragraph, explain why you think so.
3. In the early twentieth century, scientists believed that oceans and continents were geographically fixed. Write a paragraph explaining why these scientists might have thought that the oceans and continents did not move.

Extension Activities

1. Reread the passage on page 37, which describes the development of an oxidizing atmosphere and the evolution of the first living cells. Complete the flowchart on the following page.

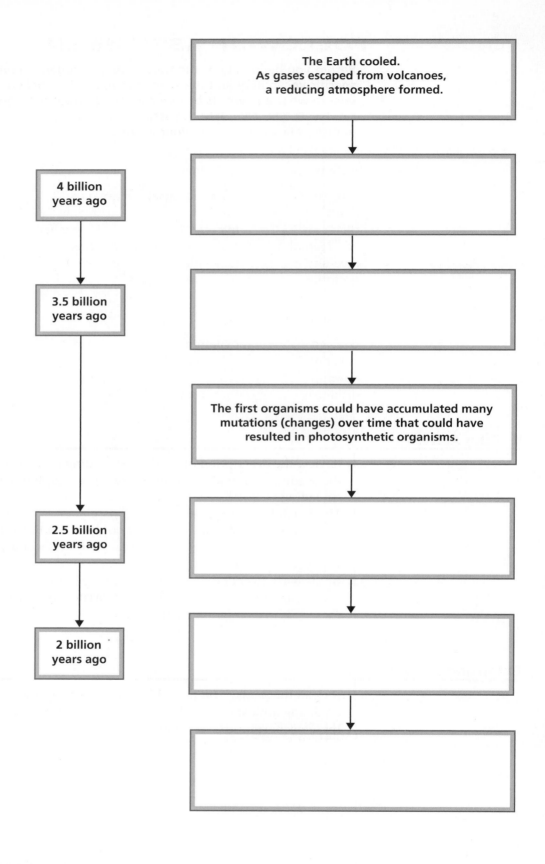

2. Reread paragraph 6 on page 37. Examine the illustration below. Use the illustration and the information in paragraph 6 to describe how life on Earth began, developed, and diversified into many thousands of different species. Write in your own words, but use the content-specific and academic vocabulary you have learned in this chapter.

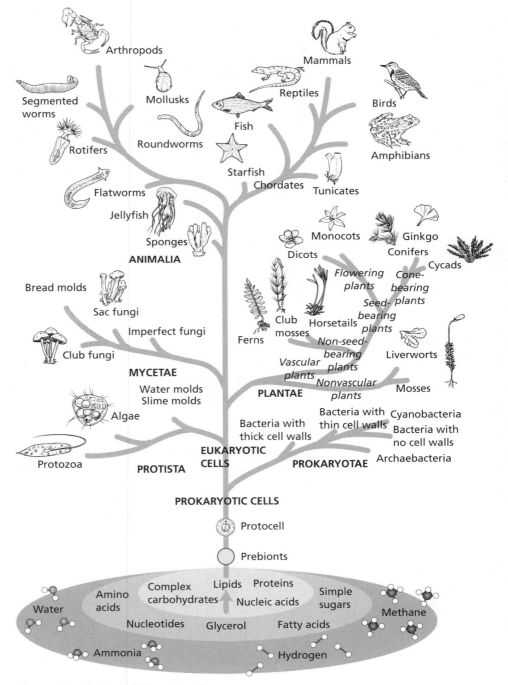

Fig. 1.2j Evolution of life on Earth

3. Examine the illustration below. Describe how the landmass on the Earth changed over the past 250 million years. Write in your own words, but use the content-specific and academic vocabulary you have learned in this chapter.

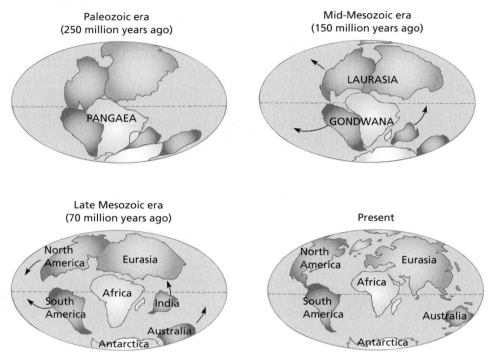

Fig. 1.2k

4. Reread the description of seafloor spreading on page 47, and examine the illustrations on the next page. Describe some of the consequences of seafloor spreading that are not mentioned in the reading. For example, how does seafloor spreading affect the size of the ocean? How does it affect the continents on either side? Where are earthquakes and volcanic eruptions most likely to occur?

Fig. 1.2l The Earth's surface, showing the world's ocean floors

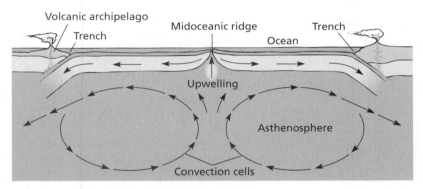

Fig. 1.2i The mechanics of seafloor spreading

Internet Research

Go online, and go to one of the websites listed below. Investigate a topic related to the information you read about in Chapter 2. Choose a topic that especially interests you. Use some of the website's search features. Search by keywords such as *Alfred Wegener, Harry Hess, continental drift, seafloor mapping, seafloor spreading, Pangaea, origins of life.*

Web page about Alfred Wegener's life and work:
   http://www.pangaea.org/wegener.htm
University of California, Berkeley Museum of Paleontology:
   http://www.ucmp.berkeley.edu
Public Broadcasting System's web page:
   http://www.pbs.org (Use PBS's Search feature.)
University of California, Berkeley's web page about continental drift:
   http://www.ucmp.berkeley.edu/geology/anim1.html
eLibrary's encyclopedia's web page:
   http://www.encyclopedia.com/ (Use the Search feature.)

WHERE DID WE COME FROM?

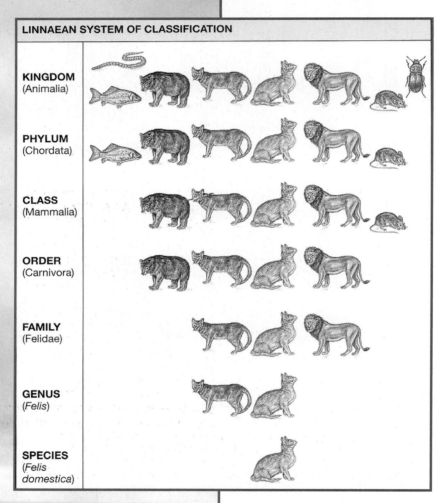

LINNAEAN SYSTEM OF CLASSIFICATION

KINGDOM
(Animalia)

PHYLUM
(Chordata)

CLASS
(Mammalia)

ORDER
(Carnivora)

FAMILY
(Felidae)

GENUS
(Felis)

SPECIES
(*Felis domestica*)

Fig. 2.0 A sample of Linnaeus's classification system

CHAPTER 3

THE NATURE OF LIFE

Skills Goals

- *Review skills from Chapters 1 and 2.*
- *Use font styles to identify and learn key vocabulary.*

Content-Specific Goals

- *Understand the Linnaean classification system.*
- *Learn the concept of evolution.*
- *Learn the theory of natural selection.*
- *Understand relationships among primates.*
- *Learn about the evolution of Homo sapiens.*
- *Learn early hominid achievements.*

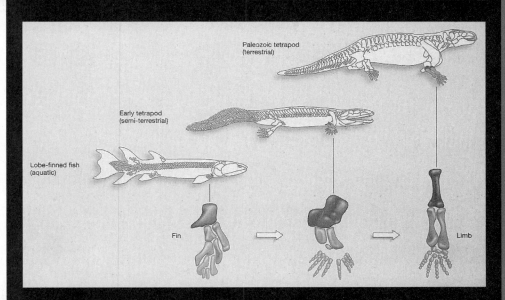

Lobe-finned fish (aquatic)

Early tetrapod (semi-terrestrial)

Paleozoic tetrapod (terrestrial)

Fin

Limb

Fig. 2.3a The evolution of the limb, showing analogous bone structure of a lobe-finned fish, an early four-legged animal, and a paleozoic four-legged animal

Chapter Readings

The Classification of Life: A Historical Overview

The Role of Natural Selection in Evolution

INTRODUCING THE READING

Activate Your Knowledge

A **Work with a partner or in a small group. Do the following activities.**

1. Think about how you would classify all the animals on Earth. What characteristics would you use to group animals into specific categories? Use the concept map below to help you organize the various ways you might classify animals. Add to the chart as you think of more ways to classify animals.

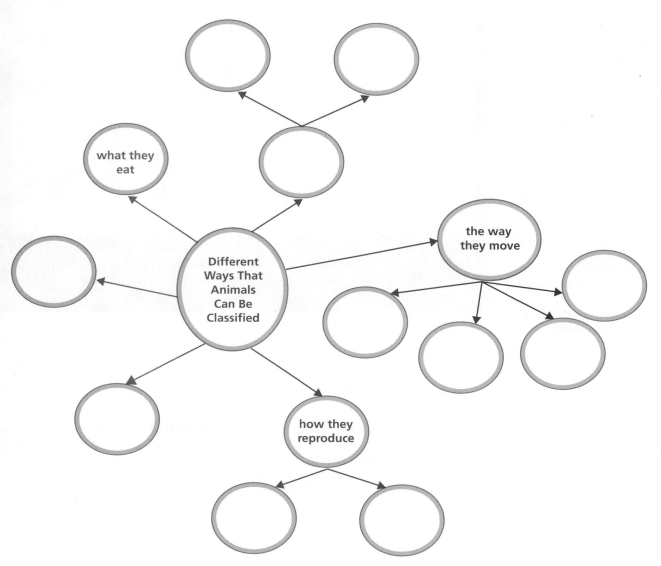

2. Read the list of organisms below. Use the chart to classify them into groups of three.

Organisms

carnation	lizard	porpoise	snake	tuna
dolphin	maple	rose	tiger	whale
leopard	oak	salmon	tortoise	
lion	pine	shark	tulip	

B Work as a class to create a chart to further classify the organisms in the previous exercise. On the board, draw a blank chart like the one below. At the bottom of the chart, list organisms that belong together, in groups of three. Once you have agreed which organisms belong together, decide on a category name for each group of three. Then decide on a name for each of the two major types of life represented in the chart. Once you have completed the chart, answer the questions below.

Type of Life	_____		_____		
Category					
Organism					

1. What guidelines (criteria) did you and your classmates use to classify these organisms?

_____

_____

2. There are millions of different plants and animals on Earth today. Using the class's guidelines, would you be able to classify them all? Why or why not?

_____

_____

PREVIEW KEY VOCABULARY

Read the list of content-specific vocabulary and check the ones you are familiar with. Leave the other spaces blank. Do not try to learn the unfamiliar items before you begin reading. You will learn them as you work with the chapter.

___ adaptation	___ *Homo sapiens*	___ organism
___ binomial	___ kingdom	___ primate
___ classify	___ Linnaeus	___ species
___ evolution	___ mammal	___ survival of the fittest
___ genetic	___ natural selection	___ taxonomy
___ genus	___ nomenclature	___ theory

USE TITLE AND HEADINGS TO PREDICT CONTENT

A **Before you work with the Introductory Reading on pages 64–66, go through it and write down the headings on the lines below.**

The Classification of Life: A Historical Overview

_____

_____

B **Read the following statements and check the ones that seem correct based on the title and headings. Then compare your answers with a classmate's. Keep in mind that you may not agree.**

1. ___ People have been interested in classifying life forms for a short time.

2. ___ People have been interested in classifying life forms for a very long time.

3. ___ Over time, people have developed many different systems for classifying life.

4. ___ Over time, people did not develop more than one system for classifying life.

5. ___ Someone named Linnaeus developed a well-known classification system.

6. ___ Someone named Linnaeus developed a little-known classification system.

7. ___ Developing a system for classifying life forms is a very simple matter.

8. ___ Developing a system for classifying life forms is a very complex matter.

⬛C **Go to page *v* in the Table of Contents. Read the brief summary of the Introductory Reading. Then review the statements above, and decide whether to change any of your predictions.**

USE FONT STYLES TO IDENTIFY AND LEARN KEY VOCABULARY

Different font styles are used in text for a variety of reasons, for example, for book titles and the names of animal species. Every content area has specific vocabulary, so when these key words are introduced, they are usually put in *italics* or **boldface** and are usually defined so the reader can understand them right away.

⬛A **Read the following selection from the Introductory Reading, and pay attention to the words in italics and boldface.**

CAROLUS LINNAEUS'S SYSTEM

The modern system of classification began in 1758 when Carolus Linnaeus (1707–1778), a Swedish doctor and botanist, published his tenth edition of *Systema Naturae*. In the previous editions, Linnaeus had used a polynomial (many-name) Latin system. However, in the tenth edition he introduced the **binomial** (two-name) **system of nomenclature**. This system used two Latin names for each species of organism. A *species* is a population of organisms capable of interbreeding and producing fertile offspring. Individual organisms are members of a species. A **genus** (plural, *genera*) is a group of closely related organisms; the species name is a word added to the genus name to identify which one of several species within the genus we are discussing. It is similar to the naming system we use with people. When you look in the phone book, you look for the last name (surname), which gets you in the correct general category. Then you look for the first name (given name) to identify the individual you wish to call. The unique name given to a particular type of organism is called its species name or scientific name. For example, in your classification chart, you put the lion, the leopard, and the tiger in the same category. They are all members of the same **genus**: *Panthera*. The lion is a specific species of *Panthera*. Its classification is *Panthera leo*. The leopard is classified as *Panthera pardus*, and the tiger is classified as *Panthera tigris*.

B Match the words in boldface or italics with their meanings.

binomial system of nomenclature　　*Panthera leo*
genera　　　　　　　　　　　　　　　　*species*
genus　　　　　　　　　　　　　　　　*Systema Naturae*

1. _____: a lion

2. _____: a group of closely related organisms

3. _____: a population of organisms capable of producing fertile offspring

4. _____: the title of a book

5. _____: groups of closely related organisms

6. _____: a two-word system for naming

C Circle one answer.

What did you observe about the words *genus* and *genera*?
a. They have opposite meanings (i.e., they are antonyms).
b. They have the same meaning (i.e., they are synonyms).
c. They are the singular and plural forms of the same word.

INTRODUCTORY READING

The following reading, "The Classification of Life: A Historical Overview," is from Concepts in Biology. *As you read, highlight the important ideas and vocabulary used to express those ideas. Highlight all italicized and* **boldfaced** *vocabulary. Monitor your comprehension by answering the Before You Continue Reading question.*

The Classification of Life: A Historical Overview

1　　　From the time we are children, we are curious about the world. We wonder where we came from, and where everything around us came from. We try to make sense of our world, and this includes trying to classify things. We often notice children who see a small dog and call it a cat, or who look at a picture of a cow and call it a horse. As children gain experience with the world, they learn to classify animals more accurately. For example, they learn to identify all kinds of "dogs," whether they see a small Chihuahua or a large Irish setter.

CLASSIFYING LIFE THROUGH THE AGES

2　　　For thousands of years, people have studied *organisms*—both plant and animal—and have tried to create a useful system for classifying them. The grouping and naming of organisms is called *taxonomy*. The Greek philosopher Aristotle (384–322 B.C.) was the first person we know of who tried to develop a logical classification system. For example, Aristotle used the size of plants to divide them into the **categories** (classifications) of trees, shrubs, and herbs.

3   We do not need to think too long about Aristotle's method to see that his taxonomy was a very simple classification system, and would not work very well because there are millions of species of plants and animals which need to be classified. [The classification activities you completed on pages 60–61 should help illustrate this point.]

4   During the Middle Ages (500–1500 A.D.), when Latin was used as a scientific language, European biologists named species using Latin words. Unfortunately, some species had Latin names that were as long as 15 words. Clearly, this system was very complex and awkward.

BEFORE YOU CONTINUE READING

According to the passage, ____.

a. *Aristotle's system worked well in classifying organisms.*

b. *Latin is better than Greek for classifying organisms.*

c. *the attempt to classify organisms has taken many forms.*

CAROLUS LINNAEUS'S SYSTEM

Fig. 2.3b Carolus Linnaeus

5   The modern system of classification began in 1758 when Carolus Linnaeus (1707–1778), a Swedish doctor and botanist, published his tenth edition of *Systema Naturae*. In the previous editions, Linnaeus had used a polynomial (many-name) Latin system. However, in the tenth edition he introduced the **binomial** (two-name) **system of nomenclature**. This system used two Latin names for each species of organism. A *species* is a population of organisms capable of interbreeding and producing fertile offspring. Individual organisms are members of a species. A **genus** (plural, *genera*) is a group of closely related organisms; the species name is a word added to the genus name to identify which one of several species within the genus we are discussing. It is similar to the naming system we use with people. When you look in the phone book, you look for the last name (surname), which gets you in the correct general category. Then you look for the first name (given name) to identify the individual you wish to call. The unique name given to a particular type of organism is called its species name or scientific name. For example, in your classification chart, you put the lion, the leopard, and the tiger in the same category. They are all members of the same **genus**: *Panthera*. The lion is a specific species of *Panthera*. Its classification is *Panthera leo*. The leopard is classified as *Panthera pardus,* and the tiger is classified as *Panthera tigris*. When biologists adopted Linnaeus's binomial method, they eliminated the confusion that was the result of using common local names. For example, with the binomial system the white water lily is known as *Nymphaea odorata*. Regardless of which of the 245 common names is used in a botanist's local area, when botanists read *Nymphaea odorata,* they know exactly which plant is being referred to.

6   In addition to assigning a specific name to each species, Linnaeus recognized a need for placing organisms into groups. His system divides all forms of life into **kingdoms**, the largest grouping used in the classification of organisms. Originally there were two kingdoms, Plantae and Animalia. Today most biologists recognize five kingdoms of life: Plantae, Animalia, Myceta (fungi), Protista (protozoa and algae), and Prokaryotae (bacteria). Each of these kingdoms is divided into smaller units and given specific names.

Checking Comprehension

A **Read the following statements. Check the correct ones. Then compare these responses with your responses on pages 62–63. Discuss your answers as a class.**

1. ___ People have been interested in classifying life forms for a short time.

2. ___ People have been interested in classifying life forms for a very long time.

3. ___ Over time, people have developed many different systems for classifying life.

4. ___ Over time, people did not develop more than one system for classifying life.

5. ___ Someone named Linnaeus developed a well-known classification system.

6. ___ Someone named Linnaeus developed a little-known classification system.

7. ___ Developing a system for classifying life forms is a very simple matter.

8. ___ Developing a system for classifying life forms is a very complex matter.

How many of your predictions on pages 62–63 were correct? ___

B **Answer the following questions in complete sentences.**

1. What was Aristotle's taxonomy (system for classifying organisms)?

_____

_____

2. What was the disadvantage, or drawback, of Aristotle's taxonomy?

_____

_____

3. During the Middle Ages, European biologists used Latin words to name species of plants and animals. Some species had names that had fifteen words.

   (1) Think of an animal, for example, a horse or a bird. What fifteen words would you use to describe this animal so another person would know exactly which animal you were referring to?

   _____

   _____

(2) What is the disadvantage (the drawback) of this system?

_____

_____

C Examine the following chart carefully. Then do the activities that follow. The chart illustrates Linnaeus's classification system. The taxonomic categories are arranged from the most inclusive (the most general) to the most exclusive (the most specific). This incomplete chart shows the classification of _Homo sapiens_, that is, humans.

TAXONOMIC CATEGORY	HUMAN CLASSIFICATION	OTHER REPRESENTATIVE ORGANISMS IN THE SAME CATEGORY
Kingdom	Animalia	• usually able to move independently • cannot produce food—must eat plants or other animals _Examples:_ insects, worms, sponges, fish, birds, reptiles, amphibians, mammals
Phylum	Chordata	• have vertebrae (i.e., backbones) _Examples:_ birds, amphibians, mammals, _____, and _____
Class	Mammalia	• have hair and mammary (milk) glands • usually give birth to live young _Examples:_ dogs, whales, humans, _____, _____
Order	Primates	• have large brains and opposable thumbs _Examples:_ gorillas, monkeys, humans, _____, _____
Family	Hominidae	• do not have a tail • have an upright posture _Examples:_ humans and extinct relatives (e.g., Neandertals)
Genus	Homo	Humans are the only surviving members of this genus, although other members of this genus existed in the past (_Homo erectus; Homo habilis_).
Species	_Homo sapiens_	humans

D Complete the chart in Exercise C by using the list below and answering the questions that follow.

baboons	horses	orangutans
chimpanzees	lions	reptiles
fish	mice	

1. Which two groups of animals belong in the phylum Chordata? Add the two groups to the chart in Exercise C.

2. Which animals belong to the class Mammalia? Add some examples to the chart.

3. Which mammals belong to the order of primates? Add the examples to the chart.

Baboons

Chimpanzees

Orangutans

Learning Vocabulary

VOCABULARY FROM CONTEXT

Reread the paragraphs indicated from the Introductory Reading to figure out the meaning of the italicized words. Then circle the correct choice to complete the sentences that follow. Circle the reason for your choice, if necessary.

1. Paragraph 2: *organism, taxonomy,* and *logical*

   (1) *Organisms* are ___.
   - **a.** large and small objects
   - **b.** living things
   - **c.** parts of the body

   (2) How did you figure out what *organism* means?
   - **a.** because many plants and animals that people study are large or small
   - **b.** because the words *plant* and *animal* are between dashes after *organism* and explain its meaning
   - **c.** because organisms need to be classified and it is a complex process

   (3) *Taxonomy* refers to ___.
   - **a.** all the different plants and animals
   - **b.** the polynomial system of naming
   - **c.** the grouping and naming of organisms

   (4) *Logical* means ___.
   - **a.** reasonable
   - **b.** connected
   - **c.** disorganized

2. Paragraph 5: *nomenclature*

(1) *Nomenclature* refers to ___.
   a. organisms in nature
   b. the editions of a book
   c. a system of grouping and naming

(2) How did you figure out what *nomenclature* means?
   a. because the explanations of polynomial and binomial are in parentheses, and both refer to a system of nomenclature
   b. because Carolus Linnaeus was trying to give Latin names to all plants and animals on Earth

USING THE DICTIONARY

Read the following sentences and dictionary entries. Select the best entry for the context, and circle the correct choice to complete the sentences that follow.

1. During the Middle Ages (500–1500 A.D.), when Latin was used as a scientific language, European biologists named species using Latin words. Unfortunately, some species had Latin names that were as long as fifteen words. Clearly, this system was very complex and *awkward*.

> **awk•ward** /ˈɔkwəd/ *adj.* **1** making you feel so embarrassed that you are not sure what to do or say: *It was really awkward, because she and Rachel don't get along.* | *an awkward silence* | *Saul's demands put Mr. McGuire* **in an awkward position** (=made it difficult for him to do or say something). **2** moving or behaving in a way that does not seem relaxed or comfortable; CLUMSY: *an awkward teenager* | *Seals are awkward on land, but graceful in the water.* **3** difficult to do, use, or handle: *Getting in and out of the water is awkward when you're wearing flippers.* | *The camera is awkward to use.* **4** not smoothly done or not skillful: *The awkward wording of the letter* **5** not convenient: *I'm sorry, have I called at an awkward time?* **6** an awkward person is deliberately unhelpful —**awkwardly** *adv.*: *"Excuse me, I mean, could you help me out?" she began awkwardly.* —**awkwardness** *n.* [U]

(1) The best definition of *awkward* in this context is number ___.

(2) Unfortunately, some species had Latin names that were as long as fifteen words. Clearly, this system was very complex and ___.
   a. made them feel embarrassed
   b. moved in a way that did not seem relaxed
   c. difficult to use

2. When biologists *adopted* Linnaeus's binomial method, they eliminated the confusion that was the result of using *common* local names. For example, with the binomial system the white water lily is known as *Nymphaea odorata*. Regardless of which of the 245 *common* names is used in a botanist's local area, when botanists read *Nymphaea odorata,* they know exactly which plant is being referred to.

a·dopt /ə'dɑpt/ *v.* **1 child** [I,T] to legally make another person's child part of your family so that he or she becomes one of your own children: *David and Sheila are unable to have children, but they're hoping to adopt.* | *My mother was adopted when she was four.* –compare FOSTER[1] **2 accept a suggestion** [T] to formally approve a proposal, especially by voting: *Congress finally adopted the law after a two-year debate.* **3 adopt an approach/strategy/policy etc.** to start to use a particular method or plan for dealing with something: *The steering committee has adopted a "wait-and-see" attitude to the proposed changes.* **4 help an organization** [T] to regularly help an organization, place etc. by giving it money, working for it etc.: *PTM Co. has adopted a neighborhood school, and employees often tutor students.* **5 style/manner** [T] to use a particular style of speaking, writing, or behaving, especially one that you do not usually use: *Kim adopts a southern accent when she speaks to her cousins.*

com·mon /kɑmən/ *adj.* [C] **1 a lot** existing in large numbers: *Olson is a very common last name in Minnesota.* | *Foxes are very common around here.* **2 happening often** happening often and to many people, or in many places: *A common reason for not hiring someone is their lack of writing skills.* | [+ **among**] *Osteoporosis, a bone disease, is common among older women.* | [**be common for sb to do sth**] *It's very common for new fathers to feel jealous of a baby.* **3 same/similar** [usually before noun, no comparative] common aims, beliefs, ideas etc. are shared by several people or groups: *Students and faculty are working toward a common goal.* | [+ **to**] *The theme of the family is common to all Engle's novels.* **4 ordinary** [only before noun, no comparative] ordinary and not special in any way: *common salt* | *The song is a tribute to* **the common man** (=ordinary people) **5 common ground** facts, opinions, and beliefs that a group of people can agree on, in a situation in which they are arguing about something: *Democrats and Republicans did find some common ground in the debates about privacy.* **6 shared by everyone** [usually before noun, no comparative] belonging to or shared by two or more people or things: *The Allies worked to defeat a common enemy.* | [+ **to**] *These problems are common to all big cities.* | *By* **common consent** (=agreed by everyone), *Joe was chosen as captain.*

(1) The best definition of *adopt* in this context is number ___.

(2) When biologists ___, they eliminated the confusion that was the result of using common local names.
   a. formally approved Linnaeus's binomial method
   b. legally made Linnaeus's binomial method part of their family
   c. started to help Linnaeus's binomial method by giving it money

(3) The best definition of *common* in this context is number ___.

(4) When biologists adopted Linnaeus's binomial method, they eliminated the confusion that was the result of using ___.
   a. ordinary local names
   b. names with common beliefs
   c. names existing in large numbers

INTRODUCING THE MAIN READING

Activate Your Knowledge

Do the following activities. Work with a partner or in a small group.

1. How are organisms selected by nature to survive and reproduce?

_____

_____

2. Write a definition of the term *evolution*.

_____

_____

3. Read the following statements. Mark whether they are True (**T**) or False (**F**).

a. ___ Evolution happened only in the past. It no longer occurs.

b. ___ Evolution has a specific aim or purpose.

c. ___ Environmental changes cause changes in organisms that help them survive.

d. ___ Individual organisms can evolve.

e. ___ Many of today's species evolved from other species that are alive today (e.g., humans evolved from gorillas).

4. The illustrations below and on the following page depict various stages in the evolution of the horse. Examine both drawings. Briefly list the changes that took place as the horse evolved.

● _____

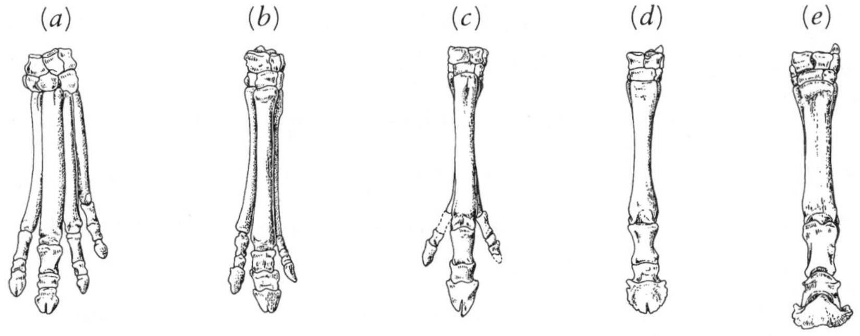

● _____

● _____

● _____

(a) *(b)* *(c)* *(d)* *(e)*

Fig. 2.3c *Evolution of the front foot of a horse from 55 million years ago (mya) to the present: (a) hyracotherium, 55 mya; (b) miohippus, 28 mya; (c) parahippus, 23 mya; (d) pliohippus, 13 mya; (e) modern horse (Equus)*

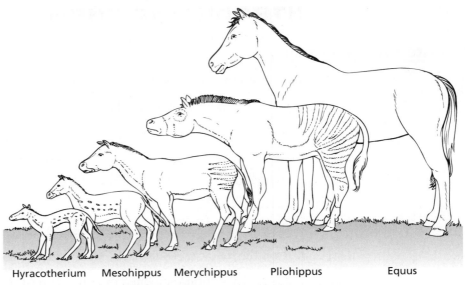

Fig. 2.3d *Several stages in the evolution of the modern horse, from the hyracotherium 55 million years ago (mya) to the present-day horse (Equus)*

Hyracotherium   Mesohippus   Merychippus   Pliohippus   Equus

Reading and Study Skill Strategies

USE TITLE AND HEADINGS TO PREDICT CONTENT

A Before you work with the Main Reading on pages 74–76, go through it and write down the headings on the lines below.

The Role of Natural Selection in Evolution

_____

_____

_____

B Read the following statements and check the ones that seem correct based on the title and headings. Then compare your answers with a classmate's. Keep in mind that you may not agree.

1. ____ Natural selection was an important factor in the evolution of life on Earth.

2. ____ Natural selection played no role in the evolution of life on Earth.

3. ____ Most people clearly understand the theory of natural selection.

4. ____ Many people do not understand the theory of natural selection very well.

5. ____ The theory of evolution is very simple, and most people understand it well.

6. ____ The theory of evolution is very complex, and many people do not understand it well.

C Go to page *v* in the Table of Contents. Read the brief summary of the Main Reading. Then review the statements on the previous page, and decide whether to change any of your predictions.

USE FONT STYLES TO IDENTIFY KEY VOCABULARY

Remember that font styles such as *italics* and **boldface** are used in text for a variety of reasons, for example, for book titles, for the names of animal species, and especially to point out content-specific vocabulary to the reader.

A Read the following excerpt from the Main Reading, and pay attention to the words in italics and boldface.

The Role of Natural Selection in Evolution

In many cultural contexts, the word *evolution* means progressive change. We talk about the evolution of economies, fashion, or musical tastes. From a biological perspective, the word has a more specific meaning. **Evolution** is the continuous genetic adaptation of a population of organisms to its environment over time. Evolution involves changes in the genes that are present in a population. By definition individual organisms are not able to evolve—only populations can. The organism's surroundings determine which characteristics favor survival and reproduction (i.e., which characteristics best fit the organism to its environment). The mechanism by which evolution occurs involves the selective passage of genes from one generation to the next through sexual reproduction. The various processes that encourage the passage of beneficial genes to future generations and discourage the passage of harmful or less valuable genes are collectively known as **natural selection**.

THE THEORY OF NATURAL SELECTION

The idea that some individuals whose gene combinations favor life in their surroundings will be most likely to survive, reproduce, and pass their genes on to the next generation is known as the **theory of natural selection**. The *theory of evolution,* however, states that populations of organisms become genetically adapted to their surroundings over time. Natural selection is the process that brings about evolution by "selecting" which genes will be passed to the next generation.

B Match the words in boldface or italics with their meanings.

> **evolution**   **natural selection**
> *theory of evolution*   **theory of natural selection**

1. _____ : the processes that encourage the passage of beneficial genes to future generations and discourage the passage of harmful/less valuable genes

2. _____ : the idea that some organisms whose gene combinations favor life in their surroundings will be most likely to survive, reproduce, and pass their genes on to the next generation

3. _____ : the continuous genetic adaptation of a population of organisms to its environment over time

4. _____ : the idea that populations of organisms become genetically adapted to their surroundings over time

MAIN READING

The Main Reading, "The Role of Natural Selection in Evolution," is also from Concepts in Biology. *As you read, highlight the important ideas and vocabulary used to express those ideas. Highlight all italicized and* **boldfaced** *vocabulary. Monitor your comprehension by answering the Before You Continue Reading questions that follow each section.*

The Role of Natural Selection in Evolution

1   In many cultural contexts, the word *evolution* means progressive change. We talk about the evolution of economies, fashion, or musical tastes. From a biological perspective, the word has a more specific meaning. **Evolution** is the continuous genetic adaptation of a population of organisms to its environment over time. Evolution involves changes in the genes that are present in a population. By definition individual organisms are not able to evolve—only populations can. The organism's surroundings determine which characteristics favor survival and reproduction (i.e., which characteristics best fit the organism to its environment). The mechanism by which evolution occurs involves the selective passage of genes from one generation to the next through sexual reproduction. The various processes that encourage the passage of beneficial genes to future generations and discourage the passage of harmful or less valuable genes are collectively known as **natural selection**.

THE THEORY OF NATURAL SELECTION

2   The idea that some individuals whose gene combinations favor life in their surroundings will be most likely to survive, reproduce, and pass their genes on to the next generation is known as the **theory of natural selection**. The *theory of evolution,* however, states that populations of organisms become genetically adapted to their surroundings over time. Natural selection is the process that brings about evolution by "selecting" which genes will be passed to the next generation.

3   You recall from Chapter One that a theory is a well-established generalization supported by many different kinds of evidence. The theory of natural selection was first proposed by Charles Darwin and Alfred Wallace and was clearly set forth in 1859 by Darwin in his book *On the Origin of Species by Means of Natural Selection, or the Preservation of Favored Races in the Struggle for Life.* Since the time it was first proposed, the theory of natural selection has been subjected to countless tests and remains the core concept for explaining how evolution occurs.

BEFORE YOU
CONTINUE
READING

1. **Natural selection and evolution ____.**

   a. *have no connection at all to each other*

   b. *are exactly the same*

   c. *both contribute to changes over time in a given population*

MISUNDERSTANDINGS OF NATURAL SELECTION

4   There are two common misinterpretations associated with the process of natural selection. The first involves the phrase *survival of the fittest.* Individual survival is certainly important because those that do not survive will not reproduce. But the more important factor is the number of descendants an organism leaves. An organism that has survived for many years but has not reproduced has not contributed any of its genes to the next generation and so has been selected against. The key, therefore, is not survival alone but survival and reproduction of the more fit organisms.

5   Second, the phrase *struggle for life* does not necessarily refer to open conflict and fighting. It is usually much more subtle than that. When a resource such as a nesting material, water, sunlight, or food is in short supply, some individuals survive and reproduce more effectively than others. For example, many kinds of birds require holes in trees as nesting places. If these are in short supply, some birds will be fortunate and find a top-quality nesting site, others will occupy less suitable holes, and some may not find any. There may or may not be fighting for possession of a site. If a site is already occupied, a bird may not necessarily try to dislodge its occupant but may just continue to search for suitable but less valuable sites. Those that successfully occupy good nesting sites will be much more successful in raising young than will those that must occupy poor sites or those that do not find any.

BEFORE YOU
CONTINUE
READING

2. *Survival of the fittest* **refers to ____.**

   a. *the survival, for many years, of strong and healthy individual animals*

   b. *the survival, for many generations, of strong and healthy individual organisms in a species*

COMMON MISCONCEPTIONS ABOUT THE THEORY OF EVOLUTION

6   Sometimes people have misconceptions not only about the theory of natural selection, but about the concept of evolution as well. The theory of evolution is complex, which may help to explain why it is so often misunderstood. Many people do not fully understand the theory of evolution. As a result, they have many misconceptions, or misunderstandings, about evolution. Here are four of the most common misunderstandings about the theory of evolution.

Evolution happened only in the past and is not occurring today. In fact, we see lots of evidence of changes in the populations of current species. An example of this is the development of resistance to pesticides by some species of insects. Suppose that, in a population of a particular species of insect, 5% of the individuals have genes that make them resistant to a specific insecticide. The first application of the insecticide could, therefore, kill 95% of the population. However, tolerant individuals would then constitute the majority of the breeding population that survived. This would mean that many insects in the second generation would be tolerant. The second use of the insecticide on this population would not be as effective as the first. With continued use of the same insecticide, each generation would become more tolerant.

Evolution has a specific goal. Natural selection selects those organisms that best fit the current environment. As the environment changes, so do the characteristics that have value. Random events such as changes in sea level, major changes in climate such as ice ages, or collisions with asteroids have had major influences on the subsequent natural selection and evolution. Evolution results in organisms that "fit" the current environment.

Individual organisms evolve. Individuals are stuck with the genes they inherited from their parents. Although individuals may adapt by changing their behavior or physiology, they cannot evolve. Only populations can change gene frequencies.

Today's species can frequently be shown to be derived from other present-day species (for example, the misconception that apes gave rise to humans). There are few examples in which it can be demonstrated that one current species gave rise to another. Apes did not become humans but apes and humans had a common ancestor several million years ago.

Checking Comprehension

A **Read the following statements. Mark whether they are True (T) or False (F). Then compare these responses with your responses on page 71.**

1. ___ Evolution happened only in the past. It no longer occurs.

2. ___ Evolution has a specific aim or purpose.

3. ___ Environmental changes cause changes in organisms that help them survive.

4. ___ Individual organisms can evolve.

5. ___ Many of today's species evolved from other species that are alive today (e.g., humans evolved from gorillas).

How many of your predictions on page 71 were correct? ___

B **Read the following statements. Check the correct ones. Then compare these responses with your responses on page 72.**

1. ___ Natural selection was an important factor in the evolution of life on Earth.

2. ___ Natural selection played no role in the evolution of life on Earth.

3. ___ Most people clearly understand the theory of natural selection.

4. ___ Many people do not understand the theory of natural selection very well.

5. ___ The theory of evolution is very simple, and most people understand it well.

6. ___ The theory of evolution is very complex, and many people do not understand it well.

How many of your predictions on page 72 were correct? ___

C **Circle the correct answers.**

1. The *theory of evolution* states that populations of organisms become genetically adapted to their surroundings over time. Natural selection is the process that brings about evolution by "selecting" which genes will be passed to the next generation.

In this context, does the word *select* mean that an organism is deliberately chosen to survive and reproduce? Yes/No

2. The *struggle for life* refers to the ability of organisms to ___.
a. successfully gain access to limited resources
b. fight other animals to get limited resources

3. *Natural selection* means that certain individuals in a species survive, reproduce, and pass on their genes to the next generation because ___.
a. they are more intelligent than other members of their species
b. they are better adapted to their environment than other members of their species
c. they are stronger than other members of their species

4. The key to evolution is ___.
a. the survival of every individual member of a species
b. both the survival and the reproduction of members of a species
c. survival and reproduction of the best adapted members of a species

D **Answer the following questions in complete sentences.**

1. What is the role of natural selection in the evolution of a species?

_____

_____

2. What effects does environment have on the evolution of a species?

_____

_____

Learning Vocabulary

VOCABULARY FROM CONTEXT

Reread the paragraphs indicated from the Main Reading to figure out the meaning of the italicized words. Then circle the correct choices to complete the sentences that follow.

1. Paragraph 4: *fittest*

   fittest means ___.
   a. smartest
   b. best adapted
   c. healthiest

2. Paragraph 5: *struggle*

   struggle means
   a. competition
   b. fight
   c. occupation

3. Paragraph 6: *misconception* and *as a result*

   (1) A *misconception* is
   a. a theory
   b. a concept
   c. a misunderstanding

   (2) *As a result* means
   a. consequently
   b. because
   c. although

USING THE DICTIONARY

Read the following sentences and dictionary entries. Select the best entry for the context, and circle the correct choice to complete the sentences that follow.

1. Many kinds of birds require holes in trees as nesting places. If these are in short supply, some birds will be fortunate and find a top-quality nesting site, others will occupy less suitable holes, and some may not find any. There may or may not be fighting for possession of a site. If a site is already occupied, a bird may not necessarily try to *dislodge* its occupant but may just continue to search for suitable but less valuable sites.

> **dis·lodge** /dɪsˈlɑdʒ/ v. [T] **1** to force or knock something out of place where it was held or stuck: *Heavy rains had dislodged a boulder at the mouth of the Thompson Canyon.* | *It was 30 minutes before rescuers could dislodge the food from his throat.* **2** to make someone leave a place or lose a position of power: *Army commanders were preparing to dislodge the militia from the capital.* —compare LODGE² (1) —**dislodgement** n. [U]

(1) In this context, the best definition of *dislodge* is number ___.

(2) If a site is already occupied, a bird may not necessarily try to ___, but may just continue to search for another suitable but less valuable site.

a. force another bird from a site which that bird held

b. make another bird leave a powerful position

2. Natural selection selects those organisms that best fit the current environment. As the environment changes, so do the characteristics that have *value*.

---

val•ue /ˈvælyu/ *n.* **1 money** **a)** [C,U] the amount of money that something is worth, or the qualities that something has that make it worth the money that it costs: *Real estate values continue to rise.* | **increase/decrease etc. in value** *The French franc has fallen in value against the dollar in recent weeks.* | *The only item* **of value** (=worth a lot of money) *was a small bronze statue.* | **value for your dollar/money** *Students today want more value for their dollar.* —see also MARKET VALUE, STREET VALUE **b)** [C] used in advertising to mean a price that is lower than usual: *Check out the values this week at Price Chopper.* | *This three-CD collection is a really* **good value** *at $25.* —see Usage Note at WORTH² **2 importance** [U] the importance or usefulness of something: *Fiber has no calories, or nutritional value.* | *The locket has great* **sentimental value** (=importance because it was a gift, it reminds you of someone etc.). | **of great/little value** *His research has been of little practical value.* **3 values** [plural] your principles about what is right and wrong, or your ideas about what is important in life: *shared cultural values* **4 math** [C] TECHNICAL a mathematical quantity shown by a letter of the alphabet or sign: *If K equals 3, what is the value of X?*

---

(1) In this context, the best definition of *value* is number ___.

(2) As the environment changes, so do the characteristics that are ___.

a. worth money

b. used in advertising

c. important or useful

d. interesting

FOLLOW-UP ASSIGNMENTS

Before you begin any of the follow-up assignments, review the content-specific vocabulary and the academic vocabulary below. If you are still unsure what any words or terms mean, go back through the chapter and review. As you complete the assignments, be sure to incorporate the appropriate vocabulary into your writing.

Content-Specific Vocabulary

adaptation	genus	natural selection	survival of the
binomial	*Homo sapiens*	nomenclature	fittest
classify	kingdom	organism	taxonomy
evolution	Linnaeus	primate	theory
genetic	mammal	species	

Academic Vocabulary

adopt	continuous	logical	role
awkward	dislodge	misconception	select
characteristics	drawback	occur	system
common	environment	reproduction	value
complex	goal		

Writing Activities

1. Reread pages 75–76. Rephrase each misconception about the theory of evolution so that it is an accurate statement. The first one has been done as an example.

   • *Evolution happened in the past and continues to take place today.*

   • _____

   • _____

   • _____

   Now write a paragraph. In the first sentence, introduce the statements you have just written. Then write the four corrected statements about the theory of evolution. Write one more sentence to conclude the paragraph.

2. Review the chart on page 67, which outlines the classification of humans. In a paragraph, describe *Homo sapiens*. Begin the paragraph with an introductory sentence. Then, in a few sentences, describe *Homo sapiens*, beginning with general information. Become more specific, until your description can apply only to *Homo sapiens* and not to any other primate. Write one more sentence to conclude your paragraph.

3. Examine the illustrations of the evolution of the horse on pages 71–72. Write two paragraphs. In the first paragraph, write an introductory

sentence, and then describe how the horse changed as it evolved. In the second paragraph, theorize why the horse might have evolved through natural selection and present some factors that might have contributed to these changes. Write one more sentence to conclude your paper.

4. Examine the illustration below. It shows the front limb of six different vertebrates. Write three paragraphs. In the first paragraph, describe how the limbs of these six vertebrates are similar. In the second paragraph, describe how the limbs differ. In the third paragraph, explain possible reasons for these similarities and differences, based on the theory of evolution.

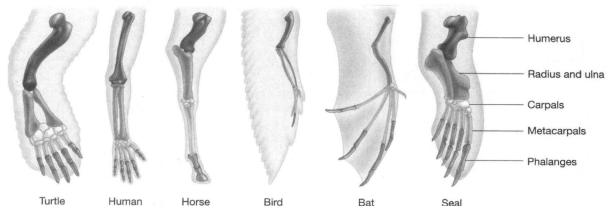

Turtle   Human   Horse   Bird   Bat   Seal

Humerus
Radius and ulna
Carpals
Metacarpals
Phalanges

Fig. 2.3e The front limbs of six different vertebrates, showing analogous bone structure

Extension Activities

1. Some animals that exist today have changed very little over many millions of years. Choose one of the following animals: coelacanth, shark, or horseshoe crab. Research this animal in books and/or through the Internet. Then prepare a presentation of five to ten minutes for the class. Describe the animal's history and evolution. Be sure to include illustrations.

2. Some animals have an especially interesting evolutionary history. Research the evolution of one of the following animals: whale, snake, seal, or bat. Then prepare a presentation. Describe the animal's history and evolution. Be sure to include illustrations.

3. The kingdom Animalia is divided into thirteen phlya. One phylum is the *Chordata*, or vertebrates. Vertebrates are further divided into seven classes: Agnatha (jawless fishes), Chondrichthyes (cartilaginous fishes), Osteichthyes (bony fishes), Mammals, Birds, Amphibians, and Reptiles. Work in groups of three or four. Each group will choose one class of vertebrates. Each student will research one animal within that class. Once you have all completed your research, work together to prepare a presentation for the class. Describe the class of animal you have chosen and present the animals within that class. Be sure to make clear why each of these animals belongs within that particular class. Use the diagram on the next page to help you organize your information.

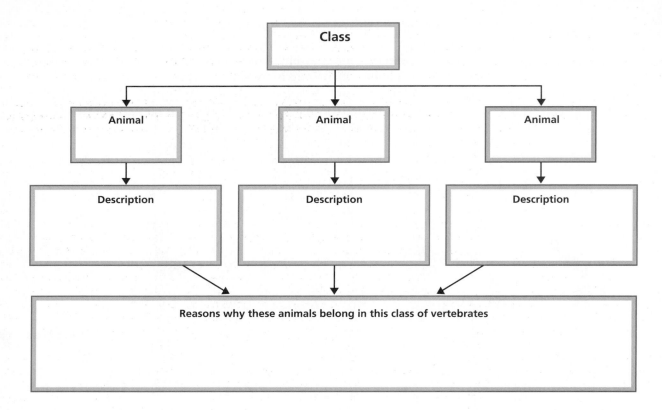

| Class |
| Animal | Animal | Animal |
| Description | Description | Description |

Reasons why these animals belong in this class of vertebrates

Internet Research

Go online, and go to one of the websites listed below. Investigate a topic related to the information you read about in Chapter 3. Choose a topic that especially interests you. Use some of the website's search features. Search by keywords such as *Linnaeus, evolution, natural selection, Charles Darwin*.

The Tree of Life Web Project:
  http://tolweb.org/tree/phylogeny.html
A Biography of Carl Linnaeus:
  http://www.ucmp.berkeley.edu/history/linnaeus.html
The Five Kingdoms of Life:
  http://waynesword.palomar.edu/trfeb98.htm
Evolution Happens website:
  http://www.evolutionhappens.net
Major Themes in Evolution:
  http://www.nap.edu/readingroom/books/evolution98/evol2.html
Public Broadcasting System's Evolution website:
  http://www.pbs.org/wgbh/evolution
British Broadcasting System's Evolution website:
  http://www.bbc.co.uk/education/darwin/index.shtml
University of Michigan's Global Change lectures website:
  http://www.globalchange.umich.edu/globalchange1/ current/lectures

CHAPTER 4

HUMAN EVOLUTION

Skills Goals

- *Review skills from Chapters 1–3.*
- *Use referents to aid in understanding text.*

Content-Specific Goals

- *Understand the relationships among primates.*
- *Understand the evolution of Homo sapiens.*
- *Learn early hominid achievements.*

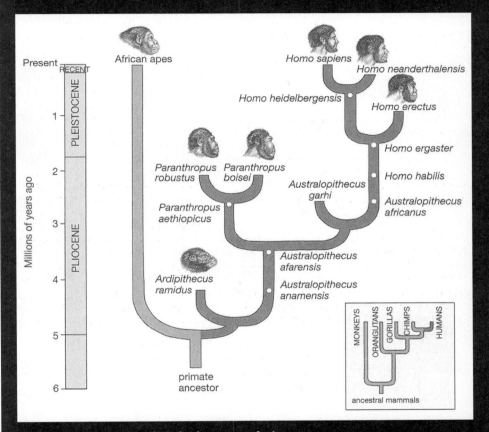

Fig. 2.4a A possible timeline for human evolution

Chapter Readings

Out of the Trees

The Evolution of Homo sapiens

INTRODUCING THE READING

Activate Your Knowledge

Work alone or in a small group. Answer the following questions. Do not worry if you do not know something. You will learn more as you work with the chapter.

1. The stone objects shown here were once used as tools. What do you think they may have been used for? Discuss your ideas.

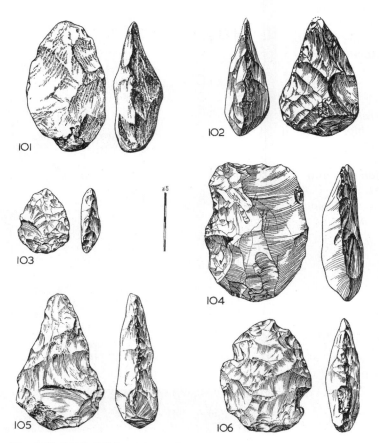

Fig. 2.4b Paleolithic stone tools

2. What are some of the similarities between human beings (*Homo sapiens*) and other primates such as chimpanzees, gorillas, bonobos, and orangutans? What are some characteristics that are unique to humans? List your ideas.

Similarities between humans and other primates	Characteristics that are unique to humans
_____	_____
_____	_____
_____	_____
_____	_____

3. *Homo sapiens* evolved from primate ancestors. List some factors that might have contributed to this evolution. Consider *natural selection* and *survival of the fittest* in your response.

_____	_____
_____	_____
_____	_____
_____	_____

Reading and Study Skill Strategies

PREVIEW KEY VOCABULARY

Read the list of content-specific vocabulary and check the words you are familiar with. Leave the other spaces blank. Do not try to learn the unfamiliar items before you begin reading. You will learn them as you work with the chapter.

___ adaptive response	___ evolution	___ precursor
___ anatomical	___ extinction	___ prehensile
___ arboreal	___ habitat	___ primate
___ bipedal	___ hominid	___ prognathism
___ cranium (*plural:* crania)	___ *Homo sapiens*	___ terrestrial
	___ hypothesize	

USE TITLE AND HEADINGS TO PREDICT CONTENT

A Before you work with the Introductory Reading on pages 87–88, go through it and write down the headings on the lines below.

Out of the Trees

_____

_____

B Read the following statements and check the ones that seem correct based on the title and headings. Then compare your answers with a classmate's. Keep in mind that you may not agree.

1. ___ The ancestors of _Homo sapiens_ developed larger brains before they became habitually bipedal.

2. ___ The ancestors of _Homo sapiens_ became habitually bipedal before they developed larger brains.

3. ___ Habitual bipedalism was an evolutionary change among a group of primates that led to humans.

4. ___ Habitual bipedalism was an evolutionary change among all primates at some time in the past.

5. ___ Major adaptive changes took place after bipedalism evolved.

6. ___ Minor adaptive changes took place after bipedalism evolved.

C Go to page _v_ in the Table of Contents. Read the brief summary of the Introductory Reading. Then review the statements above, and decide whether to change any of your predictions.

USE REFERENTS TO AID IN UNDERSTANDING TEXT

Once a word or a phrase has been mentioned in a reading, it is often replaced with a referent. For example, in the previous sentence, _it_ replaces _a word or a phrase_. Other common referents include subject, object, and possessive pronouns, as well as such words as _this, that, these, those, which, one, ones, other, another._ When you come across a referent, you need to know what it refers to if you are to understand the text.

Read the following selection from the Introductory Reading. Then complete the sentences that follow. Check your answers with a classmate. The first one has been done as an example.

THE EVOLUTION OF BIPEDALISM

[1]**Habitual bipedalism** refers to an animal's habitually (regularly) walking upright on two legs. [2]The habitual bipedalism that marks our family, **Hominidae**, seems to have evolved in response to the need of our earliest ancestors to survive in both forest and open plains environments after a climate change that dried the continent, expanding the **savannas**—the open plains of eastern and southern Africa. [3]These earliest ancestors were essentially small, bipedal apes.

[4]About 3 million years ago, a further drying trend led to two new hominid adaptive responses. [5]One gave rise to another small bipedal ape-like form, but with massive chewing bones and muscles adapted to the tough, gritty vegetation of the plains. [6]The other response was the evolution of larger brains. [7]This hominid, the first member of genus *Homo*, survived by inventing stone tools [see the illustrations on page 84], which, among other things, allowed them to scavenge the meat of the vast herds of grass eaters.

1. In sentence 5, *one* refers to <u>one of the two new hominid adaptive responses</u> .

2. In sentence 6, *the other* refers to _____ .

3. In sentence 7, *which* refers to _____ .

INTRODUCTORY READING

The following reading, "Out of the Trees," is a chapter summary from the college textbook Introducing Anthropology: An Integrated Approach. *As you read, highlight the important ideas and the vocabulary used to express those ideas. Highlight all* **boldfaced** *and italicized words. Monitor your comprehension by answering the Before You Continue Reading question. If you have trouble answering the question, reread the section before you continue reading.*

Out of the Trees

Fig. 2.4c The positions of the continents 65 million years ago (mya)

1   About 65 million years ago, a mass extinction took place on Earth. Hundreds of species of organisms died off. The best known are the various species of dinosaurs. However, many other animals and plants, both on land and in the oceans, died, too. The primates are one of the earliest of the mammal groups to evolve after the mass extinction. They appear to have arisen first in what are now North America and Europe, but the success of their adaptations allowed them to radiate over the Old World and back into the New World after the hemispheres separated. About 23 million years ago, primitive apes first appear, and from one group of African apes our family, Hominidae, branched off around 5 million years ago.

THE EVOLUTION OF BIPEDALISM

Fig. 2.4d Hand axe

2   **Habitual bipedalism** refers to an animal's habitually (regularly) walking upright on two legs. The habitual bipedalism that marks our family, **Hominidae**, seems to have evolved in response to the need of our earliest ancestors to survive in both forest and open plains environments after a climate change that dried the continent, expanding the **savannas**—the open plains of eastern and southern Africa. These earliest ancestors were essentially small, bipedal apes.

3   About 3 million years ago, a further drying trend led to two new hominid adaptive responses. One gave rise to another small bipedal ape-like form, but with massive chewing bones and muscles adapted to the tough, gritty vegetation of the plains. The other response was the evolution of larger brains. This hominid, the first member of genus *Homo,* survived by inventing stone tools [see the illustrations here and on page 84], which, among other things, allowed them to scavenge the meat of the vast herds of grass eaters.

BEFORE YOU CONTINUE READING

Primitive apes evolved about 23 million years ago. Then ____.

  a. *over a few million years, our family, the **Hominidae**, evolved larger brains and then bipedalism*

  b. *over a few million years, our family, the **Hominidae**, evolved bipedalism and then larger brains*

  c. *over many millions of years, our family, the **Hominidae**, evolved larger brains and then bipedalism*

  d. *over many millions of years, our family, the **Hominidae**, evolved bipedalism and then larger brains*

FURTHER ADAPTIVE CHANGES

Fig. 2.4e The positions of the continents today

4   From this adaptive base, the evolution of our genus accelerated. The *Homo erectus* stage, with its basically modern bodies and even larger brains, migrated all over the Old World, encountering the climatic changes of the Pleistocene, improving stone tool manufacture, and, at least in some areas, taming fire. Modern-sized brains were reached over one-half million years ago, although crania retained some primitive features. These archaic *Homo sapiens,* first seen in Africa and southern Europe, also spread all over the Old World and exhibit such typically human behaviors as burial of the dead and care of the elderly and infirm. The Neandertals are one of the best-known forms of this stage.

5   The anatomically modern *Homo sapiens* stage, first appearing in Africa around 300,000 years ago, brings with it further advances in tool-making, the clear practice of big-game hunting, and the first expressions of artistic endeavors.

Checking Comprehension

A **Read the following statements. Check the correct ones. Then compare these responses with your responses on page 86. Discuss your answers as a class.**

1. ___ The ancestors of *Homo sapiens* developed larger brains before they became habitually bipedal.

2. ___ The ancestors of *Homo sapiens* became habitually bipedal before they developed larger brains.

3. ___ Habitual bipedalism was an evolutionary change among a group of primates that led to humans.

4. ___ Habitual bipedalism was an evolutionary change among all primates at some time in the past.

5. ___ Major adaptive changes took place after bipedalism evolved.

6. ___ Minor adaptive changes took place after bipedalism evolved.

How many of your predictions on page 86 were accurate? _____

B **Refer to paragraphs 4 and 5 on page 88. Identify the referents.**

1. In paragraph 4, *its* refers to _____.

2. In paragraph 4, *these archaic Homo sapiens* refers to _____.

3. In paragraph 4, *this stage* refers to _____.

4. In paragraph 5, *it* refers to _____.

C **Answer the following questions in complete sentences.**

1. The early primates first arose in North America and Europe. How could they evolve on both these continents at the same time?

_____

_____

_____

Fig. 2.4c The positions of the continents 65 mya

2. "About 3 million years ago, a further drying trend led to two new hominid adaptive responses." Did both resulting hominid groups evolve into humans? Explain your answer.

_____

_____

_____

3. What were some of the behaviors exhibited by early members of the genus *Homo*?

_____

_____

4. Archaic *Homo sapiens* first appeared in Africa and southern Europe about half a million years ago, then spread all over the Old World. Why didn't they also spread throughout North America?

_____

_____

USE A TIME LINE TO ORGANIZE TEXT IN CHRONOLOGICAL ORDER

A time line organizes information in chronological order (the order in which events took place). When we see events summarized and organized along a time line, relationships among the events often become clearer to us. Furthermore, a time line helps us see duration of time in comparative terms.

A time line for the information on pages 87–89 has been done for you on the next page. Examine it carefully, then answer the questions that follow.

1. How much time passed from the first appearance of primates to the

first appearance of primitive apes? _____

2. How much time passed from the first appearance of primitive apes to

the first appearance of Hominidae—that is, to the evolution of

bipedalism? _____

3. How much time passed from the first appearance of the Hominidae to

the evolution of archaic *Homo sapiens*? _____

4. How much time passed from the evolution of archaic *Homo sapiens*

to the first appearance of modern *Homo sapiens*? _____

5. Review the duration of each stage of evolution from primate to *Homo*

sapiens. What do you observe? _____

_____

_____

| 65 | 23 | 5 | 3 | 0.5 | 0.3 |

A mass extinction took place on Earth; hundreds of species of plants and animals die off in the oceans and on land.

Primates evolved in what are now North America and Europe.

Primates radiated over the Old World and back into the New World after the hemispheres began to separate.

Primitive apes first appeared.

Habitual bipedalism evolved in response to a climate change that dried the African continent.

The Hominidae branched off from a group of African apes.

A further drying trend led to two new hominid adaptive responses: (1) another small bipedal apelike form with massive chewing bones and muscles (2) a hominid with a larger brain, the first of the genus *Homo*.

Modern-sized brains evolved: archaic *Homo sapiens* appeared, for example, Neandertals.

Anatomically modern *Homo sapiens* appeared.

VOCABULARY FROM CONTEXT

Reread the paragraphs indicated from the Introductory Reading to figure out the meaning of the italicized words. Then circle the correct choice to complete the sentences.

1. Paragraph 1: *arisen, radiate,* and *branched off*

    (1) *Arisen* means ___.
       a. traveled
       b. reproduced
       c. originated

    (2) *Radiate* means ___.
       a. live
       b. spread out
       c. hunt

    (3) *Branch off* means ___.
       a. separate from
       b. travel away
       c. grow taller

2. Paragraph 4: *taming*

    (1) *Taming* means ___.
       a. finding
       b. controlling
       c. fearing

USING THE DICTIONARY

Read the following sentences and dictionary entries. Select the best entry for the context. Then circle the correct choice to complete the sentences that follow.

1. The first member of genus *Homo* survived by inventing stone tools (see the illustrations here and on page 84), which, among other things, allowed them to *scavenge* the meat of the vast herds of grass eaters.

    scav•enge /ˈskævɪndʒ/ *v.* [I,T] **1** if someone scavenges, they search through things that other people do not want for food or useful objects: [+ **for**] *In the garbage dumps, women and children scavenge for glass and plastic bottles.* **2** if an animal scavenges, it eats anything that it can find —**scavenger** *n.* [C]

    (1) The best definition of *scavenge* in this context is number ___.

    (2) According to this definition, the first member of genus *Homo* ___.
       a. searched through things that others did not want
       b. ate whatever it could find

2. From this adaptive base, the evolution of our genus *accelerated*. The *Homo erectus* stage, with its basically modern bodies and even larger brains, migrated all over the Old World, encountering the climatic changes of the Pleistocene, improving stone tool manufacture, and, at least in some areas, taming fire. Modern-sized brains were reached over one-half million years ago.

> **ac·cel·er·ate** /əkˈsɛləˌreɪt/ *v.* **1** [I,T] if a process accelerates or if something accelerates it, it happens faster than usual or sooner than you expect: *Zebtech is accelerating its cost-cutting program by cutting 2,500 jobs.* **2** [I] if a vehicle or someone who is driving it accelerates, it starts to go faster: *The Ferrari can accelerate from 0 to 60 mph in 6.3 seconds.* —opposite DECELERATE

(1) The best definition of *accelerate* in this context is number ___.

(2) From the definition of *accelerate* in this context, we can understand that ___.
   a. the evolutionary process of our genus *Homo* happened faster than usual
   b. the evolutionary process of our genus *Homo* started to travel faster

INTRODUCING THE MAIN READING

Activate Your Knowledge

Work with a partner or in a small group. Answer the following questions.

1. Who are our *closest* primate relatives: monkeys, gorillas, chimpanzees, or orangutans? Why do you think so?

_____

_____

2. Humans have many characteristics that distinguish us from our primate relatives. These characteristics include large brains, small teeth, bipedalism, the ability to make tools, and the ability to control fire. Of the characteristics listed, which one is the *most important* distinguishing feature? Why do you think it is the *most* important?

_____

_____

3. Examine the human and gorilla skulls below. List the features of both. Describe the differences between them.

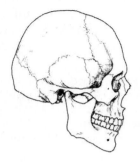 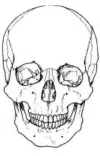 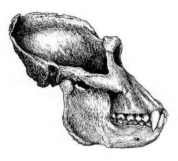 

Fig. 2.4f Modern human skull, side view; brain capacity: 1000–2000 milliliters

Fig. 2.4g Modern human skull, front view

Fig. 2.4h Male gorilla skull, side view; brain capacity: 543 milliliters

Fig. 2.4i Male gorilla skull, front view

Human Skull Features

_____

_____

_____

_____

Male Gorilla Skull Features

_____

_____

_____

_____

Major Differences between a Human Skull and a Male Gorilla Skull

_____

_____

Reading and Study Skill Strategies

USE TITLE AND HEADINGS TO PREDICT CONTENT

A Before you work with the Main Reading on pages 95–100, go through it and write down the headings on the lines below.

The Evolution of *Homo sapiens*

_____

_____

_____

_____

_____

B **Read the following statements and check which ones seem correct based on the title and headings. Then compare your answers with a classmate's. Keep in mind that you may not agree.**

1. ___ The first primates lived, or spent most of their time, in trees.

2. ___ The first primates divided their time between living in trees and on the ground.

3. ___ Continental drift helps us in understanding how early primates evolved.

4. ___ Continental drift did not affect early primate evolution.

5. ___ Primates evolved before hominids evolved.

6. ___ Hominids evolved from early primates.

7. ___ Scientists are sure how bipedalism evolved.

8. ___ Scientists have different ideas about how bipedalism evolved.

C **Go to page _v_ in the Table of Contents. Read the brief summary of the Main Reading. Then review the statements above, and decide whether to change any of your predictions.**

MAIN READING

The Main Reading, "The Evolution of Homo sapiens," *is also from* Introducing Anthropology: An Integrated Approach. *As you read, highlight the important ideas and the vocabulary used to express those ideas. Highlight all* **boldfaced** *and* italicized *words. Monitor your comprehension by answering the Before You Continue Reading questions that follow each section. If you have trouble answering a question, reread the section before you continue.*

Fig. 2.4j Notharctus, whose primatelike teeth and bones were found in Montana and Wyoming

The Evolution of *Homo sapiens*

1   The characteristic that strikes us today as the most important feature distinguishing humans from our closest primate relative is our big brains— three times the size, on average, as those of a chimp or gorilla. It is a satisfying idea that brain power is what makes us different. However, we know that the first human was not an ape with a big brain, but an ape that stood upright. Bipedalism in our line evolved millions of years before any increase in brain size. In an evolutionary sense, *it* is our most distinguishing feature. How, when, and why did it evolve? And what evolutionary trends followed?

OUT OF THE TREES

2   Before discussing how our variation of the primate theme evolved, we need to give a brief account of the evolution of the primates in general. Fossils representing the precursors of the primates may go back before the extinction of the dinosaurs 65 million years ago (mya). There are some primatelike teeth and bones found in Montana and Wyoming dated from 60 to 65 mya, but the

first undisputed primates appear about 55 mya. Their fossils are found in North America, Europe, Asia, and Africa, which at the time were in different positions than they are today [see the map on page 87].

3   These early primates, despite the modern primate arboreal theme, may not themselves have been arboreal. Rather, the primate hallmarks of prehensile hands and feet and stereoscopic vision may have evolved to aid in leaping to move through dense undergrowth and to promote fruit eating and the sight-oriented hunting of insects. As the primates continued to evolve, these basic traits proved a useful adaptive response to a more generalized life in the trees (and even, of course, set the stage for one group of terrestrial bipedal primates).

4   The earliest primates appear to come in two groups, one giving rise to the modern prosimians and the other to the anthropoid primates. By 40 mya early monkeys appear in the Old World. They expanded and began to outcompete the prosimians, pushing them into marginal areas. Most prosimians now live—as endangered species—on the island of Madagascar, which they probably reached by rafting or possibly over a land bridge.

Fig. 2.4k The lemur, a modern prosimian

THE GEOGRAPHICAL SEPARATION OF THE EARLY PRIMATES

5   Later the Eastern and Western Hemispheres (the Old World and the New World) became completely separate, dividing the early primates into two geographical groups. Although this topic is still being researched, the early New World primates were apparently replaced by more advanced monkeylike primates that rafted from Africa to the Americas when the two continents were closer together than today, floating on logs and branches or "island hopping" over a chain of volcanic islands. (As incredible as this may seem, it does happen. Recently, a group of fifteen iguanas rafted 200 miles from the Caribbean island of Guadeloupe to Anguilla, where that species was not found but has since established a small reproducing population.) All the modern New World monkeys, then, trace their ancestry to the Old World.

BEFORE YOU
CONTINUE
READING

1. What is the main idea of this section?

   a. *The early primates appeared as a single group, then branched off.*

   b. *The earliest primates arose as two groups; both groups evolved into today's primates.*

   c. *The early primates were always separate groups, and they all evolved into the primates we see today.*

---

6   Apes appear in the fossil record about 23 mya. At first, they were monkeylike but with a few anatomical details that foreshadow later, more typical apes. With the evolution of larger bodies and larger brains, they became a successful group of primates. Between 23 and 5 mya there were an estimated thirty or more types of apes throughout Europe, Africa, and Asia. Some of these species were the ancestors of modern groups. An ape from India and Pakistan, dated at 12 to 15 mya, is so similar to modern orangutans, the big red apes from Southeast Asia, that it must be ancestral to them.

Fig 2.4l "Lucy"—Australopithecus afarensis

7   We are most interested in the early African apes, however, because it is from one of them that the hominids evolved. Unfortunately, the fossil record of the African apes is scanty from about 10 mya. When we pick it up again, around 4 mya, what we see is clearly hominid. The early hominids can be exemplified by one of the most famous hominid fossils, popularly known as Lucy, found in Ethiopia and dated to 3.2 mya. Lucy is a member of the species *Australopithecus afarensis.*

THE EARLY HOMINIDS

8   Lucy (so called because her discoverers were playing the Beatles' "Lucy in the Sky with Diamonds" the night they examined her skeleton) is remarkable because, as old as her fossilized bones are, she is 40 percent complete, with all parts of the body, except the cranium, well represented. Lucy was, indeed, a female who stood about 3 feet 8 inches and weighed around 65 pounds. She and other members of her species (about 300 specimens have been found so far, representing a number of individuals of both sexes) had the brain size of a chimpanzee and in many respects resembled chimps. Their faces jutted forward, a condition called **prognathism**, and their canine teeth were pointy like an ape's. There is, in some individuals, the hint of a crest running along the top of the skull from front to back for the attachment of a major chewing muscle. Gorillas have such crests. The arms are proportionately longer than in modern humans, and the legs relatively shorter. The bones of the arms and shoulders show evidence of heavy musculature. The hands and feet are long and show curvature of the finger and toe bones.

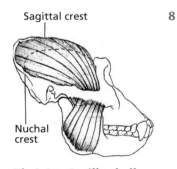

Sagittal crest

Nuchal crest

Fig 2.4m Gorilla skull, showing major chewing muscles

9   In nearly every respect, Lucy and her kin looked like apes—except that they walked bipedally. The bones of the pelvis and legs clearly show this, as does the large hole in the base of the skull from which the spinal cord emerges and around which the top of the spine attaches. This hole is underneath the skull, rather than in back, and indicates a creature that faced forward while its spine dropped straight down. Lucy was a bipedal ape and, therefore, by definition, a member of family Hominidae, the only primate family that is habitually bipedal.

BEFORE YOU CONTINUE READING

2. Answer the following questions.

   a. *What physical details characterize* Australopithecus afarensis *as an ape?*

   —————————————————————

   b. *Which single characteristic distinguishes this species from other apes?*

   —————————————————————

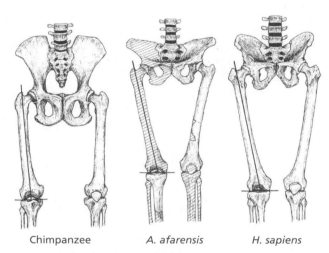

Chimpanzee   *A. afarensis*   *H. sapiens*

Fig. 2.4n *A comparison of the pelvis and leg bones of a chimpanzee,* **Australopithecus afarensis (Lucy), and Homo sapiens (modern humans)**

10   So bipedalism was the first hominid feature to evolve—millions of years before our big brains and flat faces. A major question, then, becomes why did bipedalism first evolve? What environmental circumstances would have selected for that form of locomotion while leaving the other apelike traits pretty much intact?

11   Many answers to this question are being hypothesized, and those hypotheses are being scientifically tested. Each new fossil or new date or new interpretation of ancient environments changes the outlook slightly. There is, at present, no definitive answer. But I can relate the scenario that seems to me the best supported at the moment. It is at least a reasonable one and shows how the evidence is brought to bear on the question.

HOW BIPEDALISM MAY HAVE EVOLVED

12   We may first ask what the benefits of bipedalism could be. Early hominid fossils have long been linked to the **savannas**—the open plains of eastern and southern Africa that began expanding because of climatic changes about 5 mya. In that environment, it is hypothesized, bipedalism could serve four functions. First, and probably most important, it frees the forelimbs to carry things. With food appropriate to an ape less concentrated on the plains, and with dangerous animals around more than willing to make a meal out of a small primate, the ability to search for food while possibly carrying one's offspring and to carry the food back to a safe location would certainly be a benefit. Second, by elevating the head, bipedalism provides better views of food and danger. Third, the vertical orientation helps cool the body by presenting a smaller target to the intense equatorial rays of the sun and by placing more of the body above the ground to catch cooling air currents. Fourth, bipedalism, while using a great deal of energy for running, is very efficient for walking. Long periods of steady walking in search of food require less energy if done in an upright, bipedal position. Walking bipedally, in other words, makes a lot of sense in the environment of the African savannas. Two problems have arisen with this nice connection, however.

13   First, if you look at the illustration of the bonobo, you see that bonobos are at least occasionally bipedal and they live in very dense forests. Recall, too, that the bonobo is one of our two closest relatives, separated from us modern hominids by a mere 5 million years and a mere 1.6 percent of our genes.

14   Second, recent analyses have shown that some of the earliest hominid fossils are from creatures who resided not on the open plains but in forests. And other research has indicated that there was no abrupt change in ancient East Africa from forest to savanna, but, rather, a mixture of forest and plains. Moreover, climatic changes were taking place beginning 5 mya, in an increasing range of variation, from cool to hot and moist to dry. This led to great fluctuations in water and vegetation.

15   It has been suggested, then, that the evolution of bipedalism—with the retention of long, strong arms and powerful shoulders—was an adaptation to living in an environment of *both* arboreal and terrestrial settings, giving our earliest ancestors great adaptive flexibility. As we will see, when the open plains later became the hominids' main habitat, arboreal adaptations disappeared (we're really very poor tree climbers), and bipedalism became our adaptive focus.

Fig. 2.4o Bonobos

BEFORE YOU CONTINUE READING

3. Put simply, what is the problem with the theory that bipedalism benefited early hominids?

   a. *The early hominids lived in forests, not savannas.*

   b. *Bonobos are always bipedal, too.*

   c. *The early hominids were poor tree climbers.*

16   Once we find the first evidence of habitual bipedalism—human pelvic and leg bones—a little over 4 mya, the hominid fossil record becomes more complete and more complex. Although there is much information, there is really no agreement on how it all goes together. Especially at issue is the question of just how many species of early hominids there were. Some paleoanthropologists (called "lumpers") group fossils together into a small number of species, focusing on the degree of physical variation found within modern species. Others (called "splitters") emphasize the differences among fossil specimens and interpret those as indicating different taxonomic categories. It is beyond the scope of this book to cover all the details of the debate—at least six different, and reasonable, lines of descent have been proposed—but I can give you a general idea of what we think happened.

17   The hominid fossil record begins with an enigmatic set of specimens from Ethiopia dated at 4.4 mya. The earliest well-established hominid fossils are placed in genus *Australopithecus* ("southern ape") and are often divided into as many as three species. The famous Lucy belongs to this group. Their fossils have been found in Ethiopia, Kenya, Tanzania, Chad, and south Africa and are dated at 4.2 to 2.3 mya. The australopithecines, as they are generally called, might well be described as bipedal apes. Their bones show full upright walking, but their faces are apelike, their brain sizes those of chimpanzees (around 450 ml), their bodies average about 105 pounds, and their arms are long and heavily muscled. They were probably well adapted to both arboreal as well as terrestrial environments, and microscopic analysis of their teeth indicates a mixed vegetable diet of fruits and leaves.

18   Evidently, the adaptations of early *Homo* proved so successful that hominid evolution seems to accelerate about 2 mya. Within about 800,000 years of the first evidence of stone tools in Africa, fossils of *Homo* are found as far away as Georgia (in the former Soviet Union), China, and Java. There is little agreement among anthropologists about the taxonomy and relationships during the first 2.5 million years of hominid evolution, and there is even less agreement regarding the latest 2 million years—the evolution of genus *Homo*. However, new fossil discoveries are being made, and the answers to many questions may soon be found.

Checking Comprehension

A Read the following statements. Check the correct ones. Then compare these responses with your responses on page 95.

1. ____ The first primates lived, or spent most of their time, in trees.

2. ____ The first primates divided their time between living in trees and on the ground.

3. ____ Continental drift helps us in understanding how early primates evolved.

4. ____ Continental drift did not affect early primate evolution.

5. ___ Primates evolved before hominids evolved.

6. ___ Hominids evolved from early primates.

7. ___ Scientists are sure how bipedalism evolved.

8. ___ Scientists have different ideas about how bipedalism evolved.

How many of your predictions on page 95 were correct? ___

B **Refer to paragraph 4 on page 96. Identify the referents.**

    1. *One* refers to _____.

    2. *The other* refers to _____.

    3. *They* refers to _____.

    4. *Them* refers to _____.

    5. *Which* refers to _____.

C **Answer the following questions in complete sentences.**

    1. Lucy was a member of the species *Australopithecus afarensis*. Why is this species considered a hominid and the beginning of the separation from apes?

    _____

    _____

    2. The author points out that bipedalism evolved in hominids who lived in forests. Why might forest-living primates have evolved bipedalism?

    _____

    _____

    3. Figure 2.4a on page 83 illustrates a possible time line for human evolution. Why might a different time line also be a possibility?

    _____

    _____

    _____

1. Label and date each set of skulls.
   a. *Australopithecus boisei,* 1.5 million years ago
   b. *Homo erectus,* less than 1 million years ago
   c. *Homo sapiens,* 11,000 years ago

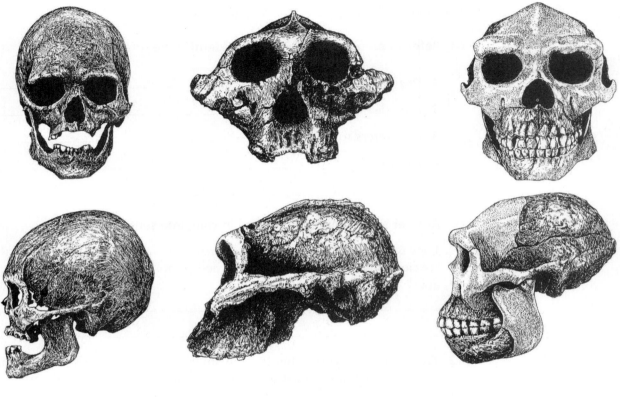

Fig. 2.4p   *Fig. 2.4q*   *Fig. 2.4r*

2. Refer to the skulls you have just labeled. Match the three skulls with the characteristics listed below.

   a. _____ has the smallest cranial capacity, a sagittal crest, a very forward-jutting face, and very pronounced cheekbones.

   b. _____ has the largest cranial capacity, no trace of a sagittal crest, almost no brow ridge, and a flat face.

   c. _____ has a somewhat larger cranial capacity, only a trace of a sagittal crest, and less pronounced cheekbones.

3. Write a paragraph. Describe the hominid skull changes as they evolved over time. As guides, use the illustrations you have just examined and labeled and the work you did in Chapter 3 on pages 71, 80, and 81.

_____

_____

_____

_____

_____

E Work in pairs or a small group. On a separate piece of paper, create a time line for the information from the Introductory Reading and the Main Reading. Use the time line on page 91 as a guide.

F Circle the correct answer based on your time line in Exercise E.

1. Which of the following mammals evolved first?
   a. apes
   b. primates
   c. hominids

2. The earliest primates ___.
   a. evolved only into species of prosimians
   b. evolved only into species of primates
   c. evolved into two groups: prosimians and primates

3. The early New World primates ___.
   a. died out
   b. spread to the Old World
   c. mixed with Old World primates

4. Where did Hominidae first appear?
   a. Europe
   b. Asia
   c. Africa
   d. India and Pakistan

5. *Australopithecus afarensis* was ___.
   a. a hominid
   b. an early ape
   c. a monkey

6. Neandertals were ___.
   a. a genus, like *Australopithecus*
   b. a species of *Australopithecus*
   c. a species of archaic *Homo sapiens*
   d. a species of modern *Homo sapiens*

Learning Vocabulary

VOCABULARY FROM CONTEXT

Reread the paragraphs indicated from the Main Reading to figure out the meaning of the italicized words. Then circle the correct choices to complete the sentences that follow, or complete the sentence.

1. Paragraph 1: *characteristic*

    (1) In this paragraph, a synonym of *characteristic* is the word ___.
    a. relative
    b. feature
    c. distinguishing

    (2) An animal that stands upright is ___.
    a. a primate
    b. a gorilla
    c. bipedal

2. Paragraph 2: *precursors*

    From this context, we can understand that the *precursors* of primates are ___.
    a. their bones
    b. their ancestors
    c. their relatives

3. Paragraph 3: *arboreal* and *terrestrial*

    (1) An *arboreal* animal generally lives ___.
    a. in trees
    b. on the ground

    (2) A *terrestrial* animal generally lives ___.
    a. in trees
    b. on the ground

4. Paragraph 8: *prognathism*

    Prognathism refers to ___.
    a. a crest running along the top of the skull
    b. pointy canine teeth
    c. a forward-jutting face

5. Paragraph 12: *savanna*

    A *savanna* is _____.

6. Paragraph 14: *moist* and *fluctuation*

    (1) A *moist* climate is a ___ climate.
    a. wet
    b. dry
    c. cool

    (2) In this paragraph, a synonym for *fluctuation* is _____.

Read the following sentences and dictionary entries. Select the best entry for the context, and circle the correct choice to complete the sentences that follow.

1. Fossils representing the precursors of the primates may go back before the extinction of the dinosaurs 65 million years ago (mya). There are some primatelike teeth and bones found in Montana and Wyoming dated from 60 to 65 mya, but the first *undisputed* primates appear about 55 mya.

   > **un·dis·put·ed** /ˌʌndɪˈspyuṭɪd./ *adj.* **1** accepted by everyone: **the undisputed leader/master/champion etc.** *In 1927 Stalin became the undisputed leader of the Soviet Union.* **2** known to be definitely true, and not argued about: *undisputed facts* | [**undisputed that**] *It is undisputed that the two were involved in a two-year relationship.*

   From this context and the dictionary entry, we can understand that *undisputed* means that the 55 million-year-old fossils that were found ____.
   a. have been accepted by everyone
   b. are known to be definitely primate fossils; no one argues about this

2. The earliest primates, despite the modern primate arboreal theme, may not themselves have been arboreal. Rather, the primate *hallmarks* of *prehensile* hands and feet and stereoscopic vision may have evolved to aid in leaping to move through dense undergrowth and to promote fruit eating and the sight-oriented hunting of insects.

   > **hall·mark** /ˈhɔlmɑrk/ *n.* [C] **1** an idea, method, or quality that is typical of a particular person or thing: [**+ of**] *Clog dancing is a hallmark of Appalachian culture.* | **has/bears all the hallmarks of sth** *Oates's new novel has all the hallmarks of her earlier work.* **2** a mark put on silver, gold, or PLATINUM that shows the quality of the metal, and where and when it was made

   > **pre·hen·sile** /priˈhɛnsəl/ *adj.* TECHNICAL a prehensile tail, foot etc. can curl around things and hold on to them

   (1) An animal with a prehensile tail ____.
   a. can hold on to a tree branch with its tail
   b. cannot hold on to a tree branch with its tail

   (2) An animal with prehensile feet ____.
   a. can hold on to objects with its feet
   b. cannot hold on to objects with its feet

(3) Primate hallmarks are prehensile hands and feet and stereoscopic vision. This means that _____.

    a. no other animals share these features; they are uniquely primate features

    b. other animals have these features, but they are especially typical of primates

FOLLOW-UP ASSIGNMENTS

Before you begin any of the follow-up assignments, review the content-specific vocabulary and the academic vocabulary below. If you are still unsure what any words or terms mean, go back through the chapter and review. As you complete the assignments and activities, be sure to incorporate the appropriate vocabulary into your writing.

Content-Specific Vocabulary

adaptive response	cranium (plural: crania)	hominid	prehensile
anatomical	evolution	*Homo sapiens*	primate
arboreal	extinction	hypothesize	prognathism
bipedal	habitat	precursor	terrestrial

Academic Vocabulary

accelerate	evidence	response	trace
arise	fluctuation	scavenge	trend
branch off	hallmark	success	undisputed
characteristic	moist	tame	unique
distinguish	radiate		

Writing Activities

1. Write a paragraph. Briefly describe the major events in the evolution and spread of *Homo sapiens* throughout the world.
2. Bipedalism evolved millions of years before hominids evolved larger brains. Write two paragraphs. In the first paragraph, write why you think that bipedalism was a successful adaptation in terms of *natural selection* and *survival of the fittest*. In the second paragraph, give evidence to support your viewpoint.
3. The habitual bipedalism that marks our family, Hominidae, first evolved about 5 million years ago. Larger brains did not evolve for another 2 million years. Write a paragraph explaining why you think these hominids' brains did not become larger for such a long time. Use the concepts of *natural selection* and *survival of the fittest*, and take into account changing environmental conditions.

Extension Activities

1. Choose one of the modern-day primates mentioned in this chapter, i.e., chimpanzee, bonobo, orangutan, gorilla. Use Linnaeus's classification system to give the animal its proper name. Create a classification chart for it, following the example of the chart on page 67 in Chapter 3. If necessary, go online to obtain the information you need (for example, go to http://www.ucmp.berkeley.edu/history/linnaeus.html). Then prepare a brief presentation for the class. Describe the animal's history and evolution. Be sure to include illustrations and perhaps a time line.

2. Research the evolution of one of the modern-day primates. How has it evolved over the past 25 million years? Prepare a brief presentation for the class. Be sure to include illustrations and perhaps a time line.

3. Prosimians and primates branched off in the late Cretaceous period. Research the evolution of prosimians, leading up to today's prosimian species. Prepare a brief presentation for the class. Be sure to include illustrations and perhaps a time line.

Internet Research

Go online, and go to one of the websites listed below. Investigate a topic related to the information you read about in Chapter 4. Choose a topic that especially interests you. Use some of the website's search features. Search by keywords such as *primate evolution*, *australopithecines, human origins, missing link.*

The United States Geologic Service website:
   www.usgs.gov
University of California, Berkeley Museum of Paleontology:
   www.ucmp.berkeley.edu
Human Prehistory: An Exhibition:
   http://users.hol.gr/%7Edilos/prehis.htm
Human Evolution website:
   http://www.ecotao.com/holism/huevo/index.html
Humboldt State University, California website:
   http://www.humboldt.edu/~mrc1/main.shtml
University of California at Santa Barbara, Department of Anthropology's website on Human Evolution in 3D (i.e., three dimensional):
   http://www.anth.ucsb.edu/projects/human/#
The Smithsonian Institution Human Origins Program:
   http://www.mnh.si.edu/anthro/humanorigins/
Public Broadcasting System's Human Origins website:
   http://www.pbs.org/wgbh/aso/tryit/evolution/

WHERE DID CIVILIZATION FIRST DEVELOP?

Fig. 3.0 Ruins of Elamite Ziggurat, 1250 B.C.

CHAPTER 5

FIRST STEPS TOWARD CIVILIZATION

Skills Goals

- *Review skills from Chapters 1–4.*
- *Learn word forms.*

Content-Specific Goals

- *Understand factors leading up to the development of civilization.*
- *Learn how humans first settled into villages.*
- *Learn how humans developed agriculture.*

Fig. 3.5a Farmers using a scratch plow

Chapter Readings

The Early Accomplishments of Homo sapiens

Setting the Stage for Civilization: The Origins of Food Production

INTRODUCING THE READING

Activate Your Knowledge

A Work alone or in a small group. Do the following activities.

1. The map below shows the extent of ice sheets during the last Ice Age (35,000 to 12,000 B.C.E.[1]). How might the climate during the Ice Age have affected the way people lived during that time? List your ideas.

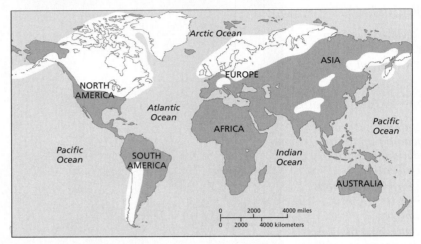

Fig 3.5b Maximum extent of the ice sheets in the last Ice Age, about 18,000 years ago

_____

_____

_____

2. In Chapter 4 you learned that anatomically modern *Homo sapiens* first appeared around 300,000 years ago. These early *Homo sapiens* made tools, practiced big game hunting, cared for the elderly and the sick, and buried the dead. By about 35,000 years ago, *Homo sapiens* had advanced still further. What were some of the accomplishments of *Homo sapiens* at this time? List your ideas.

_____   _____

_____   _____

_____   _____

B Work as a class to develop a list on the board using ideas from your lists in Exercise A.

---

[1] B.C.E. is the abbreviation for the term "before the common era." Therefore, 12,000 B.C.E. is 14,000 years ago.

PREVIEW KEY VOCABULARY

Read the list of content-specific vocabulary and check the ones you are familiar with. Leave the other spaces blank. Do not try to learn the unfamiliar items before you begin reading. You will learn them as you work with the chapter.

___ agriculture   ___ harvest   ___ mural

___ anatomical   ___ hunting-gathering   ___ nomadic

___ civilization   ___ Ice Age   ___ sedentary

___ differentiation of labor   ___ implement   ___ subsistence

___ domesticate   ___ migrate   ___ transition

___ forage

USE TITLE AND HEADINGS TO PREDICT CONTENT

In the previous four chapters, you previewed the title and headings of the readings as they appeared in the text. Another way of previewing the title and headings is by creating a diagram.

A Before you read the Introductory Reading on pages 113–114, go through it and write down the headings in the diagram below. Some of the diagram has already been filled in. Then as a class, draw the diagram on the board and add your ideas to it.

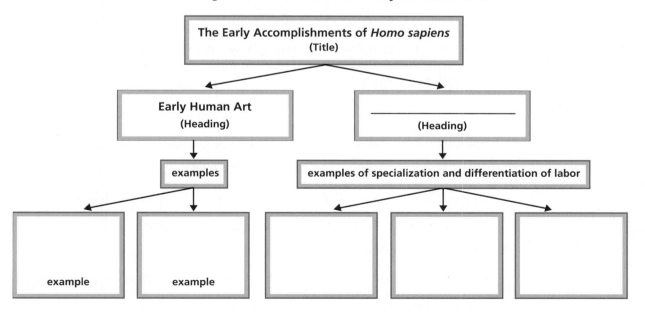

The Early Accomplishments of *Homo sapiens*
(Title)

Early Human Art
(Heading)

_____
(Heading)

examples

examples of specialization and differentiation of labor

example   example

B Go to page *v* in the Table of Contents. Read the brief summary of the Introductory Reading. Then review your diagram above, and decide whether to make any changes to it.

LEARN AND USE WORD FORMS

You can expand your English vocabulary by learning the various forms that words have.

A Study the following chart which contains words from the Introductory Reading. Note the spelling changes. Pay attention to the words as they are used in the Introductory Reading.

VERB	NOUN	ADJECTIVE	ADVERB
add	addition	additional	additionally
colonize	colonization colony	colonial	
connect	connection	connected	
evolve	evolution	evolutionary evolving/evolved	
inhabit	habitation habitat	inhabited	
indicate	indication	indicative	
migrate	migration	migratory	
populate	population	populated	
preserve	preservation	preserved	
specialize	specialization	specialized	

B Complete the following paragraph by circling the correct form of the word in parentheses. When you are done, check your answers by reading paragraph 1 on page 113.

Between 40,000 and 30,000 years ago the Eastern Hemisphere was (population / populated / populating) by human beings anatomically just
1.
like us. Concurrently the newly (evolution / evolved / evolutionary) human
2.
species (migration / migrated / migratory) into the Western Hemisphere,
3.
needing no boats for this because there was then a land
(connection / connected / connecting) between Siberia and Alaska. Since
4.
Australia was (colony / colonization / colonized) (in still mysterious ways)
5.
before 30,000 years ago, the entire globe then knew human
(habitation / habitat / inhabited) more or less as it does today.
6.

INTRODUCTORY READING

The following reading, "The Early Accomplishments of Homo sapiens," *is from the college textbook* World Civilizations: Their History and Their Culture, Volume One. *As you read, highlight the important ideas and vocabulary used to express those ideas.*

The Early Accomplishments of *Homo sapiens*

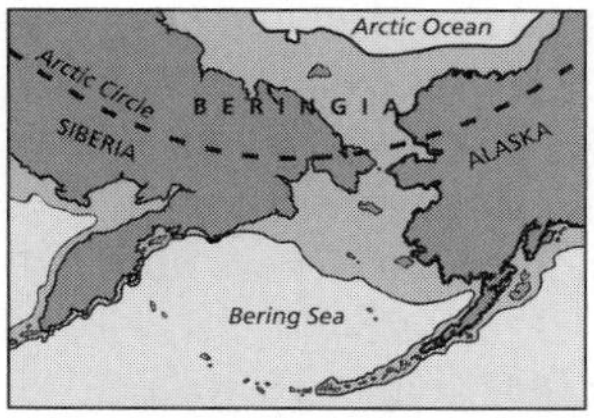

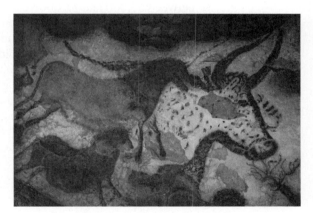

Fig. 3.5c The ancient land connection between Asia and North America

1   Between 40,000 and 30,000 years ago the Eastern Hemisphere was populated by human beings anatomically just like us. Concurrently the newly evolved human species migrated into the Western Hemisphere, needing no boats for this because there was then a land connection between Siberia and Alaska. Since Australia was colonized (in still mysterious ways) before 30,000 years ago, the entire globe then knew human habitation more or less as it does today.

EARLY HUMAN ART

2   One of the first things modern humans accomplished was the creation of some of the most stunning paintings known in the entire history of human art—the famous cave murals of southern France and northern Spain executed between 30,000 and 12,000 years ago. In over 200 caves so far discovered (the most famous of which are the cave of Lascaux in southern France and that of Altamira in Spain), the earliest known artists painted breathtaking murals of prancing animals—bison, bulls, horses, ponies, and stags. The emphasis in this cave art was unquestionably on movement. Almost all of the murals depict proud game species running, leaping, or facing the hunter at bay.

Fig. 3.5d A cave painting, Lascaux, France

BEFORE YOU CONTINUE READING

In the first two paragraphs, what is the most significant information about modern human beings?

_____

EARLY HUMAN HUNTING SOCIETY

3   It is certain that the early human hunting society that produced the cave paintings was one that had arrived at extensive specialization and differentiation of labor. Handicraft workers in the same societies concurrently developed extraordinary facility in fashioning tools, not just from stones and bones but also from antlers and ivory. Examples of the implements they added to the ancient human tool kit include fishhooks, harpoons, bows and arrows, and needles for sewing together animal skins.

4   Hunting in the period between 30,000 and 12,000 years ago would have called for specialized training since artful new techniques were being added to the hunting repertoire. Specifically, with darts and arrows hunters of that time learned how to bring down birds, with harpoons and fishhooks they learned how to catch fish, and by studying the instinctive movements of game animals they learned how to stampede and trap herds. Since they relied on game most of all, they migrated with game herds and there is some evidence that they followed preservation rules by not killing everything that they could. Nonetheless, masses of charred bones found regularly at archeological sites dating from this period indicate that huge quantities of game were killed and then roasted in community feasts, proving that the peoples in question not only knew how to paint and how to hunt, but also how to share.

5   [1]Around 12,000 years ago (10,000 B.C.E.), hunting feasts occurred rarely or not at all for a simple reason—the herds were vanishing. [2]The era between 35,000 and 12,000 years ago had been an "Ice Age": daytime temperatures in the Mediterranean regions of Europe and western Asia averaged about 60°F (16°C) in the summer and about 30°F (–1°C) in the winter. [3]Accordingly, herds of cold-loving game species such as reindeer, elk, wild boar, European bison, and various kinds of mountain goats roamed the hills and valleys. [4]But as the last glaciers receded northwards such species retreated with them. [5]Some humans may have moved north with the game but others stayed behind, creating an extremely different sort of world in comparatively short order.

Checking Comprehension

A Reread pages 113–114 and complete the diagram below. Then compare this diagram with your work on page 111.

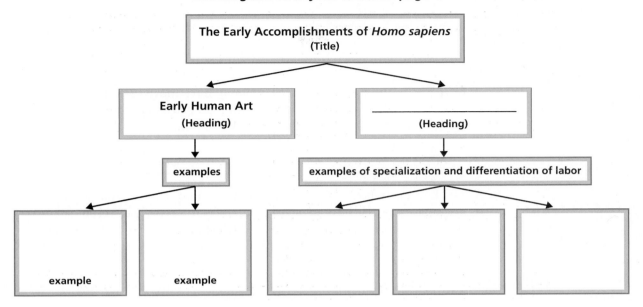

How much of your diagram on page 111 was accurate? _____

Fig. 3.5e A painting of a bison from a cave at Altamira, Spain

B Refer to paragraph 5 in the Introductory Reading on page 114. Identify the referents.

1. In the fourth sentence, *such species* refers to _____.

2. In the fourth sentence, *them* refers to _____.

3. In the fifth sentence, *others* refers to _____.

C **Answer the following questions in complete sentences.**

1. The early human hunting societies had division and specialization of labor. What kinds of specialized work did people do in these societies?

_____

_____

2. "As the last glaciers receded northwards, many cold-loving species retreated with them. Some humans may have moved north with the game but others stayed behind, creating an extremely different sort of world in comparatively short order." Which one of these two groups remained hunters?

_____

3. The humans who stayed behind and became sedentary, that is, settled in one place, are the humans who created "an extremely different sort of world in comparatively short order." In what ways do you think the world they created might have been different from their previous way of life? Why do you think so?

_____

_____

_____

Learning Vocabulary

VOCABULARY FROM CONTEXT

Reread the paragraphs indicated from the Introductory Reading to figure out the meaning of the italicized words. Then circle the correct choice to complete the sentences.

1. Paragraph 1: *anatomically* and *colonized*

   (1) From this context, we can understand that if these human beings were *anatomically* like us, then they ___.
   a. spoke like us
   b. looked like us
   c. thought like us

   (2) *Anatomically* refers to ___.
   a. physical characteristics
   b. language characteristics
   c. thought processes

   (3) *Colonized* means ___.
   a. conquered
   b. explored
   c. populated

2. Paragraph 3: *implements*

In this context, a synonym for *implements* is ___.
a. tools
b. bones
c. stones

3. Paragraph 4: *migrated*

In this context, *migrated* means ___.
a. hunted
b. walked
c. traveled

USING THE DICTIONARY

Read the following sentences and dictionary entries. Select the best entry for the context. Then circle the correct choice to complete the sentences that follow.

1. Hunting in the period between 30,000 and 12,000 years ago would have called for specialized training since artful new techniques were being added to the hunting *repertoire*. Specifically, with darts and arrows hunters of that time learned how to bring down birds, with harpoons and fishhooks they learned how to catch fish, and by studying the instinctive movements of game animals they learned how to stampede and trap herds.

> **rep·er·toire** /ˈrɛpɚˌtwɑr/ *n.* [C usually singular] **1** all of the plays, pieces of music etc. that a performer or group has learned and can perform **2** the total number of things that someone or something is able to do: *Kate shouldn't have any problem finding a job with her repertoire of skills.*

(1) In this context, the best definition of *repertoire* is number ___.

(2) Artful new techniques were being added to ___.
a. the pieces of music that these people played
b. the list of things that these people were able to do
c. the plays that these people learned to perform

2. Around 12,000 years ago (10,000 B.C.E.), hunting feasts occurred rarely or not at all for a simple reason—the herds were *vanishing*. The era between 35,000 and 12,000 years ago had been an "Ice Age": daytime temperatures in the Mediterranean regions of Europe and western Asia averaged about 60°F (16°C) in the summer and about 30°F (–1°C) in the winter. Accordingly, herds of cold-loving game species such as reindeer, elk, wild boar, European bison, and various kinds of mountain goats roamed the hills and valleys. But as the last glaciers *receded* northwards such species retreated with them. Some humans may have moved north with the game but others stayed behind, creating an extremely different sort of world in comparatively short order.

> **van·ish** /ˈvænɪʃ/ *v.* [I] **1** to disappear suddenly, especially in a way that cannot easily be explained: *Before she could scream, the man had vanished into the night.* | *Earhart **vanished without a trace** (=disappeared so that no sign remained) on July 2, 1937.* —see also **disappear/vanish into thin air** (THIN¹ (13)) **2** to stop existing, especially suddenly: *Statistics show that Santa Clara's farmland is vanishing.* **3 a vanishing act** INFORMAL a situation in which something disappears suddenly in a way that is not expected or explained

> **re·cede** /rɪˈsid/ *v.* [I] **1** if something you can see or hear recedes, it gets further and further away until it disappears: *She walked away, her footsteps receding down the hall.* | [**+ into/from**] *The two figures receded into the mist.* **2** if a memory, feeling, or possibilty recedes, it gradually goes away: *As the threat of attack receded, village life returned to normal.* | [**+ into/from**] *The postwar division of Europe is receding into the past.* **3** if water recedes, it moves back from an area that it was covering: *Flood waters finally began to recede in November.* **4** if your hair recedes, you gradually lose the hair at the front of your head: *He has a fuzzy beard and a receding hairline.* **5 receding chin** a chin that slopes backward

(1) In this context, the best definition of *vanish* is number ___.

(2) Around 12,000 years ago, the game herds ___.
  a. disappeared suddenly
  b. stopped existing

(3) In this context, the best definition for *recede* is number ___.

(4) The cold-loving game species ___.
  a. got further away until they stopped existing
  b. moved away from the area they had lived in

LEARN AND USE WORD FORMS

Complete the sentences below with the correct form of the word from the box. Refer to the word form chart on page 112. Be sure to use the correct tense of verbs. Use each word only once.

add	indicate	specialize
colonize	preserve	

1. Hunting in the period between 30,000 and 12,000 years ago would have called for _____ training.

2. Examples of the implements they _____ to the ancient human tool kit include fishhooks, harpoons, bows and arrows, and needles for sewing together animal skins.

3. There is some evidence that they followed _____ rules by not killing everything that they could.

4. Masses of charred bones found regularly at archeological sites dating from this period _____ that game was killed and roasted in community feasts.

5. No one is sure how humans _____ Australia, but we do know that humans arrived there about 30,000 years ago.

INTRODUCING THE MAIN READING

Activate Your Knowledge

Work with a partner or in a small group. Answer the following questions.

What types of social organization might have been necessary for people to develop farming? For instance, what types of specialized labor might have been needed? Brainstorm answers and list them below. Then use the diagram on the following page to help you organize your ideas; do not hesitate to change the diagram in any way that helps you.

_____

_____

_____

_____

_____

_____

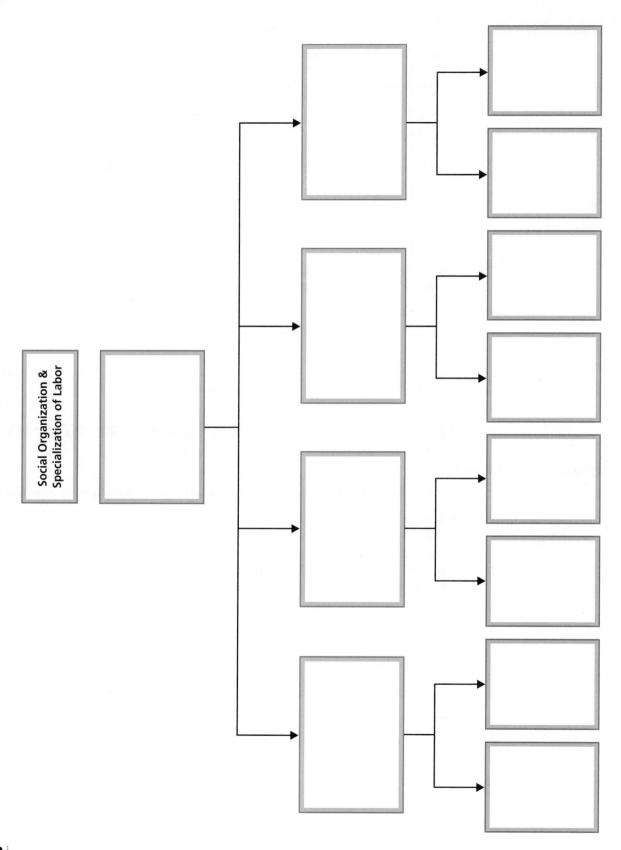

USE TITLE AND HEADINGS TO PREDICT CONTENT

In the Introductory Reading, you previewed the title and headings of a reading by creating a diagram. Another way of previewing the title and headings is by creating a flowchart.

A **Before you work with the Main Reading on pages 123–127, go through it and write down the headings on the lines in the flowchart below.**

Setting the Stage for Civilization: The Origins of Food Production

---

_____

Possible Reasons for This Developing Need:
-
-
-

↓ This need led to

_____

Steps in the Transition:
1.

2.

3.

4.

5.

6.

7.

8.

This transition from gathering to production led to

↓

_____

This way of life enabled

↓

_____

B Work with a partner in a small group. Answer the questions and complete the diagram. When you are done, share your ideas as a class, and put everyone's ideas for the diagram on the board.

What are the steps that you think humans took in order to make the transition from food gathering to food production? Write your ideas in the diagram on page 121.

C Go to page *vi* in the Table of Contents. Read the brief summary of the Main Reading. Then review your diagram on page 121, and decide whether to change any of your predictions.

D On a separate piece of paper, write a paragraph describing how a society based on hunting and gathering food might have developed villages, trade, and, eventually, civilization.

LEARN AND USE WORD FORMS

Remember that you can expand your vocabulary in English by learning word forms.

A Study the following chart, which contains words from the Main Reading. Note the spelling changes. Pay attention to the words as they are used in the Main Reading.

VERB	NOUN	ADJECTIVE	ADVERB
accelerate	acceleration	accelerating accelerated	
colonize	colonization colony	colonial	
domesticate	domestication	domesticated	
justify	justification	justified	
organize	organization	organized	
produce	production product	productive	productively
stimulate	stimulation	stimulating	
appear	appearance		
emerge	emergence	emerging	
exist	existence	existing	
maintain	maintenance	maintained	
subsist	subsistence	subsistence	

B Complete the following paragraph by circling the correct form of the word in parentheses. When you are done, check your answers by reading paragraph 9 on page 127.

Focusing here on developments in western Asia after the switch from food-gathering to food (production / produce / productive), the next steps in
1.
the region's (acceleration / accelerate / accelerating) evolution toward
2.
civilization were the (emergence / emerge / emerging) of villages, the rise of
3.
long-distance trade, and the onset of bitter warfare. Villages constituted the most advanced form of human (organization / organized) in western Asia
4.
from about 6500 to about 3500–3000 B.C.E., when some villages gradually became cities. Village organization inevitably brought about long-distance trade, and it just as inevitably provoked the growth of war. No doubt warfare has been the bane of human (existence / exist / existing), with famine and
5.
disease, at least since the (appearance / appear) of agricultural villages, but
6.
since the growth of warfare in ancient times
(stimulation / stimulated / stimulating) the growth of economic and social
7.
complexity, it nonetheless must be counted as a step toward the emergence of civilization.

MAIN READING

The Main Reading, "Setting the Stage for Civilization: The Origins of Food Production," is also from World Civilizations: Their History and Their Culture, Volume One. *As you read, highlight the important ideas and vocabulary used to express those ideas. For this reading, be sure to highlight and number the steps in the process that humans took in their transition from food-gathering to food production. The highlighting and numbering will help you complete a flowchart when you have finished reading.*

Setting the Stage for Civilization: The Origins of Food Production

1   The era between 35,000 and 12,000 years ago had been an Ice Age. Within about 3,000 to 4,000 years after the end of the Ice Age, humans in western Asia had accomplished one of the most momentous revolutions ever accomplished by any humans: a switch from subsistence by means of food-gathering to subsistence by means of food-producing. For roughly two million years humanlike species and humans had gained their sustenance by

foraging, or by combined foraging and hunting. These modes of existence meant that such peoples could never stay very long in one place because they continually ate their way through local supplies of plant food, and, if they were hunters, they were forced to follow the movements of herds.

2   But "suddenly" (that is, in terms of the comparative time spans involved) substantial numbers of humans began to domesticate animals and raise crops, thereby settling down. As soon as this shift was accomplished, villages were founded, trade developed, and populations in areas of sedentary habitation started increasing by leaps and bounds. Then, when villages began evolving into cities, civilization was born. "The rest is history" in a very literal sense, for human history—as opposed to prehistory—really began with the birth of civilization.

BEFORE YOU CONTINUE READING

1. After 2 million years of living by hunting or hunting and gathering, humans began to domesticate animals, raise crops, establish villages, and develop trade. About how long was the process that took them from hunting/gathering to civilization?

    a. *millions of years*

    b. *thousands of years*

    c. *hundreds of years*

THE GRADUALLY DEVELOPING NEED FOR RELIABLE FOOD SOURCES

3   To say that some humans became food producers all of a sudden is of course justifiable only in terms of the broadest chronological picture. Seen from the perspective of modern historical change, wherein technological revolutions transpire in a few decades or years, the change in western Asia from food-gathering to food production was an extremely gradual one. Not only did the transition take place over the course of some 3,000 to 4,000 years (c. 10,000 to c. 7000/6000 B.C.E.), but it was so gradual that the peoples involved hardly knew themselves what was happening.

4   The story of how humans became food producers is roughly as follows. Around 10,000 B.C.E. most of the larger game herds had left western Asia. Yet people in coastal areas were not starving; on the contrary, they were surrounded by plenty because the melting glaciers had raised water levels and thereby had introduced huge quantities of fish, shellfish, and water fowl in newly created bays and swamps. Excavations near Mount Carmel and at the site of Jericho in modern-day Israel—locations not far from the Mediterranean Sea—prove that wildlife and vegetation in that area between about 10,000 and 9000 B.C.E. were so lush that people could sustain themselves in permanent settlements in an unprecedented fashion, easily catching fish and fowl, and picking fruits off trees as if they were in the Garden of Eden. But the plenty of Mount Carmel and Jericho had its costs in terms of population trends. Modern nomadic hunting peoples have low birthrates, and the same is presumed to have been true of prehistoric peoples.

The given in this regard is that a woman can trek with one baby in her arms but hardly with two; hence nature finds ways to limit nomadic births for each woman to one every three or four years. Once people became sedentary in Eden-like environments, however, their reproductive rates began to increase, until, over the course of centuries, there were too many people for the lush coastal terrains.

BEFORE YOU CONTINUE READING

2. What were some of the negative consequences of a sedentary (non-nomadic) lifestyle?

> **a.** *The population increased rapidly, and people did not have enough food.*
>
> **b.** *People had plenty of food to eat and had permanent homes to live in.*

THE GRADUAL TRANSITION FROM FOOD GATHERING TO FOOD PRODUCTION

5
[1]Accordingly, paleoanthropologists posit, or hypothesize, that around 9000 B.C.E. excess populations in western Asia started migrating inland to territories where wildlife and plant foods were less plentiful, and where they were forced to return to the nomadic ways of hunter-gatherers. [2]What is certain is that between 9000 and 8000 B.C.E. some humans in Iran had taken the first known step toward food production by domesticating animals—in this case, sheep and goats. [3]This would have been no more than the equivalent of taking out a small insurance policy. [4]People seeking to avoid overreliance on one particular food source, and starvation if that source failed, captured live animals and gradually bred them so that they had meat on the hoof, available whenever the need arose. [5]Owning a few sheep or goats did not inhibit the people who first domesticated them from continuing in their nomadic way of life (it is easier to travel with trained goats than with babies). [6]But it did make them accustomed to the notion of actively manipulating their environments.

6
Producing plant food came next. After the glaciers had receded, wild wheat and wild barley had begun to grow in scattered hilly parts of inland western Asia. Accustomed to gathering all sorts of seeds, hunter-gatherers between about 9000 and 8000 B.C.E. gladly drew on the wheat and barley because when these plants were ripe, gatherers could reap large amounts of seeds from them within as little as three weeks and then move on to other pursuits. Archeological discoveries reveal that the peoples in question developed flint sickles to accelerate their harvesting, mortars for grinding their harvested grain into flour, and—most significantly for future developments—lined storage pits for preserving their grain or flour. In other words, these peoples had not only begun to pay special attention to harvesting wild grain, but they were saving their harvests for use over time. Again, people were manipulating their environments instead of merely adjusting to them.

Fig. 3.5f Reaping grain with flint sickles (in ancient Egypt)

BEFORE YOU CONTINUE READING

3. About 10,000 years ago, the hunter-gatherers ____.

a. *collected seeds, planted them, cared for them, harvested them, prepared them, and stored them*

b. *developed simple technologies for harvesting, preparing, and storing seeds, but did not plant the seeds*

THE TRANSITION TO A SEDENTARY WAY OF LIFE

7   Still nomads, the same people most likely would have been content to gather their grain and other foods forever. But since grain could be stored particularly well, some groups of grain gatherers may have come gradually to rely on it more and more. In such cases they would have been adversely affected by a poor growing year or by gradual depletion caused by excessive harvesting. Then, paying more attention to keeping their wild grain growing profusely, they would have noticed that the grain would grow better if rival plants (weeds) were removed, still better if the soil were scratched so that falling seeds could take root more easily, and still better if they themselves sprinkled some seeds into sparser patches of soil. The people who did these things were more influential discoverers and explorers in terms of the origins of our own modern existence than Columbus or Copernicus, yet from their point of view they were merely adjusting some of the details of their ongoing hunting and gathering way of life.

8   Imperceptibly, however, they became "hooked" and surrendered their nomadic ways for sedentary ones. Already having small herds as "insurance policies," they must have decided at some point that it would be equally sensible to be able to count on having patches of planted grain awaiting them when they reached a given area on seasonal nomadic rounds. And then they would have

learned that planting could be done better at a different time of year than harvesting, and then that their livestock might graze well on harvested stubble, and then that they might grow more than one crop a year in the same place. Meanwhile they would have become more and more accustomed to storing and would have seen less and less reason to move away from their fields and their stores. And so sedentary plant-food production, or agriculture, was invented.

BEFORE YOU CONTINUE READING

4. About 8,000 years ago, ____.

   a. *these people were no longer hunter-gatherers; they were farmers who knew how to plant seeds, grow crops, and raise animals*

   b. *these people were still hunter-gatherers, but they understood how to plant seeds, grow crops, and raise animals*

Fig. 3.5g Illustration of a reconstructed prehistoric house

THE EMERGENCE OF VILLAGES, TRADE, AND CIVILIZATION

9   Focusing here on developments in western Asia after the switch from food-gathering to food production, the next steps in the region's accelerating evolution toward civilization were the emergence of villages, the rise of long-distance trade, and the onset of bitter warfare. Villages constituted the most advanced form of human organization in western Asia from about 6500 to about 3500–3000 B.C.E., when some villages gradually became cities. Village organization inevitably brought about long-distance trade, and it just as inevitably provoked the growth of war. No doubt warfare has been the bane of human existence, with famine and disease, at least since the appearance of agricultural villages, but since the growth of warfare in ancient times stimulated the growth of economic and social complexity it nonetheless must be counted as a step toward the emergence of civilization.

Checking Comprehension

A Complete the flowchart below according to the information on pages 123–127.

Setting the Stage for Civilization: The Origins of Food Production

_____

Possible Reasons for This Developing Need:

-
-
-

This need led to

⬇

_____

Steps in the Transition:

1.

2.

3.

4.

5.

6.

7.

8.

This transition from gathering to production led to

⬇

_____

This way of life enabled

⬇

_____

Compare this flowchart with the one you completed on page 121. What information do you have that you did not have before?

_____

B Refer to paragraph 5 on page 125. Identify the referents.

1. In the first sentence, *they* refers to _____.

2. In the third sentence, *this* refers to _____.

3. In the fourth sentence, *that source* refers to _____.

4. In the last sentence, *it* refers to _____.

C Circle the correct answers.

1. How long did the transition from food gathering to agriculture take?
a. about eight or nine thousand years
b. about three or four thousand years
c. about one or two thousand years

2. According to the passage, which one of the following discoveries was the most important?
a. Columbus's discovery of America
b. Copernicus's discovery that the Earth and planets revolve around the sun
c. Humans' discovery of agriculture

D Answer the following questions in complete sentences.

1. When people found food by foraging and hunting, was their food supply dependable, or was it irregular? Why?

_____

_____

2. Hunter-gatherers were constantly moving, looking for food, and following the herds. Then they gradually switched to producing food instead of looking for it. In what ways did this change affect their way of life?

_____

_____

3. Why does the author call the domestication of animals a type of insurance policy?

_____

_____

4. What were some of the effects of the emergence of villages?

_____

_____

VOCABULARY FROM CONTEXT

Reread the paragraphs indicated from the Main Reading to figure out the meaning of the italicized words. Then circle the correct choice to complete the sentences that follow.

1. Paragraph 1: *subsistence* and *foraging*

   (1) From this context, we can understand that *subsistence* means
   ___.
   a. survival
   b. travel
   c. cooking

   (2) From the context, we can also understand that ___ is similar in meaning to *subsistence.*
   a. following the herds
   b. eating local plants
   c. gaining sustenance

   (3) When early humans *foraged,* they ___.
   a. searched for plants
   b. hunted for animals
   c. grew plants for food

2. Paragraph 2: *suddenly*

   The word *"suddenly"* is in quotation marks because the transition from searching for food to producing food ___.
   a. really happened very quickly
   b. really happened very slowly

3. Paragraph 3: *transition*

   (1) In this context, we can understand that a *transition* is ___.
   a. a completely new idea
   b. a revolution in technology
   c. a change from one thing to another thing

   (2) In this paragraph, a synonym for *transition* is the word ___.
   a. shift
   b. perspective
   c. production

4. Paragraph 8: *sedentary*

   (1) When people *settle down,* they ___.
   a. move from place to place
   b. stay in one place

   (2) When people settle down, they become ___.
   a. civilized
   b. farmers
   c. sedentary

USING THE DICTIONARY

Read the following sentences and dictionary entries. Select the best entry for the context, and circle the correct choice to complete the sentences that follow.

1. But "suddenly" substantial numbers of humans began to domesticate animals and raise crops, thereby settling down. As soon as this shift was accomplished, villages were *founded*, trade developed, and populations in areas of sedentary habitation started increasing by leaps and bounds.

> **found** *v.* [T] **1** to start something such as an organization, institution, company or city: *Founded in 1935 in Ohio, Alcoholics Anonymous is now a worldwide organization.* | *Mr. Packard was instrumental in founding the Stanford Industrial Park in the 1950s.* **2 to be founded on/upon sth a)** to base your ideas, beliefs etc. on something: *Racism is not founded on rational thought, but on fear.* | *The Soviet Union was originally founded on Socialism.* **b)** to be the solid layer of CEMENT, stones etc. that a building is built on: *The castle is founded on solid rock.* **3** TECHNICAL to melt metal and pour it into a MOLD (=a hollow shape), to make things such as tools, parts for machines etc. —**founding** *n.* [U] *the founding of the University of Chicago* —see also FOUNDATION, WELL-FOUNDED

(1) In this context, the best definition for *found* is number ____.

(2) According to the sentence, villages were ____.
a. based on people's ideas and beliefs
b. made of layers of cement and stones
c. started by people after the shift to sedentary habitation

2. To say that some humans became food producers all of a sudden is of course justifiable only in terms of the broadest chronological picture. Seen from the perspective of modern historical change, wherein technological *revolutions* transpire in a few decades or years, the change in western Asia from food-gathering to food production was an extremely gradual one.

> **rev·o·lu·tion** /ˌrɛvəˈluʃən/ *n.* **1** [C] a complete change in ways of thinking, methods of working etc.: *Penicillin began a revolution in the treatment of infectious disease.* | *the technological revolution* —see also INDUSTRIAL REVOLUTION **2** [C,U] a time of great, usually sudden, social and political change, especially the changing of a ruler or political system by force: *the Bolshevik Revolution of 1917* —compare REBELLION —see also COUNTERREVOLUTION **3** [C,U] one complete circular movement, or continued circular movement, around a certain point: *The Earth makes one revolution around the sun each year.* **4** [C] one complete circular spinning movement, made by something such as a wheel fastened on a central point: *a speed of 100 revolutions per minute* —see also REVOLVE

(1) In this context, the best definition of *revolution* is number ____.

(2) The gradual change from food-gathering to food production ___.
   a. involved a complete change in people's methods of working
   b. was a time of great and sudden social and political change
   c. involved complete circular movements to harvest crops

3. Archeological discoveries reveal that the peoples in question developed flint sickles to accelerate their harvesting, mortars for grinding their harvested grain into flour, and—most significantly for future developments—lined storage pits for preserving their grain or flour. In other words, these peoples had not only begun to pay special attention to harvesting wild grain, but they were saving their harvests for use over time. Again, people were manipulating their environments instead of merely adjusting to them.

> **ma·nip·u·late** /məˈnɪpyəˌleɪt/ *v.* [T] **1** DISAPPROVING to make someone do what you want by deceiving or influencing them: *Students were outraged that someone could use their newspaper to manipulate them.* **2** DISAPPROVING to dishonestly change information or influence an event or situation: *Local people were unwilling to believe that the police had manipulated evidence.* **3** to work with or change informaton, systems etc. to achieve the result that you want: *The images can be manipulated and stored on disk.* | *Developing a budget involves manipulating numbers and requires strong analytical skills.* **4** to make something move or turn in a way that you want, especially using your hands: *Babies investigate their world by manipulating objects.* | *Players manipulate characters on the screen using a joystick.* **5** TECHNICAL to skillfully move and press a joint or bone into the correct position —**manipulation** /məˌnɪpyəˈleɪʃən/ *n.* [U]

(1) In this context, the best definition of *manipulate* is number ___.

(2) Over time, these people learned to ___.
   a. influence the environment to do what they wanted it to do
   b. dishonestly change the environment to achieve the results they wanted
   c. change the environment with their hands to achieve the result they wanted
   d. make the environment move or turn in the way they wanted, especially by using their hands

LEARN AND USE WORD FORMS

Complete the sentences below with the correct form of the word from the box. Refer to the word forms chart on page 122. Be sure to use the correct tense of verbs. Use each word only once.

domesticate	maintain	subsist
justify	produce	

1. Anthropologists' hypotheses are probably _____, given the strong evidence they have found so far in support of their theories.

2. When people _____ only on the food they could find, their lives were very difficult.

3. Once people learned to remove weeds, scratch the soil, and sprinkle the seeds themselves, the land became much more _____, and people had more to eat.

4. The first _____ animals were probably sheep and goats.

5. For a population to grow, and for villages to emerge, people need to _____ a steady food supply in reliable ways by farming and raising animals.

FOLLOW-UP ASSIGNMENTS

Before you begin any of the follow-up assignments, review the content-specific vocabulary and the academic vocabulary below. Read over the vocabulary in the word forms lists on pages 112 and 122. If you are still unsure what any words or terms mean, go back through the chapter and review. As you complete the assignments, be sure to incorporate the appropriate vocabulary in your writing.

Content-Specific Vocabulary

agriculture	domesticate	Ice Age	nomadic
anatomical	forage	implement	sedentary
civilization	harvest	migrate	subsistence
differentiation of labor	hunting-gathering	mural	transition

Academic Vocabulary

colonize	recede	settle	switch
found (verb)	reliable	shift	technique
hypothesize	repertoire	source	tool
gather	revolution	sustain	vanish
manipulate			

Writing Exercises

1. Write a paragraph describing how people made the transition from food gathering to food-producing, that is, to farming (agriculture).
2. Write a paragraph describing what you imagine people's lives were like during the last Ice Age, that is, between 30,000 and 12,000 B.C.E.
3. Think about the two groups of people mentioned in the reading: "Some humans may have moved north with the game but others stayed behind, creating an extremely different sort of world in comparatively short order." Write two paragraphs. In the first paragraph, describe the world that the hunters had. In the second paragraph, describe the "extremely different sort of world" created by the group that stayed behind.

Extension Activities

1. Reread pages 113–114 and pages 123–127. Complete the time line on the following page. When you have finished the time line, answer the questions that follow.

   a. Do the dates on the time line indicate the exact dates that something began, happened, or was invented? Explain your answer.

   _____

   _____

   b. Do you think the people living in the ancient past understood the passage of time in the same way we do today? Explain your answer.

   _____

   _____

   c. In the period before 300,000 B.C.E., early humans invented stone tools, tamed fire, and began to care for their elderly and infirm. Did people stop doing these things after 300,000 B.C.E.? Did people stop creating cave art after 12,000 B.C.E.? Explain your answer.

   _____

   _____

2. Hunting-gathering societies still exist in the world today. Other societies maintained a hunting-gathering way of life until recently. Research one of these societies. Prepare a brief presentation describing this society. Be sure to include illustrations.

Time Line of *Homo sapiens* Development

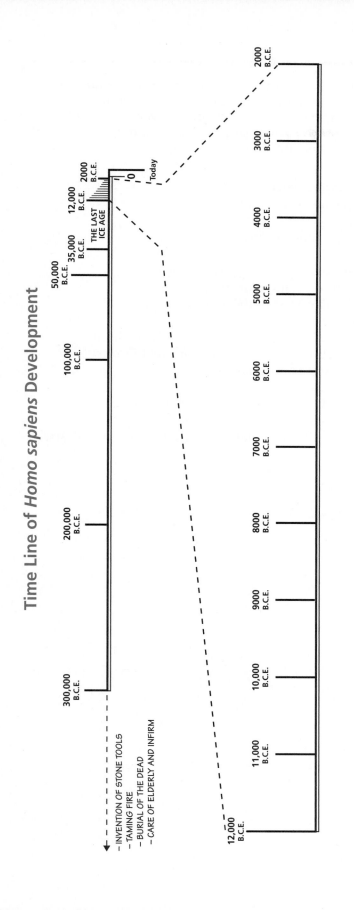

Go online, and go to one of the websites listed below. Investigate a topic related to the information you read about in Chapter 5. Choose a topic that especially interests you. Use some of the website's search features. Search by keywords such as *cave art, Ice Age, domestication of plants, domestication of animals.*

University of Reading, England, History of Agriculture website:
http://www.ecifm.rdg.ac.uk/history.htm
TryAgain website:
http://www.tryagain.com/humcivil/index.htm
Hyper History Online:
http://www.hyperhistory.com/online_n2/History_n2/a.html
A Definition of Civilization by Philip Atkinson:
http://www.users.bigpond.com/smartboard/civdef.htm
Poppa's World History: The Near East:
http://victorian.fortunecity.com/kensington/207/mideast0.html
Great Archeological Sites (grands sites archéologiques) of France:
http://www.culture.fr/culture/arcnat/lascaux/en
http://www.culture.fr/culture/arcnat/chauvet/en
Tourist Information for the Cantabria Region of Spain website:
http://www.turcantabria.com
Go to this website, then click on "English," click on "History and Art," then click on "caves."

EARLY CIVILIZATION

Fig. 3.6a Sumerian statuettes of three male worshippers

Chapter Readings

Mesopotamia: The First Civilization

Ancient Sumer: The World of the First Cities

INTRODUCING THE READING

Activate Your Knowledge

A **Work alone or in a small group. Do the following activities.**

What does a civilization consist of? In other words, what are some criteria (requirements) for a civilization? List your ideas.

_____   _____

_____   _____

_____   _____

_____   _____

B **Work as a class to develop a list on the board using ideas from the lists in the exercise above.**

C **Discuss the following questions with a partner or in a small group.**

1. What are some of the uses of a wheel?

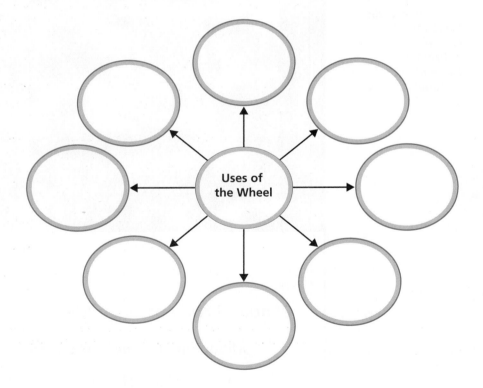

2. What are some of the uses of writing?

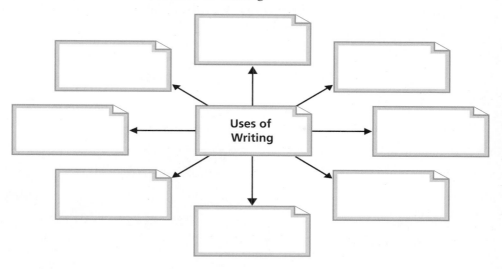

3. On the map below, locate the Tigris and the Euphrates rivers, and circle them. What is the climate in this area of the world? _____

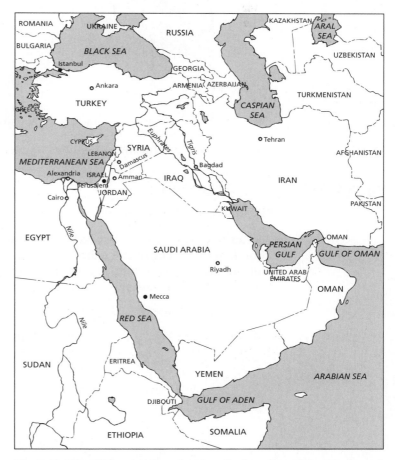

Fig. 3.6b The Mideast today, showing the location of the Tigris and Euphrates rivers.

4. The map below is an enlargement of the area you circled on the map in the previous activity. Examine this map. What features, or characteristics, of this area do you observe that might have made it an ideal location for a civilization to emerge?

_____   _____

_____   _____

_____   _____

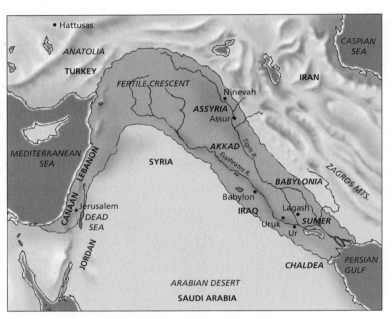

Fig. 3.6c The area around the Tigris and Euphrates rivers

Reading and Study Skill Strategies

PREVIEW KEY VOCABULARY

Read the list of content-specific vocabulary and check the ones you are familiar with. Leave the other spaces blank. Do not try to learn the unfamiliar items before you begin reading. You will learn them as you work with the chapter.

___ Babylon   ___ fertile   ___ invention

___ city-states   ___ Hammurabi   ___ irrigation

___ civilization   ___ harvest   ___ jurisprudence

___ code of law   ___ history   ___ Sargon

___ cuneiform   ___ inhabit   ___ social stratification

___ dynasty   ___ innovation   ___ Sumer

USE TITLE AND HEADINGS TO PREDICT CONTENT

A Work with a partner or in a small group. Before you work with the Introductory Reading on pages 143–144, go through it and write down the heading on the line below. Then try to answer the following questions about the title and the heading.

Mesopotamia: The First Civilization

_____

1. Write a definition of *invention*.

   _____

   _____

2. Write a definition of *innovation*.

   _____

   _____

3. What do you think the Mesopotamians invented? Make a list.

   _____   _____

   _____   _____

4. What innovations do you think the Mesopotamians were the first to develop? Make a list.

   _____   _____

   _____   _____

B Go to page *vi* in the Table of Contents. Read the brief summary of the Introductory Reading. Then review your responses above, and decide whether to change any of them.

LEARN AND USE WORD FORMS

A Study the following chart which contains words from the Introductory Reading. Note the spelling changes. Pay attention to the words as they are used in the Introductory Reading.

VERB	NOUN	ADJECTIVE	ADVERB
civilize	civilization	civilized	
contribute	contribution contributor		
express	expression	expressive	expressively
inhabit	inhabitant	inhabited	
invent	invention inventor	inventive	
narrate	narration narrative	narrative narrated	
document	document	documented	
form	form	formative	formatively
function	function	functional	functionally
influence	influence	influential	influentially
pioneer	pioneer	pioneering	
record	record	recorded	

B Complete the following paragraph by writing the correct form of the word in parentheses. When you are done, check your answers by reading paragraph 1 on page 143.

Mesopotamia: The First Civilization

History begins in Sumer. Modern knowledge of the first 35,000 years of human life is based entirely on archeological _____, for until only a little more than 5,000 years
1. (record)
ago humans left behind many things but no words. Around 3200 B.C.E., however, in a region of Mesopotamia known as Sumer, the earliest forms of writing _____ and "history began" in the sense that
2. (invent)
words _____ that help current scholars understand
3. (record)
what men and women were doing.

Obviously the _____ of writing alone would
                    4. (invent)
earn the ancient Mesopotamians a prominent place among the most

_____ and _____ peoples who
        5. (invent)   6. (influence)
contributed to the forward movement of humankind. But amazingly the

peoples who _____ Mesopotamia in the centuries
                    7. (inhabit)
between roughly 3200 and roughly 500 B.C.E. _____
                                                        8. (contribute)
much more.

INTRODUCTORY READING

The following reading, "Mesopotamia: The First Civilization," is from World
Civilizations: Their History and Their Culture, Volume One. *As you read,
highlight the important ideas and the vocabulary used to express those
ideas. Monitor your comprehension by answering the Before You Continue
Reading question.*

Mesopotamia: The First Civilization

1   History begins in Sumer. Modern knowledge of the first 35,000 years
of human life is based entirely on archeological records, for until only a little
more than 5,000 years ago humans left behind many things but no words.
Around 3200 B.C.E., however, in a region of Mesopotamia known as Sumer,
the earliest forms of writing were invented and "history began" in the sense
that words were recorded that help current scholars understand what men and
women were doing.

BEFORE YOU	**History begins when people ____.**
CONTINUE	**a.** *begin to have something important to record*
READING	**b.** *begin to keep written records*
	c. *help scholars understand what people are doing*

MESOPOTAMIAN INVENTIONS AND INNOVATIONS

2   [1]Obviously the invention of writing alone would earn the ancient
Mesopotamians a prominent place among the most inventive and influential
peoples who ever contributed to the forward movement of humankind. [2]But
amazingly the peoples who inhabited Mesopotamia in the centuries between
roughly 3200 and roughly 500 B.C.E. contributed much more. [3]We sometimes
forget that somebody had to have invented the wheel, but somebody did, and
he or she was a Mesopotamian who lived around 3000 B.C.E. [4]Somebody had
to invent the calendar too, and somebody had to invent the mathematical
functions of multiplication and division, and those persons also were ancient
Mesopotamians. [5]Aside from arriving at such inventions, the Mesopotamians
were profound thinkers who pioneered in the life of the mind to such an

extent that their innovations in theology, jurisprudence, astronomy, and narrative literature all became fundamental for subsequent developments in these areas of thought and expression. [6]Assuredly the ancient Mesopotamians had their unattractive qualities; for example, their rulers were usually ruthless militarists, and their art often seems frigid or fierce. [7]Nevertheless, the "first chapter of history," which the Mesopotamians wrote by their exploits and their documents, was surely one of the most important chapters in the entire book of human events.

Fig. 3.6d Art from the Mesopotamian era

Checking Comprehension

A **Reread pages 143–144. Make a list of the Mesopotamians' inventions and innovations.**

_____ _____ _____

_____ _____ _____

How accurate were your guesses on page 141? _____

B **Refer to paragraph 2 in the Introductory Reading on pages 143–144. Identify the referents.**

1. In the third sentence, *we* refers to _____ .

2. In the third sentence, *he or she* refers to _____ .

3. In the fourth sentence, *those persons* refers to _____ .

4. In the last sentence, *which* refers to _____ .

C **Answer the following questions in complete sentences.**

1. Why does the author say that "history began" in Sumer in about 3200 B.C.E.?

_____

_____

2. Which invention or innovation of the Mesopotamians do you think is the most important? Why do you think so?

_____

_____

VOCABULARY FROM CONTEXT

Reread the paragraphs indicated from the Introductory Reading to figure out the meaning of the italicized words. Then circle the correct choice to complete the sentences.

1. Paragraph 1: *history*

   It is clear from this context that the term *history* refers to ___.
   a. archeological records of human life
   b. the many things that humans have left behind
   c. the written record of human events

2. Paragraph 2: *prominent* and *inhabited*

   (1) In this context, *prominent* means ___.
   a. special
   b. clear
   c. mythical

   (2) In this context, *inhabited* means ___.
   a. discovered
   b. lived in
   c. worked in

USING THE DICTIONARY

Read the following sentences and dictionary entries. Select the best entry for the context. Then circle the correct choice to complete the sentence that follows.

The Mesopotamians were *profound* thinkers who *pioneered* in the life of the mind to such an extent that their *innovations* in theology, jurisprudence, astronomy, and narrative literature all became fundamental for subsequent developments in these areas of thought and expression.

> **pro·found** /prəˈfaʊnd/ *adj.* **1** important and having a strong influence or effect: *The impact of these changes will be profound.* | *a book with profound social implications* **2** showing strong serious feelings: *Her death left me with a profound sense of sadness.* **3** showing great knowledge and understanding: *a profound remark* | *Much of what he had to say was very profound.* **4** complete; TOTAL: *profound deafness* | *There was a profound silence after his remark.* **5** LITERARY deep or far below the surface of something —**profoundly** *adv.*: *profoundly disturbing news*

pi·o·neer /ˌpaɪəˈnɪr/ *n.* [C] **1** one of the first people to do something that other people will later develop or continue to do: [+ **of/in**] *Dr. DeBakey was one of the pioneers of heart-transplant surgery.* | *pioneers in special education* | **pioneer photographer/geologist etc.** (=one of the first people to develop the skill of photography etc.) **2** one of the first people to travel to a new country or area and begin living there, farming etc.: *Many of the early pioneers left after a long cold winter.*

in·no·va·tion /ˌɪnəˈveɪʃən/ *n.* **1** [C] a new idea, method, or invention: *Anti-lock brakes have been a major safety innovation.* **2** [U] the introduction of new ideas, methods, or inventions: *Innovation and hard work are the cornerstones of this company.*

(1) The most appropriate definition of *profound* in this context is number ___.

(2) The thinking of the Mesopotamians ___ many areas of thought and expression.
   a. was important and had a strong influence on
   b. showed strong serious feelings on
   c. was complete in

(3) The appropriate definition of *pioneer* in this context is number ___.

(4) The Mesopotamians were the first people to ___.
   a. travel to the area between the Tigris and Euphrates rivers
   b. develop theology, astronomy, jurisprudence, and literature

LEARN AND USE WORD FORMS

Complete the sentences below with the correct form of the word in the box. Refer to the word form chart on page 142. Be sure to use the correct tense of verbs. Use each word only once.

express	invent	pioneer
inhabit	narrate	

1. Ancient Mesopotamians were _____ of the wheel, writing, and mathematical functions.

2. The ancient _____ of Mesopotamia contributed much that we still use in our modern world.

3. The ancient Mesopotamians had a _____ spirit in many areas including mathematics and law.

4. Mesopotamian literature is often very _____. These ancient people wrote very vividly about their feelings.

5. The story of Gilgamesh is a Mesopotamian _____ that has been translated into many languages.

INTRODUCING THE MAIN READING

Activate Your Knowledge

Work with a partner or in a small group. Answer the following questions.

1. What do you think is the most outstanding characteristic of a civilization? Explain your answer.

   _____

   _____

2. Who were the Sumerians?

   _____

   _____

3. Describe the writing system that the Sumerians invented. For example, was it pictographic like Chinese characters? Was it alphabetic like English or Korean?

   _____

   _____

4. What do you think happened to the Sumerians? Explain your answer.

   _____

   _____

Reading and Study Skill Strategies

USE TITLES AND HEADINGS TO PREDICT CONTENT

A **Work with a partner or in a small group. Before you work with the Main Reading, go through it and write down the headings in the outline on the following page. Then write what you think you will read about under each heading. Some ideas have already been listed. Share your ideas as a class, and put together an outline on the board.**

Ancient Sumer: The World of the First Cities

I. Sumerian Inventions and Innovations

    A. _____

    B. _____

    C. _____

II. _____

    A. Pictorial conventions

    B. _____

    C. _____

III. _____

    A. The main cause was _____

    B. _____

IV. _____

    A. One distinction was _____

    B. The second distinction was _____

V. _____

    A. One law was _____

    B. Another law was _____

VI. _____

    A. They used tables for _____

    B. They also used tables for _____

    C. A precedent we still use today is _____

B Go to page _vi_ in the Table of Contents. Read the brief summary of the Main Reading. Then review your outline above, and decide whether to change any of your predictions.

LEARN AND USE WORD FORMS

A Study the chart on the following page, which contains words from the Main Reading. Note the spelling changes. Pay attention to the words as they are used in the Main Reading.

VERB	NOUN	ADJECTIVE	ADVERB
appreciate	appreciation	appreciative	appreciatively
conclude	conclusion	concluding	
deteriorate	deterioration	deteriorating	
determine	determination	determined	
irrigate	irrigation		
retaliate	retaliation	retaliatory	
stratify	stratification	stratified	
unify	unification	unified/unifying	
chronicle	chronicle	chronicled	
harvest	harvest	harvested	
last	last	lasting	
rule	rule/ruler	ruled/ruling	

B **Complete the following paragraph by writing the correct form of the word in parentheses. When you are done, check your answers by reading paragraph 1 on page 150.**

Ancient Sumer: The World of the First Cities

Between 3500 and 3200 B.C.E., Mesopotamia, the land between the Tigris and Euphrates rivers, became the first civilized territory on the globe in the sense that its society and culture rested on the existence of cities. We may call the historical period that ensued, _____
1. (last)
from about 3200 B.C.E. to about 2000 B.C.E., the "Sumerian era." During the first nine centuries of the Sumerian era no _____
2. (unify)
government existed in Sumer; instead, the region was dotted with numerous independent city-states. Then, around 2320 B.C.E., all Sumer was conquered by a mighty warrior from Akkad, the part of Mesopotamia lying directly to the north. This warrior's birth name does not survive, but contemporaries called him "Sargon the Great." Mesopotamian _____
3. (chronicle)
record that Sargon gained control of Sumer by winning thirty-four battles. For almost two centuries Sargon the Great's dynasty

_____ an empire consisting of Akkad and Sumer.
4. (rule)

MAIN READING

The Main Reading, "Ancient Sumer: The World of the First Cities," is also from World Civilizations: Their History and Their Culture, Volume One. *As you read, highlight the important ideas and the vocabulary used to express those ideas. Remember to highlight all the italicized and **boldfaced** vocabulary.*

Ancient Sumer: The World of the First Cities

1   Between 3500 and 3200 B.C.E., Mesopotamia, the land between the Tigris and Euphrates rivers [see the maps on pages 139 and 140], became the first civilized territory on the globe in the sense that its society and culture rested on the existence of cities. We may call the historical period that ensued, lasting from about 3200 B.C.E. to about 2000 B.C.E., the "Sumerian era" because the most advanced part of Mesopotamia was then its southernmost territory, Sumer, a region of mud flats, which was roughly the size of Massachusetts. During the first nine centuries of the Sumerian era no unified government existed in Sumer; instead, the region was dotted with numerous independent city-states, the most important of which were Uruk, Ur, and Lagash. Then, around 2320 B.C.E., all Sumer was conquered by a mighty warrior from Akkad, the part of Mesopotamia lying directly to the north. This warrior's birth name does not survive, but we know that he took the title of "Sargon," which means "true king," and that contemporaries called him "Sargon the Great." Mesopotamian chronicles record that Sargon gained control of Sumer by winning thirty-four battles; when his victories finally brought him to "the lower sea" (the Persian Gulf), he washed his weapons in its waters to signify the end of struggle. For almost two centuries thereafter Sargon the Great's dynasty ruled an empire consisting of Akkad and Sumer. But around 2130 B.C.E. Sumer regained its independence and enjoyed a "revival" that lasted until roughly 2000 B.C.E., during which time most of the region was ruled by kings who resided in Ur. The Sumerians' accomplishments during this revival were truly extraordinary.

Fig. 3.6e Sargon the Great

SUMERIAN INVENTIONS AND INNOVATIONS

2   Sumer's accomplishments were preponderantly influenced by its climate and geography. Although the soil between the southern Tigris and southern Euphrates was extremely fertile, irrigation was essential because there was almost no rainfall for eight months of each year and torrential spring showers came too late to water the main crops that had to be harvested in April. (The summer months were not productive in Sumer because temperatures then rose to a soil-parching 125°F.) Collective work on irrigation projects demanded careful planning and assertive leadership, which in turn led to social stratification, professional specialization, and the emergence of cities. The situation in Sumer was further determined by the fact that southern Mesopotamia was entirely lacking in natural resources such as stone, minerals, and even trees. This meant that Sumer's inhabitants were forced to rely heavily on trade and to be very alert to any possible means of redressing economic imbalances to their advantage. In other words, the Sumerians had to subdue nature rather than live off its plenty.

3   One of the Sumerians' most remarkable inventions, which they perfected about the time the Sumerian era was opening (around 3200 B.C.E.),

was wheeled transport. To appreciate how advanced this invention was from a comparative perspective, it should be noted that wheeled transport was unknown in Egypt until about 1700 B.C.E. and that wheels were unknown in the Western Hemisphere (except for Peruvian children's toys) until they were introduced by Europeans. Probably the first Sumerian to think of employing a circular device turning on an axis for purposes of conveyance had seen a potter's wheel, for as early as about 4000 B.C.E., wheels were used in pottery-making in Iran, from whence they entered Sumer about 500 years later. The process of extending the principle of the wheel from pottery-making to transport was by no means obvious; the Egyptians knew the potter's wheel by at least 2700 B.C.E., but they did not use the wheel for transport until a millennium later, and even then they probably did not "reinvent the wheel" but learned of it from contacts with Mesopotamia. Thus the unknown Sumerian who first attached wheels to a sledge to make a better transportation vehicle really does have to be counted among the greatest technological geniuses of all time.

THE INVENTION OF WRITING

4   Ranking together with the wheel and the calendar as one of Sumer's three most precious gifts to succeeding Western civilizations was the invention of writing. To say that writing was "invented" is slightly misleading inasmuch as the emergence of writing in Sumer was gradual, evolving over the course of a millennium (c. 3500 to c. 2500 B.C.E.) from the representation of ideas by means of pictorial conventions to writing (albeit not alphabetic writing) as we currently know it. Around 3500 B.C.E. Sumerians had begun to carve pictures in stone or to stamp them on clay as ownership marks: a picture might have stood for a person's nickname (perhaps a rock for "Rocky") or dwelling (a house by a tree). Some five centuries later the evolution toward writing had advanced vastly farther. By then Sumerian temple administrators were using many standardized schematic pictures in combination with each other to preserve records of temple property and business transactions. Although the script of this period was still pictographic, it had advanced beyond pictures standing for people and tangible things to pictures standing for abstractions: a bowl meant any kind of food and a

Fig. 3.6f Sign for "fish" in (1) pictographic form, c. 3000 B.C.E. (2) cuneiform, c. 2400 B.C.E. and (3) 650 B.C.E.

head with a bowl conveyed the concept of eating [see the lower left corner of the clay tablet in Figure 3.6g]. After five more centuries full-fledged writing had taken over, for by then the original pictures had become so schematized that they were no longer recognizable as pictures but had to be learned purely as signs, and many of these signs no longer represented specific words but had become symbols of syllables that turned into words when combined with other such signs.

Fig. 3.6g A cuneiform clay tablet, about 3000 B.C.E.

5   The writing system that reached its fully developed form in Sumer around 2500 B.C.E. is known as *cuneiform* because it was based on wedge-shaped characters (*cuneus* is Latin for wedge) impressed on wet clay by a reed stylus with a triangular point. In total there were about 500 cuneiform characters, and many of these had multiple meanings (the "right one" could only be identified in context), making the system much more difficult to learn than subsequent writing

systems based on alphabets. Nonetheless, cuneiform served well enough to be used as the sole writing system of Mesopotamia for two millennia and even to become the standard medium of commercial transactions throughout most of western Asia until about 500 B.C.E.

BEFORE YOU CONTINUE READING

1. What were the Sumerians' three most significant innovations and inventions?

a. _____

b. _____

c. _____

THE DECLINE OF SUMERIAN DOMINANCE

6   [1]Although the Sumerians achieved marvels in mastering their physical environment, an ecological problem that escaped their attention was the steady deterioration of their soil caused by mounting salt content, a process technically known as salinization. [2]The irrigation of the dry soil of Sumer from the nearby rivers brought moisture, but it also brought salt, and the salt remained when the river water evaporated. [3]On a year-by-year basis the quantities of salt thus introduced into Sumer's soil were insignificant, but on a century-by-century basis they became deleterious to its fertility. [4]Study of surviving cuneiform tablets has shown that arable lands were becoming less productive in parts of Sumer by as early as 2350 B.C.E., a fact that may help to account for Sargon of Akkad's ability to conquer the whole region. [5]Sumer was not yet so weak that it could not rise up to overthrow the Akkadians two centuries later, but by around 2000 B.C.E. the region was sinking into permanent economic eclipse. [6]Unable to produce agricultural surpluses, Sumer's cities could no longer support their priests, administrators, and armies, and the area gradually yielded primacy in Mesopotamia to territories lying farther north.

THE OLD BABYLONIAN ERA

7   The Sumerian era of Mesopotamian history was followed by the Old Babylonian era, which lasted from about 2000 to about 1600 B.C.E. It must be emphasized that the first date is chosen arbitrarily, for nothing dramatic happened in the year 2000 to make a break from one era to another. Indeed, not only was the transition from Sumerian to Old Babylonian dominance in Mesopotamia gradual, but even when the Old Babylonian era had come to its fullest flowering around 1770 B.C.E., its culture was not dramatically different from the Sumerian culture that had preceded it. Two criteria alone allow for drawing any sharp distinctions between Sumerians and Old Babylonians: geography and language. We have seen that the most prosperous and culturally advanced cities in Mesopotamia during the Sumerian era were those that lay farthest to the south; during the succeeding 400 years, on the other hand, the weight of civilization shifted northwards to Akkad, where for much of the time it became centered on the newly founded city of Babylon. In addition, unlike the Sumerians who had spoken a language unrelated to any other, the peoples who held sway in Mesopotamia during the Old Babylonian era spoke languages that belonged to the Semitic language group (Arabic, Hebrew, for example).

BEFORE YOU
CONTINUE
READING

2. According to this paragraph, ＿.

    a. *the Sumerian era ended and the Old Babylonian era began; the two eras were very similar except for the language the people spoke and their location in the area*

    b. *the Sumerian era ended and the Old Babylonian era began; they were very similar because the people spoke the same language and lived in the same area*

HAMMURABI'S CODE OF LAW

8   The founder of the Old Babylonian empire was Hammurabi (1792–1750 B.C.E.[1]) Scholars agree that the **Code of Hammurabi**, a stone document containing 282 laws, was based on Sumerian legal principles with an admixture of Semitic innovations. The two most famous principles underlying Hammurabi's code are "an eye for an eye" and "let the buyer beware." At first both seem dreadfully primitive. In offering the recompense of exact retaliation ("if a man destroy the eye of another, his eye shall be destroyed"), the code never considers whether the initial injury may have been accidental. The "buyer beware" principle is less chilling but hardly seems like law. Hammurabi's code becomes more intelligible only if we recognize that it aimed at different ends than modern jurisprudence. The Mesopotamians promulgated laws primarily to stop fights. Thus they thought—and by no means without reason—that a person tempted to act violently might refrain from such behavior if he remembered that whatever wound he inflicted on another would probably be inflicted upon himself.

Fig. 3.6h Hammurabi's code; the top shows the king paying tribute to the seated god of justice

BEFORE YOU
CONTINUE
READING

3. The main purpose of Hammurabi's code of law was ＿.

    a. *to ensure fair treatment of everyone under the law*

    b. *to discourage people from fighting*

---

[1]Dates following a ruler's name refer to dates of reign.

BABYLONIAN MATHEMATICS

9   A final remarkable aspect of Old Babylonian culture lies in a very different area: mathematics. It is difficult to ascertain how far Old Babylonian accomplishments were indebted to Sumerian ones because the earliest records pertaining to the knowledge of mathematics in Mesopotamia are all Old Babylonian. Yet these display arithmetical and algebraic concepts that are so advanced that they must have been based on Sumerian foundations. As that may be, Old Babylonian temple scribes around 1800 B.C.E. were employing tables for multiplication and division, and also for calculating square roots, cube roots, reciprocals, and exponential functions. So impressive were these achievements that if only a single Old Babylonian mathematical tablet had survived it would still allow the conclusion that the Old Babylonians were the most accomplished arithmeticians in antiquity. A basic aspect of modern daily life that derives from Old Babylonian mathematical precedents is our division of the day into two sets of twelve hours, the hour into sixty minutes, and the minute into sixty seconds. When one stops to think of it, working with multiples of ten would be easier, but the Old Babylonians based their arithmetic on multiples of twelve (apparently because their most fundamental reckoning was that of twelve lunar cycles to a year), and all Western civilizations have adhered to Old Babylonian *duodecimal* time reckonings (those based on units of twelve) ever since.

Checking Comprehension

A **Complete the outline below according to the information on pages 150–154. Then compare this outline with your outline on page 148.**

Ancient Sumer: The World of the First Cities

I. Sumerian Inventions and Innovations

   A. _____

   B. _____

   C. _____

II. _____

   A. Pictorial conventions

   B. _____

   C. _____

III. _____

   A. The main cause was _____

   B. _____

IV. _____

    A. One distinction was _____

    B. The second distinction was _____

V. _____

    A. One law was _____

    B. Another law was _____

VI. _____

    A. They used tables for _____

    B. They also used tables for _____

    C. A precedent we still use today is _____

How much of your outline on page 148 was accurate? _____

B **Refer to paragraph 6 in the Main Reading on page 152. Identify the referents.**

  1. In the first sentence, _their_ refers to _____.

  2. In the second sentence, _it_ refers to _____.

  3. In the third sentence, _they_ refers to _____.

C **Circle the correct answers.**

  1. In Sumer, writing evolved from pictographic to syllabic form. How long did this process take?
    a. 3,500 years
    b. 1,000 years
    c. 500 years

  2. For how long did the cuneiform system of writing remain in use?
    a. 2,000 years
    b. 3,500 years
    c. 1,000 years

  3. What were the major differences between the Sumerian and the Old Babylonian eras? Circle all that apply.
    a. language
    b. culture
    c. writing system
    d. geography
    e. religion

D **Answer the following questions in complete sentences.**

1. What was Sargon's main accomplishment?

   _____

   _____

2. What were the major environmental influences on the Sumerian
   civilization? How did these natural features affect the development of
   Sumerian social organization and its economy?

   _____

   _____

3. Why does the author state that writing was not really "invented"?

   _____

   _____

4. What were some of the major accomplishments of the Sumerian
   civilization that we still use today?

   _____

   _____

5. Why did the Sumerian civilization fall?

   _____

   _____

6. One of Hammurabi's codes was "an eye for an eye." If a man killed
   another man, what would his punishment be, according to this law?

   _____

   _____

7. Another of Hammurabi's codes was "let the buyer beware." If a
   Babylonian bought a cow from another Babylonian, and the cow died the
   next day, what could the buyer do? Explain your reason for your answer.

   _____

   _____

VOCABULARY FROM CONTEXT

Reread the paragraphs indicated from the Main Reading to figure out the meaning of the italicized words. Then circle the correct choice to complete the sentences that follow.

1. Paragraph 1: *ensued, lasting,* and *unified*

   (1) From this context, we can understand that *ensued* means ___.
   a. happened
   b. followed
   c. civilized

   (2) From this context, we can understand that *lasting* means ___.
   a. continuing
   b. finishing
   c. recording

   (3) From this context, we can understand that *unified* means ___.
   a. strong
   b. democratic
   c. united

2. Paragraph 4: *dwelling, tangible,* and *abstract*

   (1) From this context, we can understand that a *dwelling* is a ___.
   a. tree
   b. home
   c. nickname

   (2) *Tangible* refers to something ___.
   a. real
   b. conceptual
   c. pictographic

   (3) *Abstract* refers to something ___.
   a. real
   b. pictographic
   c. conceptual

Fig. 3.6i Cuneiform pictograph for "eat"

3. Paragraph 6: *deterioration*

   (1) From this context, we can understand that *deterioration* ___.
   a. is a fast process
   b. is a slow process

   (2) From this context, we can understand that *deterioration* refers to ___.
   a. a process whereby something becomes worse
   b. a process whereby something becomes better
   c. a process whereby something stays the same

USING THE DICTIONARY

Read the following sentences and dictionary entries. Select the best entry for the context, and circle the correct choice to complete the sentences that follow.

1. Mesopotamian chronicles record that Sargon gained control of Sumer by winning thirty-four battles; when his victories finally brought him to "the lower sea" (the Persian Gulf), he washed his weapons in its waters to signify the end of struggle. For almost two centuries thereafter Sargon the Great's *dynasty* ruled an empire consisting of Akkad and Sumer.

> **dy•nas•ty** /ˈdaɪnəsti/ *n. plural* **dynasties** [C] **1** a family of kings or other rulers whose parents, grandparents etc. have ruled the country for many years: *The Habsburg dynasty ruled in Austria from 1278 to 1918.* **2** a period of time when a particular family ruled a country or area: *the Ming dynasty* **3** INFORMAL a group or family that controls a particular business or organization for a long period of time —**dynastic** /daɪˈnæstɪk/ *adj.*

   (1) In this context, the best definition for *dynasty* is number ___.

   (2) After Sargon the Great died, the rulers of the empire that he had created were ___.
   a. members of other families in the empire
   b. other kings in the area who claimed the empire
   c. his children, grandchildren, and great-grandchildren

2. Sumer was not yet so weak that it could not rise up to overthrow the Akkadians two centuries later, but by around 2000 B.C.E. the region was sinking into permanent economic *eclipse*. Unable to produce agricultural surpluses, Sumer's cities could no longer support their priests, administrators, and armies, and the area gradually yielded primacy in Mesopotamia to territories lying farther north.

> **e•clipse** /ɪˈklɪps/ **1** [C] an occasion when the sun or the moon cannot be seen because one of them is passing between the other one and the Earth: *I've never seen a **total eclipse of the sun*** (=an occasion when the sun is completely blocked by the moon so that the sun cannot be seen). —see also LUNAR ECLIPSE, SOLAR ECLIPSE **2** [U] FORMAL a situation in which someone or something else has become more powerful than or famous: *the eclipse of Europe's prestige after World War I* **3** **be in eclipse/go into eclipse** FORMAL to be or become less famous or powerful than before: *Left-wing political ideas seem to be in eclipse among young people.*

   (1) In this context, the best definition for *eclipse* is number ___.

   (2) By around 2000 B.C.E., the Sumerian region ___.
   a. could not see the moon or the sun
   b. became less important economically than it had been before
   c. lost its economic power and fame to another area

3. Not only was the transition from Sumerian to Old Babylonian dominance in Mesopotamia gradual, but even when the Old Babylonian era had come to its fullest *flowering* around 1770 B.C.E., its culture was not dramatically different from the Sumerian culture that had preceded it.

> **flow·er·ing** /ˈflaʊərɪŋ/ *n.* **the flowering of sth** a successful period in the development of something: *Reforms paved the way for a flowering of democracy in Eastern Europe.*

From this dictionary entry for the word *flowering,* we can understand that, at around 1770 B.C.E., ___.
a. Old Babylonia reached its highest level of achievement
b. Old Babylonia produced flowers to improve its economy
c. Sumer reached its highest level of achievement
d. Sumer produced flowers to improve its economy

LEARN AND USE WORD FORMS

Complete the sentences below with the correct form of the word in the box. Refer to the word forms chart on page 149. Be sure to use the correct tense of verbs. Use each word only once.

deteriorate	retaliate	unify
irrigate	stratify	

1. The Mesopotamians _____ their dry soil with water from the nearby rivers.

2. Hammurabi's law, "an eye for an eye," was _____ in nature. If someone injured another person's leg, then his leg would be injured.

3. Societies are often _____ by levels of power, wealth, prestige, or a combination of the three.

4. Sargon the Great _____ several independent city-states into one nation.

5. The Sumerians did not realize that their soil _____ because the salt content of the soil increased gradually over centuries.

FOLLOW-UP ASSIGNMENTS

Before you begin any of the follow-up assignments, review the content-specific vocabulary and the academic vocabulary below, and look over the vocabulary in the word forms lists on pages 142 and 149. If you are still unsure what any words or terms mean, go back through the chapter and review. As you complete the assignments, be sure to incorporate the appropriate vocabulary in your writing.

Content-Specific Vocabulary

Babylon	dynasty	inhabit	Sargon
city-states	fertile	innovation	social
civilization	Hammurabi	invention	stratification
code of law	harvest	irrigation	Sumer
cuneiform	history	jurisprudence	

Academic Vocabulary

abstract	deteriorate	to flower	rank
criteria (sg.	dominant	to last	salinization
criterion)	dwelling	pioneer	tangible
decline	to eclipse	profound	unify
deleterious	ensue	prominent	

Writing Activities

1. Write three paragraphs. In the first paragraph, describe the inventions and innovations of the ancient Sumerians. In the second paragraph, describe those of the Old Babylonians. In the third paragraph, describe the ones that we still rely on today, and speculate on why you think they have been in use for so many thousands of years.

2. The first civilization developed in Mesopotamia, but civilizations developed in other places as well, including the Western Hemisphere. Choose one of the following civilizations and research it in books and/or online: Egyptian, Hebrew, Greek, Indian, Chinese, Hittite, Etruscan, Phoenician, Roman, Incan, Aztecan. Focus on the civilization's inventions and innovations. Then write three paragraphs. In the first paragraph, summarize the inventions and innovations of the Mesopotamians. In the second paragraph, summarize the inventions and innovations of the civilization you chose. In the third paragraph, describe which inventions and innovations of both civilizations were particularly valuable, and explain why.

3. The ancient Mesopotamians expressed themselves in literature. Read one of their poems, which appears on the following page.

Little girl who sits in the ashes
Little girl with such a kind heart.
Your relatives forget you—all but your mother
Alas! Oh Alas! Your mother has been cremated.
Pious that you are little girl.
Though they throw you to the ashes
Your fairy comes to bless you.
Dance the night away.
Leave, but not forever, your prince will find you.
When the midnight hour strikes, the magic is undone
Your prince finds you home,
You become his bride.

What story does this poem remind you of? Why? _____

_____

Extension Activities

1. Examine the Mesopotamian clay tablet in Figure 3.6g. It is the earliest known form of writing and dates from about 3000 B.C.E.

Fig. 3.6g The earliest form of writing on clay tablets from Mesopotamia; about 3000 B.C.E.

   a. What do you think the round holes represent?
   b. Refer to the pictographs in Figure 3.6j below. Which symbols can you recognize in the tablet above?

Eat   Head   Hand   Date-palm   Barley   Orchard   Water   Well   Mountains

Fig. 3.6j Cuneiform pictographs

   c. What do you think was the purpose of this particular tablet? In other words, what do you think the writer recorded? Why do you think so?

2. As a class, choose two or three of the civilizations that you and your classmates researched. Using the chart below as a guide, compare these two or three civilizations to the Mesopotamian civilization. You will use this information later on, in Chapter 8.

CIVILIZATION	INVENTIONS	INNOVATIONS	INVENTIONS AND INNOVATIONS WE STILL USE TODAY

Internet Research

Go online, and go to one of the websites listed below. Investigate a topic related to the information you read about in Chapter 6. Choose a topic that especially interests you. Use some of the website's search features. Search by keywords such as *ancient history, Mesopotamia, Sumer, early civilizations, inventions.*

About.com website:
    http://ancienthistory.about.com/cs/mesoptimelines/index.htm
University of San Francisco, California, website:
    http://www.usfca.edu/westciv/Mesochro.html
The British Museum website:
    http://www.mesopotamia.co.uk/menu.html
Providence College, Providence, Rhode Island, website:
    http://www.providence.edu/dwc/mesopot1.htm
Metropolitan Museum of Art, New York, website:
    http://www.metmuseum.org/toah/ht/02/wam/ht02wam.htm

HOW HAVE PEOPLE REPRESENTED THE WORLD AROUND THEM?

(Left) Fig. 4.0a **Whirpool and Waves at Naruto, Awa Province** *by Hiroshige Utagawa, ca. 1797–1858, Japan*

(Below) Fig. 4.0b **Hunters in the Snow (January)** *by Peter Brueghel the Elder, 1565, The Netherlands*

(Above) Fig. 4.0c **Chimu Gold Funerary Mask,** *ca. 1100, Peru*

(Right) 4.0d **Dancing Apsara on Column in Angkor Thorn,** *ca. 1100, Cambodia*

CHAPTER 7

DEFINITION AND CONTEXT IN ART

Skills Goals

- *Review skills from Chapters 1–6.*
- *Annotate text.*

Content-Specific Goals

- *Understand the nature of art.*
- *Learn the part that imagination plays in art.*
- *Gain an understanding of the creative process.*
- *Learn about specific works of art.*

Chapter Readings

Art and the Artist

Creativity, Meaning, and Style

INTRODUCING THE READING

Activate Your Knowledge

A Work in a small group. Do the following activity.

What is art? Think about what defines art. Use the concept map below to help you organize your ideas. When you are finished, work as a class to put all the groups' ideas on the board. Decide on a definition of "art."

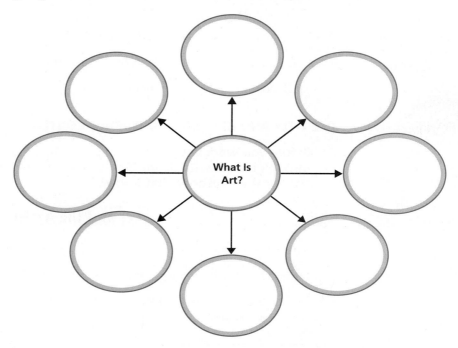

B On your own, think of a work of art that you particularly like. If possible, find a picture of it, or draw one if you can. Otherwise, describe the picture. Use the chart below to help you organize your information about the work of art. When you have finished, work with your group. Take turns describing the works of art. Take notes.

ARTIST'S NAME AND TITLE OF THE WORK	DESCRIPTION OF THE WORK	WHY YOU LIKE IT	HOW IT MEETS THE CLASS'S CRITERIA FOR "ART"

PREVIEW KEY VOCABULARY

Read the list of content-specific vocabulary and check the ones you are familiar with. Leave the other spaces blank. Do not try to learn the unfamiliar items before you begin reading. You will learn them as you work with the chapter.

___ aesthetic	___ genius	___ Michelangelo
___ artisan	___ imagination	___ Picasso
___ artist	___ intrinsic value	___ sculpture
___ craftsman	___ leap of the imagination	___ style
___ creativity	___ metaphor	___ talent

USE TITLE AND HEADINGS TO PREDICT CONTENT

A Before you work with the Introductory Reading on pages 169–170, go through it and write down the headings on the lines below. Then try to answer the questions that follow.

Art and the Artist

_____

_____

1. What connection is the author going to make between art and the artist who creates art?

_____

_____

2. In art, what is the role of the imagination?

_____

_____

3. For how long have people been creating art? In what ways is art uniquely human?

_____

_____

B Go to page *vi* in the Table of Contents. Read the brief summary of the Introductory Reading. Then review your answers above, and decide whether to change any of them.

LEARN AND USE WORD FORMS

A Study the following chart which contains words from the Introductory Reading. Note the spelling changes. Pay attention to the words as they are used in the Introductory Reading.

VERB	NOUN	ADJECTIVE	ADVERB
aspire to	aspiration	aspiring	
create	creation	creative	creatively
culminate	culmination	culminating	
define	definition	definitive	definitively
determine	determination	determined	
evolve	evolution	evolutionary	
express	expression	expressive	expressively
imagine	imagination	imaginative	imaginatively
separate	separation	separate	separately
acknowledge	acknowledgment	acknowledged	
develop	development	developmental	
judge	judgment	judgmental	

B Complete the following paragraph by writing the correct form of the word in parentheses. When you are done, check your answers by reading paragraph 4 on page 170.

Art as Uniquely Human

_____ is a fundamental part of our makeup,
1. (imagine)
though we share it with other creatures. By contrast, the urge to make art is

unique to us. It _____ us from all other creatures
2. (separate)
across an unbridgeable gap. The ability to make art must have been acquired

relatively recently in the course of _____. Human
3. (evolve)
creatures have been walking upright on Earth for some 4.4 million years,

but the oldest prehistoric art that we know of was made only about 35,000

years ago. It was undoubtedly the _____ of a long
4. (culminate)
_____ no longer traceable, since the record of the
5. (develop)
earliest art is lost to us.

ANNOTATE TEXT

Annotating text means writing brief notes in the margin. These notes might be a definition of a new word, a simple outline of a paragraph, key words, questions you have about what you have read, or comments you have about the text. Annotating may also include paraphrasing—putting pieces of important information into your own words. Annotating text helps you remember what you have read and makes it easy for you to find important words, phrases, or ideas when you are reviewing.

A **Read the following excerpt from the Introductory Reading, and study the annotation in the margin.**

Purpose of art—

- *helps us understand ourselves*
- *reaches deep into our being*

Artists—articulators (meaning?) of shared beliefs/values

> Art plays a special role in human personality. Like science and religion, art fulfills a universal urge to comprehend ourselves and the universe. This function makes art especially significant and, hence, worthy of our attention. Art has the power to reach the core of our being, which recognizes itself in the creative act. For that reason, art represents its creators' deepest understanding and highest aspirations. At the same time, artists often act as the articulators of shared beliefs and values, which they express through an ongoing tradition to us, their audience.

B **Annotate the following excerpt from the Introductory Reading.**

> "What is art?" Few questions provoke such heated debate and provide so few satisfactory answers. If we cannot come to any definitive conclusions, there is still quite a lot we can say. *Art* is first of all a *word,* one that acknowledges both the idea and the fact of art. Without the word, we might well ask whether art exists in the first place. The term, after all, is not found in the vocabulary of every society. Yet art is *made* everywhere. Art, therefore, is also an object, but not just any kind of object. Art is an *aesthetic object.* It is meant to be looked at and appreciated for its intrinsic value. Its special qualities set art apart, so that it is often placed away from everyday life, in museums, churches, or caves.

C **Work with a classmate and compare your annotations. Then compare your annotations with the annotations in paragraph 1 on page 169 when you begin reading. Keep in mind that your annotation does not have to be exactly the same. Annotating has been done for you in the entire Introductory Reading, as an example.**

INTRODUCTORY READING

The following reading, "Art and the Artist," is from A Basic History of Art. *As you read, highlight the important ideas and the vocabulary used to express those ideas. Study the annotations in the margin.*

Art and the Artist

Art—

1   "What is art?" Few questions provoke such heated debate and provide so few satisfactory answers. If we cannot come to any definitive conclusions, there is still quite a lot we can say. Art is first of all a word, one that acknowledges both the idea and the fact of art. Without the word, we might well ask whether art exists in the first place. The term, after all, is not found in the vocabulary of every society. Yet art is *made* everywhere. Art, therefore, is also an object, but not just any kind of object. Art is an *aesthetic object*. It is meant to be looked at and appreciated for its intrinsic value. Its special qualities set art apart, so that it is often placed away from everyday life, in museums, churches, or caves. What do we mean by aesthetic? By definition, **aesthetic** is "that which concerns the beautiful." Of course, not all art is beautiful to our eyes, but it is art nonetheless.

• made everywhere

• an aesthetic object

• appreciated for intrinsic (meaning?) value

aesthetic— concerns the beautiful, even if it isn't beautiful

2   People the world over make much the same fundamental judgments. Our brains and nervous systems are the same, because, according to recent theory, we all descend from one woman in Africa who lived about a quarter-million years ago. Taste, however, is conditioned by culture, which is so varied that it is impossible to reduce art to any one set of laws. It would seem, therefore, that absolute qualities in art must elude us, and that we cannot escape viewing works of art in the context of time and circumstance, whether past or present.

taste—conditioned by culture

time & circumstance affect art

BEFORE YOU CONTINUE READING

1. **According to the first two paragraphs, _____.**

   a. *a society with no word for art in its vocabulary does not have art*

   b. *art must be considered in the context of culture, time, and circumstance*

   c. *people around the world agree on what is beautiful art*

IMAGINATION

Humans can describe what we imagine

Imagination—

• connects conscious & subconscious

3   [1]We all dream. [2]That is imagination at work. [3]To imagine means simply to make an image—a picture—in our minds. [4]Human beings are not the only creatures who have imagination. [5]Even animals dream. [6]There is, however, a profound difference between human and animal imagination. [7]Humans are the only creatures who can tell one another about imagination in stories or pictures. [8]The imagination is one of our most mysterious facets, or features. [9]It can be regarded as the connector between the conscious and the subconscious, where most of our brain activity takes place. [10]It is the very glue that holds our personality, intellect, and spirituality together. [11]Because the imagination responds to all three, it acts in lawful, if unpredictable, ways that are determined by the psyche and the mind. [12]The imagination is important, as it allows us to conceive of all kinds of possibilities in the future and to understand the past in a way that has real survival value.

• opens us to possibilities!

2. Why is human imagination so essential? _____

_____

ART AS UNIQUELY HUMAN

Art—

4

• only humans make art

• recent for humans (Yes! Ch. 5 had cave paintings)

Imagination is a fundamental part of our makeup, though we share it with other creatures. By contrast, the urge to make art is unique to us. It separates us from all other creatures across an unbridgeable gap. The ability to make art must have been acquired relatively recently in the course of evolution. Human creatures have been walking upright on Earth for some 4.4 million years, but the oldest prehistoric art that we know of was made only about 35,000 years ago. It was undoubtedly the culmination of a long development no longer traceable, since the record of the earliest art is lost to us.

Purpose of art—

5

• helps us understand ourselves & world

• reaches deep into our being

Artists—

articulators (meaning?) of shared beliefs/values

Art plays a special role in human personality. Like science and religion, art fulfills a universal urge to comprehend ourselves and the universe. This function makes art especially significant and, hence, worthy of our attention. Art has the power to reach the core of our being, which recognizes itself in the creative act. For that reason, art represents its creators' deepest understanding and highest aspirations. At the same time, artists often act as the articulators of shared beliefs and values, which they express through an ongoing tradition to us, their audience.

Checking Comprehension

A **Answer the following questions.**

1. What connection does the author make between art and the artist?

_____

_____

2. In art, what is the role of the imagination?

_____

_____

3. In what ways is art uniquely human?

_____

_____

4. Compare these answers with your answers on page 166. What ideas from the reading were included in your answers above, but not on page 166?

_____

_____

B Refer to paragraph 3 in the Introductory Reading on pages 169–170. Identify the referents.

1. In the second sentence, *that* refers to _____.

2. In the ninth sentence, *where* refers to _____.

3. In the eleventh sentence, *all three* refers to _____

_____.

4. In the last sentence, *it* refers to _____.

C Write a few sentences to answer each of the following questions.

1. The author states that "we cannot escape viewing works of art in the context of time and circumstance, whether past or present." What does the author mean by this statement?

_____

_____

_____

2. According to the author, why do people create art?

_____

_____

Learning Vocabulary

VOCABULARY FROM CONTEXT

Reread the paragraphs indicated from the Introductory Reading to figure out the meaning of the italicized words. Then circle the correct answer to complete each sentence that follows.

1. Paragraph 1: *aesthetic object, intrinsic value,* and *nonetheless*

   (1) From this context, we can understand that *aesthetic objects* are usually ___.
   a. very valuable
   b. pleasing to look at
   c. never in people's homes

   (2) The *intrinsic value* of an artwork—or of anything—is its __ value.
   a. inherent
   b. monetary
   c. resale

   (3) From this context, we can understand that *nonetheless* means ___.
   a. no less than
   b. not at all
   c. just the same

(4) What does the last sentence in this paragraph mean?
  a. Art that is not beautiful to our eyes isn't really art.
  b. Art that is not beautiful to our eyes is still art.

2. Paragraph 3: *conceive of*

  (1) From this context, we can understand that *conceive of* means ___.
    a. understand
    b. plan
    c. imagine

3. Paragraph 4: *urge* and *unique*

  (1) When we have an *urge* to do something, ___.
    a. we have a strong need to do it
    b. we have a strong desire to do it

  (2) If something is *unique* to humans, ___.
    a. no other creature has it
    b. some other creatures may have it

4. Paragraph 5: *articulators*

  From this context, we can figure out that *articulators* ___ about shared beliefs and values.
  a. express what they think or feel
  b. make a tradition of what they think or feel
  c. study what they think or feel

USING THE DICTIONARY

Read the following sentences and dictionary entries. Select the best entry for the context. Then circle the correct choice to complete the sentence that follows.

1. "What is art?" Few questions *provoke* such heated debate and provide so few satisfactory answers. If we cannot come to any definitive conclusions, there is still quite a lot we can say.

> **pro·voke** /prəˈvoʊk/ *v.* [T] **1** to make someone very angry, especially by annoying them: *The dog would not have attacked if it hadn't been provoked.* | [**provoke sb into (doing) sth**] *Paul tried unsuccessfully to provoke Fletch into a fight.* **2** to cause a reaction or feeling, especially a sudden one: *Dole's comments provoked laughter from the press.* | [**provoke sb to do sth**] *His criticisms only provoked her to work harder.* | [**provoke sb into (doing) sth**] *She hopes her editorial will provoke readers into thinking seriously about the issue.* —see also THOUGHT-PROVOKING

  (1) The best definition in this context for *provoke* is number ___.

  (2) A question that provokes heated debate ___.
    a. causes people to have very strong reactions
    b. makes people ask questions that cannot be answered
    c. creates arguments that have no clear conclusions

2. People the world over make much the same fundamental judgments. Our brains and nervous systems are the same, because, according to recent theory, we all descend from one woman in Africa who lived about a quarter-million years ago. *Taste,* however, is conditioned by culture, which is so varied that it is impossible to reduce art to any one set of laws. It would seem, therefore, that absolute qualities in art must *elude* us, and that we cannot escape viewing works of art in the context of time and circumstance, whether past or present.

taste /teɪst/ *n.* **1 food** [singular,U] the special feeling that is produced by a particular food or drink when you put it in your mouth: *The flour gives a faintly sweet taste to the crust.* | [+ of] *Noriko doesn't like the taste of American coffee.* —compare FLAVOR¹ (1) **2 judgment** [U] someone's judgment about what is good or appropriate when they choose clothes, music, art etc.: *No one with any taste would buy a painting like that.* | *Rubin has shown good taste in the roles she has chosen to play.* **3 sth you like** [C,U] the type of thing that you tend to like or like to do: *The resort caters to people with expensive tastes.* | [+ for] *A rafting trip through the Grand Canyon will satisfy your taste for adventure.* | [+ in] *Nick admits he has a bizarre taste in clothing.* | *She had the whole house redecorated to her taste.* **4 small amount of food** [C usually singular] a small amount of food or drink that you put in your mouth to try it: *Can I have a taste of your sundae?* **5 experience** [C usually singular] a small example or short experience of something, especially something that you want more of: [+ of] *I parked my car and started walking to get a taste of Chinatown.* | *Begley got his first taste of fame on the 1970s television show.*

e·lude /ɪ'lud/ *v.* [T] **1** to avoid being found or caught by someone, especially by tricking them: *Jones eluded the police for six weeks.* | **elude arrest/capture/ discovery etc.** *She hid in the bushes to elude detection.* **2** if something that you want eludes you, you fail to find, catch, or achieve it: *Til now a college degree has eluded her.* **3** if a fact, idea etc. eludes you, you cannot completely understand it: *The distinction between the two philosophies largely eludes me.*

(1) In this context, the best definition for *taste* is number ___.

(2) We can conclude that a painting by an artist ___ because people from different cultures have different tastes.
　　a. will be considered art in every country and culture
　　b. may be considered art in one culture, but not considered art in another culture

(3) In this context, the best definition for *elude* is number ___.

(4) The author is saying that absolute qualities in art ___.
　　a. avoid being found or caught by people
　　b. cannot be completely understood

LEARN AND USE WORD FORMS

Complete the sentences below with the correct form of the word in the box. Refer to the word forms chart on page 167. Be sure to use the correct tense of verbs. Use each word only once.

acknowledge	create	express
aspire	determine	

1. Artistic expression through painting or sculpture, for example, is an intense, _____ process.

2. Artistic _____ may show itself in painting, sculpture, architecture, or other ways.

3. Who finally _____ whether a work is art?

4. Many _____ artists struggle for years to create work that comes from their imagination.

5. Placing a painting or sculpture in a museum is a clear _____ that the work is, in fact, considered art.

INTRODUCING THE MAIN READING

Activate Your Knowledge

Work with a partner or in a small group. Answer the following questions.

1. Write a definition of *creativity*. When you are finished, work as a class to put all the definitions on the board. Use them to write a single definition of *creativity*.

   _____

   _____

Fig. 4.7a

2. Look at the sculpture on the left. What does it represent? What is its meaning? Does this sculpture fit the class's definition of creativity? Explain your answer.

   _____

   _____

Fig. 4.7b

3. Look at the sculpture on the left. Answer the questions.

    a. What does it represent? What is its meaning? Does this sculpture fit the class's definition of creativity? Explain your answer.

    _____

    _____

    b. The artist who began this sculpture never finished it. Why do you think he didn't finish his sculpture?

    _____

    _____

    c. This sculpture is unfinished. In your opinion, is it still a work of art? Explain your answer.

    _____

    _____

4. Work in a small group. Write what you know about Picasso and Michelangelo. When you have finished, put the chart on the board. Work as a class to combine the information of all the groups.

	PABLO PICASSO	MICHELANGELO
where he lived		
when he lived		
what types of work he created (painting, sculpture, architecture, etc.)		
examples (names) of some of the art he created		

Reading and Study Skill Strategies

USE TITLE AND HEADINGS TO PREDICT CONTENT

A Work with a partner or in a small group. Before you work with the Main Reading on pages 178–182, go through it and write down the headings on the lines below. Then answer the questions that follow.

Creativity, Meaning, and Style

_____

_____

_____

_____

1. Write your class definition of *creativity*.

_____

_____

2. Write a definition of *style*.

_____

_____

3. In art, how are creativity, meaning, and style connected?

_____

_____

B Go to page *vi* in the Table of Contents. Read the brief summary of the Main Reading. Then review your responses above, and decide whether to change any of your predictions.

LEARN AND USE WORD FORMS

A Study the following chart, which contains words from the Main Reading. Note the spelling changes. Pay attention to the words as they are used in the Main Reading.

VERB	NOUN	ADJECTIVE	ADVERB
absorb	absorption	absorbed	
connect	connection	connecting/connected	
describe	description	descriptive	descriptively
explain	explanation	explanatory	
fabricate	fabrication	fabricated	
impress	impression	impressive	impressively
inspire	inspiration	inspiring/inspired	
liberate	liberation	liberating/liberated	
visualize	visualization	visual	visually
attempt	attempt	attempted	
experience	experience	experienced	
shape	shape	shaped	

B Complete the following paragraph by writing the correct form of the word in parentheses. When you are done, check your answers by reading paragraph 4 on page 179.

Creativity

Our *Bull's Head* is, of course, an ideally simple case, involving only one major _____ and a manual act in response to it.
1. (connect)
Once the seat had been properly placed on the handlebars and then cast in bronze, the job was done. Ordinarily, artists do not work with ready-made parts but with materials that have little or no shape of their own. The creative process generally consists of a long series of leaps of the imagination and the artist's _____ to give them form
2. (attempt)
by _____ the material accordingly. In this way, by a
3. (shape)
constant flow of impulses back and forth between the mind and the partly

_____ material, the artist gradually defines more and
4. (shape)
more of the image, until at last all of it has been given visible form. Needless to say, artistic creation is too subtle and intimate an experience to permit an exact step-by-step _____. Only artists can observe it
5. (describe)
fully, but they are so _____ by it that they have great
6. (absorb)
difficulty _____ it to us.
7. (explain)

ANNOTATE TEXT

As you may recall from the previous reading, annotating text means writing brief notes in the margin to help you remember what you have read and to make it easy for you to find important words, phrases, or ideas when you review. The margin is also a useful space for paraphrasing and for writing comments or questions you might have as you read.

Read the following excerpt from the Main Reading, and annotate it in the margin.

MEANING AND STYLE

Why do we create art? Surely one reason is an irresistible urge to adorn ourselves and to decorate the world around us. Both impulses are part of a larger desire, not to remake the world in our image but to recast ourselves and our environment in *ideal* form. Art is, however, much more than decoration, for it is laden with (i.e., full of) meaning, even if that content is sometimes slender or obscure. Art enables us to communicate our understanding in ways that cannot be expressed otherwise. Truly a painting (or any work of art) is worth a thousand words, not only in its descriptive value but also in its symbolic significance. In art, as in language, we are above all inventors of symbols that convey complex thoughts in new ways. However, we must think of art in terms not of everyday prose but of poetry, which is free to rearrange conventional vocabulary and syntax in order to convey new, often multiple, meanings and moods.

Work with a classmate and compare your annotations. Then compare your annotations with the annotations in paragraph 9 on page 181 when you begin reading.

MAIN READING

The Main Reading, "Creativity, Meaning, and Style," is also from **A Basic History of Art.** *As you read, highlight the important ideas and vocabulary used to express those ideas. Study the annotations in the margin. (Annotating has been done for you in the entire Main Reading, as an example.)*

Creativity, Meaning, and Style

Art—made by human hands   1   What do we mean by *making*? If we concentrate on the visual arts, we might say that a work of art must be a tangible thing shaped by human hands. This definition at least eliminates the confusion of treating as works of art such natural phenomena as flowers, seashells, or sunsets. It is a far from sufficient definition, to be sure, since human beings make many things other than works of art. Still, it will serve as a starting point.

CREATIVITY

2   Now let us look at the striking *Bull's Head* by Pablo Picasso, which seems to consist of nothing but the seat and handlebars of an old bicycle. How meaningful is our definition here? Of course the materials Picasso used are fabricated, but it would be absurd to insist that he must share the credit with the manufacturer, since the seat and handlebars in themselves are not works of art.

¹While we feel a certain jolt when we first recognize the ingredients of this visual pun, we also sense that it was a stroke of genius to put them together in this unique way, and we cannot very well deny that it is a work of art. ²Nevertheless, the actual handiwork of mounting the seat on the handlebars is ridiculously simple. ³What is far from simple is the leap of the imagination by which Picasso recognized a bull's head in these unlikely objects. ⁴The leap of the imagination is sometimes experienced as a flash of inspiration, but only rarely does a new idea emerge full-blown like Athena from the head of Zeus. ⁵Instead, it is usually preceded by a long gestation period in which all the hard work is done without finding the key to the solution to the problem. ⁶At the critical point, the imagination makes connections between seemingly unrelated parts and recombines them.

Our *Bull's Head* is, of course, an ideally simple case, involving only one major connection and a manual act in response to it. Once the seat had been properly placed on the handlebars and then cast in bronze, the job was done. Ordinarily, artists do not work with ready-made parts but with materials that have little or no shape of their own. The creative process generally consists of a long series of leaps of the imagination and the artist's attempts to give them form by shaping the material accordingly. In this way, by a constant flow of impulses back and forth between the mind and the partly shaped material, the artist gradually defines more and more of the image, until at last all of it has been given visible form. Needless to say, artistic creation is too subtle and intimate an experience to permit an exact step-by-step description. Only artists can observe it fully, but they are so absorbed by it that they have great difficulty explaining it to us.

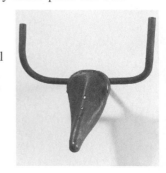

Fig. 4.7a Pablo Picasso, Bull's Head. 1943. Bronze cast bicycle parts.

BEFORE YOU CONTINUE READING

1. Picasso's *Bull's Head* is an example of creativity because _____.

a. *using bicycle parts as art is a very interesting and unusual idea*

b. *it is not a natural phenomenon such as a flower or a sunset*

c. *it required a leap of the imagination to "see" a bull's head in something like bicycle parts*

THE CREATIVE PROCESS

The creative process has been likened to birth, a metaphor (comparison) that comes closer to the truth than would a description cast in terms of a transfer or projection of the image from the artist's mind. The making of a work of art is both joyous and painful, and full of surprises. We have, moreover, ample testimony that artists themselves tend to look upon their creations as living things. Perhaps that is why creativity was once a concept reserved for God, as the only one who could give material form to an idea. Indeed, the artist's labors are much like the Creation told in the Bible.

Michelangelo—creative
process liberated figure from
marble prison

His process—

* visualized figure inside
  stone
* concept of figure became
  clearer as he carved
* freed figure if guess was
  correct
* could not liberate St.
  Matthew

This divine ability was not realized until Michelangelo, who described the anguish and glory of the creative experience when he spoke of "liberating the figure from the marble that imprisons it." We may translate this to mean that he started the process of carving a statue by trying to visualize a figure in the rough, rectilinear block as it came to him from the quarry. It seems fair to assume that at first Michelangelo did not see the figure any more clearly than one can see an unborn child inside the womb, but we may believe that he could see isolated "signs of life" within the marble. Once he started carving, every stroke of the chisel would commit him more and more to a specific conception of the figure hidden in the block, and the marble would permit him to free the figure whole only if his guess as to its shape was correct. Sometimes he did not guess well enough, and the stone refused to give up some essential part of its prisoner.

Fig. 4.7b Michelangelo's Saint Matthew. 1506. Marble.

Michelangelo, defeated, left the work unfinished, as he did with *Saint Matthew,* whose very gesture seems to record the vain struggle for liberation. Looking at the block, we may get some inkling of Michelangelo's difficulties here. But could he not have finished the statue in *some* fashion? Surely there is enough material left for that. He probably could have, but perhaps not in the way he wanted. In that case the defeat would have been even more stinging.

make and create are very
different

artist tries to find the art

Picasso found bull in bicycle
parts

Michelangelo sought figure in
stone

Artisan—attempts the
possible

Artist—attempts the
impossible

artisan = craftsmanship

Clearly, then, the making of a work of art has little in common with what we ordinarily mean by "making." It is a strange and risky business in which the makers never quite know what they are making until it has actually been made: or, put it another way, it is a game of find-and-seek in which the seekers are not fully sure what they are looking for until they have found it. In the case of the *Bull's Head,* it is the bold "finding" that impresses us most; in the *Saint Matthew,* the strenuous "seeking." To the nonartist, it seems hard to believe that this uncertainty, this need to take a chance, should be the essence of the artist's work. We all tend to think of "making" in terms of artisans or manufacturers who know exactly what they want to produce from the very outset. There is thus comparatively little risk, but also little adventure, in such handiwork, which as a consequence tends to become routine. Whereas the artisan attempts only what is known to be possible, the artist is always driven to attempt the impossible, at least the improbable or unimaginable. No wonder the artist's way of working is so resistant to any set rules, while the craftsperson's encourages standardization and regularity. We acknowledge this difference when we speak of the artist as *creating* instead of merely *making* something. Clearly, then, we must be careful not to confuse the making of a work of art with manual skill or craftsmanship. Some works of art may demand a great deal of technical discipline; others do not. Even the most painstaking piece of craft does not deserve to be called a work of art unless it involves a leap of the imagination.

8   Needless to say, there have always been many more craftspeople than artists among us, since our need for the familiar and expected far exceeds our capacity to absorb the original but often deeply unsettling experiences we get from works of art. The urge to discover unknown realms, to achieve something original, may be felt by every one of us now and then. What sets the real artist apart is not so much the desire to *seek*, but that mysterious ability to *find*, which we call **talent**. We also speak of it as a **gift**, implying that it is a sort of present from some higher power; or as **genius**, a term which originally meant a higher power (a kind of "good demon") that inhabits and acts through the artist.

We all have urge to discover. The real artist has ability to find—talent! It's a gift.

BEFORE YOU CONTINUE READING

2. The creative process ___ .

a. *is difficult, because the artist is never quite sure what the work will look like until it has been completed*

b. *is easy, because the artist knows exactly what the work will look like when it is completed*

MEANING AND STYLE

Why create art?
- *to adorn ourselves*
- *to decorate the world*

9   Why do we create art? Surely one reason is an irresistible urge to adorn ourselves and to decorate the world around us. Both impulses are part of a larger desire, not to remake the world in our image but to recast ourselves and our environment in *ideal* form. Art is, however, much more than decoration, for it is laden with (i.e., full of) meaning, even if that content is sometimes slender or obscure. Art enables us to communicate our understanding in ways that cannot be expressed otherwise. Truly a painting (or any work of art) is worth a thousand words, not only in its descriptive value but also in its symbolic significance. In art, as in language, we are above all inventors of symbols that convey complex thoughts in new ways. However, we must think of art in terms not of everyday prose but of poetry, which is free to rearrange conventional vocabulary and syntax in order to convey new, often multiple, meanings and moods. A work of art likewise suggests much more than it states. It communicates partly by implying meanings through pose, facial expression, allegory, and the like. As in poetry, the value of art lies equally in what it says and how it says it.

Art—
- *lets us communicate in a special way*
- *has symbolic significance*
- *implies meanings*

meaning of art (iconography)

art cannot be separated from style

10   But what is the *meaning* of art—its iconography? What is it trying to say? Artists often provide no clear explanation, since the work is the statement itself. Nonetheless, even the most private artistic statements can be understood on some level, even if only an intuitive one. The meaning, or content, of art is inseparable from its formal qualities, its *style*. In the visual arts, style means the particular way in which the forms that make up any given work of art are chosen and fitted together. To art historians the study of styles is of central importance. It not only enables them to find out, by means of careful analysis and comparison, when, where, and often by whom a given work was produced, but it also leads them to understand the artist's intention as expressed through the style of the work. This intention depends on both the artist's personality and the context of time and place. Accordingly, we speak of "period styles." Thus art, like language, requires that we learn the style and outlook of a country, period, and artist if we are to understand it properly.

art historians—study of styles is essential
- *when, where, who created the art*
- *artist's intention depends on*
  —personality
  —context of time & place

11   Nevertheless, our faith in the very existence of period style has been severely shaken, even though we keep referring to them as a convenient way of discussing the past. They seem to be a matter of perspective: the more remote or alien the period, the more clear-cut the period style—and the more limited our knowledge and understanding. The nearer we come to the present, the more apt we are to see diversity rather than unity. Yet we cannot deny that works of art created at the same time and in the same place do have something in common. What they share is a social and cultural environment, which must have affected artist and patron alike to some degree. We have also come to realize, however, that these environmental factors often do not influence all the arts in the same way or to the same extent. Nor can artistic developments be fully understood as direct responses to such factors. Insofar as "art comes from art," its history is directed by the force of its own traditions, which tend to resist the pressure of external events or circumstances.

style is clearer when period is further away & stranger

art created in same time & place share social & cultural environments

environments influence artists differently

Checking Comprehension

A   **Reread pages 178–182. Answer the following questions.**

   1. Write a definition of *creativity*.

      _____

      _____

   2. Write a definition of *style*.

      _____

      _____

   3. In art, how are creativity, meaning, and style connected?

      _____

      _____

   4. Compare your responses above with your responses on page 176. What ideas from the reading were included in your answers above, but not on page 176?

      _____

      _____

B   **Refer to paragraphs 2 and 3 in the Main Reading on pages 178–179. Identify the referents.**

   1. In the first sentence in paragraph 2, *us* refers to _____.

   2. In the second sentence in paragraph 2, *here* refers to _____.

   3. In the first sentence in paragraph 3, *them* refers to _____.

4. In the third sentence in paragraph 3, *which* refers to _____ .

5. In the third sentence in paragraph 3, *these unlikely objects* refers to

_____ .

C **Answer the following questions in complete sentences.**

1. Why is Picasso's *Bull's Head* considered to be a work of art? Do you agree?

_____

_____

2. Briefly describe the creative process.

_____

_____

3. How did Michelangelo create a sculpture from a block of stone?

_____

_____

4. What is meant by an artistic style?

_____

_____

5. In what ways do "period styles" help us understand art?

_____

_____

Learning Vocabulary

VOCABULARY FROM CONTEXT

Reread the paragraphs indicated from the Main Reading to figure out the meaning of the italicized words. Then circle the correct choice to complete the sentences that follow, or write the correct answer in the blank.

1. Paragraph 5: *likened to* and *metaphor*

(1) In this context, *likened to* means ___.
a. compared to
b. wished for
c. enjoyed as

(2) A *metaphor* is ___.
   a. a birth
   b. a work of art
   c. a comparison

2. Paragraph 9: *urge, adorn, laden with,* and *convey*

   (1) When we have an *urge* to do something, we have ___.
      a. a strong desire to do it
      b. a strong need to do it

   (2) In this paragraph, the word that is a synonym for *adorn* is the word _____.

   (3) In this paragraph, the synonym for *laden with* is _____.

   (4) In this paragraph, a synonym for *convey* is _____.

3. Paragraph 11: *apt to*

   From the context, we can understand that *apt to* means ___.
   a. easy to
   b. happy to
   c. likely to

USING THE DICTIONARY

Read the following sentences and dictionary entries. Select the best entry for the context. Then circle the correct choice to complete the sentence that follows.

1. What do we mean by *making*? If we concentrate on the visual arts, we might say that a work of art must be a *tangible* thing shaped by human hands. This definition at least eliminates the confusion of treating as works of art such natural *phenomena* as flowers, seashells, or sunsets.

   > **tan·gi·ble** /ˈtændʒəbəl/ *adj.* **1 tangible proof/results/evidence etc.** proof, results etc. that are easy to see so that there is no doubt: *We won't see tangible benefits from the new system before next year.* —opposite INTANGIBLE **2** FORMAL able to be seen and touched: *tangible personal property* —**tangibly** *adv.* —**tangibility** /ˌtændʒəˈbɪləti/ *n.* [U]

   > **phe·nom·e·non** /fɪˈnɑmənən, -ˌnɑn/ *n.* plural **phenomena** /-nə/ [C]
   > **1** something that happens or exists in society, science, or nature, often something that people discuss or study because it is difficult to understand: *It's a TV program about strange natural phenomena.* | [+ of] *the phenomenon of international terrorism* | *Homelessness is not **a new phenomenon.*** **2** [usually singular] something or someone that is very unusual, because of a rare quality or ability that they have: *Still walking five miles a day at the age of 95, the woman was an absolute phenomenon.*

   (1) In this context, the best definition for *tangible* is number ___.

(2) The part of a work of art that is tangible is ___.
  a. the artist's creative plan for it
  b. the artwork itself

(3) In this context, the best definition for *phenomenon* is number ___.

(4) A work of art and a sunset are both *phenomena* because they both ___.
  a. exist and are studied and discussed by people
  b. are very unusual because of their rare qualities

2. Needless to say, artistic creation is too subtle and intimate an experience to permit an exact step-by-step description. Only artists can observe it fully, but they are so *absorbed* by it that they have great difficulty explaining it to us.

   There have always been many more craftspeople than artists among us, since our need for the familiar and expected far exceeds our capacity to *absorb* the original but often deeply unsettling experiences we get from works of art.

> **ab·sorb** /əbˈsɔrb, -ˈzɔrb/ *v.* [T] **1 liquid/substance** if something absorbs a liquid or other substance, it takes the substance into itself from the surface or space around it: *Lead that gets into your body is absorbed into the bones.* | *Simmer the rice for 20 minutes until all the liquid is absorbed.* **2 interest** to interest someone very much, often so that you do not notice other things happening around you: [absorb sb in sth] *You could tell he was absorbed in his conversation, and not paying much attention to the road.* **3 information** to read or hear a large amount of new information and understand it: *I keep the lesson simple because small kids can't absorb that much.* **4 become part of** to make a smaller country, company, or group of people become part of your country, company or group: *In the last 10 years, California has absorbed 35% of all legal immigrants to the U.S.* | *Azerbaijan was absorbed into the Soviet Union in the 1920s.*

(1) The best meaning of *absorb* as it is used in the first paragraph above is definition number ___.

(2) The most appropriate meaning of *absorb* as it is used in the second paragraph above is definition number ___.

LEARN AND USE WORD FORMS

Complete the sentences below with the correct form of the word in the box. Refer to the word forms chart on page 176. Be sure to use the correct tense of verbs. Use each word only once.

experience	impress	liberate
fabricate	inspire	

1. Like Picasso, many artists also _____ works of art from previously manufactured objects.

2. For Michelangelo, creating a work of art from marble was a _____ act.

3. Many of us feel _____ by the work of artists. It may lead us to create paintings, or poetry, or music.

4. It takes years of _____ looking at art before we really begin to appreciate artists' skills.

5. Although Michelangelo never completed the *Saint Matthew* piece, it remains a very _____ work of art.

FOLLOW-UP ASSIGNMENTS

Before you begin any of the follow-up assignments, review the content-specific vocabulary and the academic vocabulary below, and look over the vocabulary in the word forms lists on pages 167 and 176. If you are still unsure what any words or terms mean, go back through the chapter and review. As you complete the assignments, be sure to incorporate the appropriate vocabulary in your writing.

Content-Specific Vocabulary

aesthetic	creativity	leap of the imagination	Picasso
artisan	genius	metaphor	sculpture
artist	imagination	Michelangelo	style
craftsman	intrinsic value		talent

Academic Vocabulary

apt to	culture	nonetheless	taste
articulate	elude	phenomenon	unique
conceive of	fundamental	provoke	urge
context	intrinsic	tangible	value
convey	liken to		

Writing Activities

1. Write two paragraphs. In the first paragraph, explain how a person who views a work of art can know what the artist intended. In the second paragraph, explain why different people might view the same work of art differently.

2. Write a paragraph in which you explain why you do or do not consider Picasso's *Bull's Head* a work of art.

3. Write a paragraph explaining why you do or do not consider Michelangelo's unfinished sculpture, *Saint Matthew*, a work of art.

4. On page 179, the author states that "the creative process generally consists of a long series of leaps of the imagination and the artist's attempts to give them form by shaping the material accordingly." Artists are not the only people who have such flashes of inspiration—we all do at one time or another. In a paragraph, describe a time that you experienced the creative process. What were you trying to do? How did you experience leaps of the imagination? What did you finally create?

5. On page 181, the author states "What sets the real artist apart is not so much the desire to *seek*, but that mysterious ability to *find*, which we call **talent**." Write a paragraph explaining why you agree or disagree with this statement.

Extension Activities

1. Research a particular work of art that you like. You might want to research one of the works of art on page 163. What was the process by which the artist created this work of art? Find a picture of the work of art, and prepare a presentation for the class. Be sure to bring in a copy of the artist's work (for example, in a book from the library).

2. Many authors refer to works of literature in their writing. For instance, an author might take a quote from Shakespeare. Authors do this because they assume that their audience understands the reference, and that the reference will make it easier for the audience to understand an idea. On page 179, the author refers to Greek mythology and mentions Athena and Zeus. Research the Greek myth of Athena and Zeus. Present your findings to your class.

3. Michelangelo did not finish his sculpture, *Saint Matthew*. Research the work of Michelangelo. Why did he leave *Saint Matthew* unfinished? Did he leave any other work unfinished? Present your findings to the class. Be sure to bring in examples of the artist's work.

4. Research one particular period style of art that you are interested in. Write a description of the style, and outline the historical context of this particular style. Include pictures of artwork that represent this style, and present your information to the class.

Internet Research

Go online, and go to one of the websites listed below. Investigate a topic related to the information you read about in Chapter 7. Choose a topic that especially interests you. Use some of the website's search features. Search by keywords such as the name of an artist, a style of art (e.g., *impressionist, abstract*), or a period.

Artlex Art Dictionary website:
    http://www.artlex.com/
Metropolitan Museum of Art, New York, website:
    http://www.metmuseum.org
Metropolitan Museum of Art's Mesopotamian website:
    http://www.metmuseum.org/toah/ht/02/wam/ht02wam.htm
Museum of Modern Art, New York, website:
    http://moma.org
Art Institute of Chicago website:
    http://artic.edu

CHAPTER 8

THE INFLUENCE OF HISTORY ON ART

Skills Goal

- *Review skills from Chapters 1–7.*

Content-Specific Goals

- *Understand how to look at a work of art.*
- *Learn the purposes of ancient Egyptian art.*
- *Experience Egyptian art and understand it in its historical context.*

Fig. 4.8a Egyptian Eighteenth Dynasty bas-relief wall painting of Horemheb, ca 1348–1320 B.C.

Chapter Readings

Looking at Art

Experiencing Ancient Egyptian Art

INTRODUCING THE READING

Activate Your Knowledge

Work alone or in a small group. Do the following activities.

1. Paintings and sculpture are examples of art forms. What are some other forms of art?

   _____

   _____

   _____

2. What are some of the purposes of art? Use the diagram below to organize your ideas.

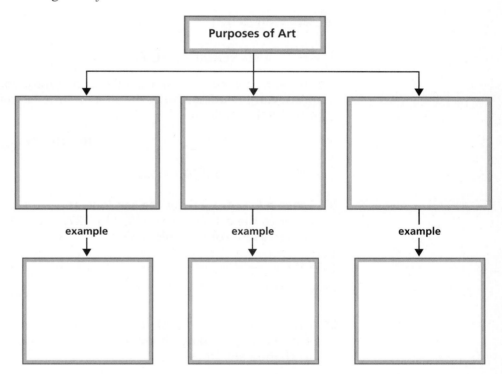

PREVIEW KEY VOCABULARY

Read the list of content-specific vocabulary and check the ones you are familiar with. Leave the other spaces blank. Do not try to learn the unfamiliar items before you begin reading. You will learn them as you work with the chapter.

___ aesthetic	___ *ka*	___ static
___ carving	___ look at	___ transition
___ conservatism	___ pharaoh	___ unprecedented
___ formulaic	___ replica	___ visual background noise
___ image	___ sculpture	
___ innovation	___ see	___ visual elements

USE TITLE AND HEADINGS TO PREDICT CONTENT

Work with a partner or in a small group. Before you work with the Introductory Reading, study the title and the heading, then do the activities that follow.

Looking at Art

Understanding Works of Art

A **Make a list of the ways we can look at a work of art and understand it. Refer to the art on pages 113, 115, 137, 150, 163, 179, and 180 as points of departure for your discussion.**

_____   _____   _____

_____   _____   _____

B **Go to page *vi* in the Table of Contents. Read the brief summary of the Introductory Reading. Then review your list above, and decide whether to change any items.**

LEARN AND USE WORD FORMS

A Study the chart below which contains words from the Introductory Reading. Note the spelling changes. Pay attention to the words as they are used in the Introductory Reading.

Verb	Noun	Adjective	Adverb
appreciate	appreciation	appreciative	appreciatively
civilize	civilization	civilized/civilizing	
decorate	decoration	decorative	
explode	explosion	explosive	explosively
limit	limitation	limiting/limited	
reproduce	reproduction	reproductive	
reveal	revelation	revealing/revealed	
visualize	visualization	visual	visually
achieve	achievement	achievable	
enjoy	enjoyment	enjoyable	enjoyably
formulate	formula	formulaic	
trivialize	trivia	trivial trivialized	

B Complete the following paragraph by writing the correct form of the word in parentheses. When you are done, check your answers by reading paragraph 3 on pages 192–193.

    Visual analysis can help us _____ the beauty
                                         1. (appreciate)

of a masterpiece, but we must be careful not to _____
                                                   2. (trivialize)

it with a _____ approach. Every aesthetic "law"
                          3. (formulate)

advanced so far has proven of dubious value and usually gets in the way of

our understanding. Even if a valid "law" were to be found—and none has yet

been discovered—it would probably be so elementary as to prove useless in

the face of art's complexity. We must also bear in mind (remember) that art

_____ is more than mere
            4. (appreciate)

_____ of aesthetics. It is learning to understand the
            5. (enjoy)

meaning (or iconography) of a work of art. Finally, let us remember that no

work can be understood outside its historical context.

INTRODUCTORY READING

The following reading, "Looking at Art," is from **A Basic History of Art.** *As you read, highlight the important ideas and vocabulary used to express those ideas. Annotate the second and third paragraphs of the text.*

Looking at Art

visual background noise—

1   We live in a sea of images conveying the culture and learning of modern civilization. Fostered by an unprecedented media explosion, this *visual background noise* has become so much a part of our daily lives that we take it for granted. In the process, we have become desensitized to art as well. Anyone can buy cheap paintings and reproductions to decorate a room, where they often hang virtually unnoticed, perhaps deservedly so. It is small wonder that we look at the art in museums with equal casualness. We pass rapidly from one object to another, sampling them like dishes in a smorgasbord. We may pause briefly before a famous masterpiece that we have been told we are supposed to admire, then ignore the gallery full of equally beautiful and important works around it. We will have *seen* the art but not really *looked at* it. Indeed, looking at great art is not an easy task, for art rarely reveals its secrets readily. While the experience of a work can be immediately electrifying, we sometimes do not realize its impact until time has let it filter through the recesses of our imaginations. It even happens that something that at first repelled or confounded us emerges only many years later as one of the most important artistic events of our lives.

we are surrounded by images; we take them for granted

● *We don't take time to look at art*

● *Really understanding a work of art might take years!!*

BEFORE YOU CONTINUE READING

What is the main idea of the first paragraph?

a. *We enjoy the art that we see around us everywhere.*

b. *We do not pay attention to the art that we see around us everywhere.*

c. *The decorations in our homes and the art in museums are equally valuable.*

UNDERSTANDING WORKS OF ART

2   Understanding a work of art begins with a sensitive appreciation of its appearance. Art may be approached and appreciated for its purely visual elements: line, color, light, composition, form, and space. These may be shared by any work of art; their effects, however, vary widely according to medium (the physical materials of which the artwork is made) and technique, which together help determine the possibilities and limitations of what the artist can achieve.

3   Visual analysis can help us appreciate the beauty of a masterpiece, but we must be careful not to trivialize it with a formulaic approach. Every aesthetic "law" advanced so far has proven of dubious value and usually gets in the way of our understanding. Even if a valid "law" were to be found—and none has yet been discovered—it would probably be so elementary as to prove useless in the face of art's complexity. We must also bear in mind (remember) that art appreciation is more than mere enjoyment of aesthetics. It is learning to understand the meaning (or iconography) of a work of art. Finally, let us remember that no work can be understood outside its historical context.

Checking Comprehension

A **Answer the following questions.**

1. What are some of the ways we can look at art and understand it?

   _____

   _____

2. Compare this answer with your list on page 190. How many ways of looking at art were on your list?

   _____

   _____

B **Refer to paragraph 1 in the Introductory Reading on page 192. Identify the referents.**

1. In the first sentence, *we* refers to _____.

2. In the second sentence, *this visual background noise* refers to

   _____.

3. In the sixth sentence, *them* refers to _____.

C **Answer the following questions in complete sentences.**

1. Why do we pay so little attention to art, both in our homes and in museums?

   _____

   _____

2. What is the difference between *seeing* art and *looking at* art?

   _____

   _____

3. We can begin to understand art through a visual analysis, that is, an analysis of its appearance.
   a. What are the advantages of this approach?

   _____

   b. What are the disadvantages of this approach?

   _____

4. What is an essential factor in understanding the meaning of a work of art?

   _____

D Review your annotations on page 192. Do you have any questions that have not been answered? If so, discuss them now with your classmates or your instructor.

Learning Vocabulary

VOCABULARY FROM CONTEXT

Reread paragraph 1 on page 192 in the Introductory Reading to figure out the meaning of the following italicized words: *conveying, desensitized,* and *smorgasbord.* Then circle the correct choice to complete the sentences.

1. In this context, *conveying* means ___.
   a. decorating
   b. selling
   c. expressing

2. From this context, we can understand that when we are *desensitized* to something, ___.
   a. we make it very cheaply
   b. we respond less strongly to it
   c. we make it part of our lives

3. "Visual background noise" refers to images that ___.
   a. we see, but do not pay attention to
   b. we see and pay attention to

4. From this context, we can understand that a *smorgasbord* is ___.
   a. a formal "sit-down" dinner where a preselected meal is served to you
   b. an informal buffet dinner where you select what you want to eat

5. The author uses the word *smorgasbord* in referring to the art in museums in order to help us understand ___.
   a. how many works of art are in an art museum
   b. that too many works of art in a museum is not a good idea
   c. how we sometimes move from one object to another without really appreciating anything

USING THE DICTIONARY

Read the following sentences and dictionary entries. Sometimes an entry has only one definition. In such cases, read the definition for that specific meaning. When an entry has more than one definition, select the best entry for the context. In both cases, circle the correct choice to complete the sentence that follows.

1. We live in a sea of images conveying the culture and learning of modern civilization. *Fostered* by an *unprecedented* media explosion, this visual background noise has become so much a part of our daily lives that we take it for granted. In the process, we have become desensitized to art as well.

fos·ter /ˈfɔstɚ, ˈfɑ-/ v. **1** [T] FORMAL to help to develop a skill, feeling, idea etc. over a period of time: *The workshops can foster better communication between husbands and wives.* **2** [I,T] to take care of someone else's child for a period of time and have them live with you, without becoming their legal parent: *The Hammonds fostered a little Romanian boy for a few months.* —compare ADOPT (1)

un·prec·e·dent·ed /ʌnˈprɛsəˌdɛntɪd/ adj. [C] never having happened before, or never having happened so much: *unprecendented success*

(1) In this context, the best definition for *foster* is number ___.

(2) The second sentence means that ___.
  a. we no longer pay attention to what we see around us because we see so much of it all the time. As a result, we do not pay attention to art, either.
  b. we no longer pay attention to art because so much art is around us all the time in the media.

2. While the experience of a work can be immediately electrifying, we sometimes do not realize its impact until time has let it filter through the recesses of our imaginations. It even happens that something that at first *repelled* or *confounded* us *emerges* only many years later as one of the most important artistic events of our lives.

re·pel /rɪˈpɛl/ v. **repelled, repelling 1** [T] if something repels you, you want to avoid it because you do not like it: *Her heavy make-up and cheap perfume repelled him.* **2** [T] to fight a group or military force and make them stop attacking you: *Guerrilla fighters were soon able to repel the army's attack.* **3** [T] to keep something or someone away from you: *Use cedar or citronella candles to repel biting insects.* **4** [I,T] TECHNICAL if two things repel each other they push each other away with an electrical force

con·found /kənˈfaʊnd/ v. [T] **1** to confuse and surprise people by being unexpected: *Dan's speedy recovery confounded the medical experts.* **2** if a problem, question etc. confounds you, you cannot understand it or explain it: *Even travel agents are confounded by the logic of airline ticket pricing.* **3** LITERARY to defeat an enemy, plan etc. **4 confound it/him/them etc.** OLD-FASHIONED used to show that you are annoyed: *Confound it! What did I do with my glasses?*

e·merge /ɪˈmɚdʒ/ v. [I] **1** to appear or come out from somewhere: *Insects emerge in the spring and start multiplying rapidly.* | [+ **from**] *The sun emerged from behind the clouds.* **2** if facts emerge, they become known after being hidden or secret: *New evidence emerged to contradict earlier claims.* | [**it emerges that**] *After the crash, it emerged that bomb warnings had been issued to airlines.* **3** to come out of a difficult experience, often with a new quality or position: [+ **from**] *She emerged from the divorce a stronger person.* **4** to begin to be known or noticed: *Marlena Fischer is emerging as a top fundraiser for the charity.* —see also EMERGENT, EMERGING

(1) In this context, the best definition for *repel* is number ___.

(2) In this context, the best definition for *confound* is number ___.

(3) In this context, the best definition for *emerge* is number ___.

(4) The second sentence means that we may experience a work of art, ___.

    a. then try to avoid it for many years because we do not like it and because it confuses us

    b. and have a strong reaction to it, but many years later we understand how impressed we were by it

3. Visual analysis can help us appreciate the beauty of a masterpiece, but we must be careful not to *trivialize* it with a *formulaic* approach. Every aesthetic "law" advanced so far has proven of dubious value and usually gets in the way of our understanding. Even if a valid "law" were to be found—and none has yet been discovered—it would probably be so elementary as to prove useless in the face of art's complexity.

> **triv·i·al·ize** /ˈtrɪviə,laɪz/ *v.* [T] to make an important subject seem less important than it really is: *The media also has trivialized the peace movement and its leaders.* —**trivialization** /ˌtrɪviələˈzeɪʃən/ *n.* [U]

> **for·mu·la·ic** /ˌfɔrmyəˌleɪ-ɪk/ *adj.* FORMAL, DISAPPROVING containing or made from ideas or expressions that have been used many times before and are therefore not very new or interesting: *a formulaic mystery novel*

The authors are saying that ___.

    a. we will make the work of art seem unimportant if we analyze it according to overused ideas about art

    b. we will make the work of art seem very important if we analyze it according to ideas that have been used many times before

LEARN AND USE WORD FORMS

Complete the sentences below with the correct form of the word in the box. Refer to the word forms chart on page 191. Be sure to use the correct tense of verbs. Use each word only once.

achieve	reproduce	visualize
decorate	reveal	

1. Sometimes a work of art we have seen years earlier emerges as one of the most important artistic events of our lives, and we experience an artistic _____.

2. Museum gift shops often _____ and sell copies of priceless works of art.

3. An artist's _____ may extend beyond painting and sculpture to include architecture.

4. Michelangelo _____ a figure within marble, then cut away the marble to reveal the figure within.

5. When we use art for purely _____ purposes, we tend to ignore it, and it becomes visual background noise.

INTRODUCING THE MAIN READING

Activate Your Knowledge

Work with a partner or in a small group. Do the following activities.

1. Examine the map below. Locate the Nile River, and draw a circle around it. Describe the climate in this area of the world. _____

_____

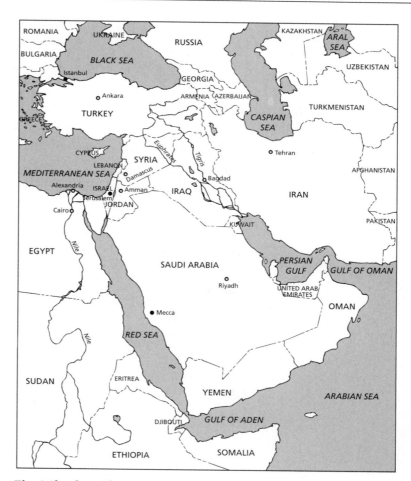

Fig. 4.8b The Mideast today, with Egypt and the Nile River

2. The map below is an enlargement of the area you circled in the map on the previous page. Examine it carefully. What do you observe about ancient Egypt (its geography, location, etc.)? Make a list.

_____   _____

_____   _____

_____   _____

_____   _____

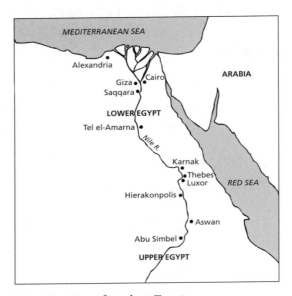

Fig. 4.8c Map of ancient Egypt

3. What do you know about ancient Egypt? Use the charts below and on the next page to help you organize your information.

History • when Egyptian civilization began • type of government • upper Egypt and lower Egypt	
Geography and Climate • significance of the Nile River • type of climate	
Art • style • purposes • examples	

Religion • beliefs	
Customs • religious • burial • •	

Fig. 4.8d

4. Look at the sculpture on the left. Describe it. Why do you think it was created?

_____

_____

_____

5. Look at the painting below. Describe it. Why do you think it was it drawn in this particular way? What does it tell you about the people of that time? What was its purpose?

Fig. 4.8e

_____

_____

_____

6. Look at the two sides of the carved piece below. What do you think the carvings illustrate?

Fig. 4.8f   *Fig. 4.8g*

_____

_____

_____

Reading and Study Skill Strategies

USE TITLE AND HEADINGS TO PREDICT CONTENT

A Work with a partner or in a small group. Before you work with the Main Reading, go through it and write down the headings on the lines below. Then answer the questions that follow.

Experiencing Ancient Egyptian Art

_____

_____

_____

1. In Chapter 6, you read about Sargon the Great's *dynasty,* which lasted for two centuries. What is a *dynasty?*

_____

_____

2. What three kinds of ancient Egyptian art do you think you are going to read about?

_____

_____

3. What do you need to know about ancient Egypt in order to understand its art?

_____

_____

B Go to page _vii_ in the Table of Contents. Read the brief summary of the Main Reading. Then review your answers above, and decide whether to change any of your predictions.

LEARN AND USE WORD FORMS

A Study the following chart which contains words from the Main Reading. Note the spelling changes. Pay attention to the words as they are used in the Main Reading.

VERB	NOUN	ADJECTIVE	ADVERB
commemorate	commemoration	commemorative	
conclude	conclusion	conclusive	conclusively
destroy	destruction	destroyed/destructive	destructively
dominate	domination	dominating	
innovate	innovation innovator	innovative	innovatively
preoccupy	preoccupation	preoccupied	
provide	provision	provided	
submit	submission	submissive	submissively
unify	unification	unified/unifying	
develop	development	developing/developed	
equip	equipment	equipped	
establish	establishment	established	

B Complete the following paragraph by writing the correct form of the word in parentheses. When you are done, check your answers by reading paragraph 3 on pages 203–204.

Tombs and Religion

Of the vast public works along the Nile nothing remains today, and very little has survived of ancient Egyptian palaces and cities. Our knowledge of early Egyptian civilization rests almost entirely on tombs and their contents. Their survival is no accident, since the tombs were built to last forever. Yet we must not make the mistake of _____
1. (conclude)
that the Egyptians viewed life on this earth mainly as a road to the grave. Their _____ with the cult of the dead is a link with
2. (preoccupy)
the Neolithic past, but the meaning they gave it was quite new and different: the dark fear of the spirits of the dead that _____
3. (dominate)
early ancestor cults seems entirely absent. Instead, the Egyptian attitude was that each person must _____ for his or her own
4. (provide)
happy afterlife. The ancient Egyptians _____ tombs
5. (equip)
as a kind of shadowy replica of their daily environment for their spirit (*ka*) to enjoy and to make sure that the *ka* had a body to dwell in (the individual's own mummified corpse or, if that should be _____, a
6. (destroy)
statue of the person).

MAIN READING

The following reading has two components. The first part, "Experiencing Ancient Egyptian Art," is from A Basic History of Art. *The second part is from* Art Past, Art Present. *As you read, highlight the important ideas and the vocabulary used to express those ideas. Annotate the text.*

Experiencing Ancient Egyptian Art

1   Egyptian civilization has long been regarded as the most rigid and conservative ever. Perhaps "enduring" and "continuous" are better descriptions of it, although at first glance all Egyptian art between 3000 and 500 B.C. does tend to have a certain sameness. In fact, the basic model of Egyptian institutions, beliefs, and artistic ideas was formed during the first few centuries of that vast span of time and kept reasserting itself until the very end. Egyptian art alternates between conservatism and innovation but is never static.

DYNASTIES

2   The history of Egypt is divided into dynasties, or families of rulers, in accordance with ancient Egyptian practice, beginning with Dynasty 1, shortly after 3000 B.C. The transition from prehistory to Dynasty 1 is referred to as the Predynastic period. The next major period, known as the Old Kingdom, lasted from about 2700 B.C. until about 2190 B.C., with the end of Dynasty 6. This method of counting historic time by dynasties conveys at once the strong Egyptian sense of continuity and the overwhelming importance of the pharaoh (king), who was not only the supreme ruler but was also revered as a god. The pharaoh transcended all people, for his kingship was not a duty or privilege derived from a superhuman source but was absolute, divine. This belief remained the key feature of Egyptian civilization and largely determined the character of Egyptian art. We do not know exactly the steps by which the early pharaohs established their claim to divinity, but we do know their historic achievements: molding the Nile Valley from the First Cataract (falls) at Aswan to the Delta into a single, effective state and increasing its fertility by regulating the river waters through dams and canals. The pharaohs also ordered the construction of great buildings, temples, and tombs, many of which survive today. They offer us a key to understanding their art and their beliefs.

BEFORE YOU CONTINUE READING

1. What was one of the most significant influences on Egyptian art?

_____

_____

TOMBS AND RELIGION

3   Of the vast public works along the Nile nothing remains today, and very little has survived of ancient Egyptian palaces and cities. Our knowledge of early Egyptian civilization rests almost entirely on tombs and their contents. Their survival is no accident, since the tombs were built to last forever. Yet we must not make the mistake of concluding that the Egyptians viewed life on this earth mainly as a road to the grave. Their preoccupation with the cult of the dead is a link with the Neolithic past, but the meaning they gave it was quite new and different: the dark fear of the spirits of the dead that dominates early ancestor cults seems entirely absent. Instead, the Egyptian attitude was that each person

Fig. 4.8h The Great Pyramids at Giza. The Old Kingdom, Dynasty 4, ca. 2601–2515 B.C.E.

must provide for his or her own happy afterlife. The ancient Egyptians equipped tombs as a kind of shadowy replica of their daily environment for their spirit (*ka*) to enjoy and to make sure that the *ka* had a body to dwell in (the individual's own mummified corpse or, if that should be destroyed, a statue of the person).

4   There is a curious blurring of the sharp line between life and death here, and perhaps that was the essential impulse behind their mock households. People who believed that their *kas*, after death, would enjoy the same pleasures they now did and who had provided these pleasures for their *kas* could look forward to active and happy lives without being haunted by fear of the great unknown. In a sense, then, the Egyptian tomb was a kind of life insurance, an investment in peace of mind. Such, at least, is the impression one gains of Old Kingdom tombs. However, the tomb paintings are not the only works that help us understand the Egyptians and their art.

BEFORE YOU CONTINUE READING

2. **What was the primary, or main, purpose of Egyptian tombs and tomb paintings?** _____

THREE EXAMPLES OF ANCIENT EGYPTIAN ART

5   In the past, important historical developments often led to the creation of objects that commemorated or interpreted the event. One of the earliest surviving works of Egyptian art, the *Votive Palette of King Narmer,* was apparently created to mark the unification of Egypt. Narmer,

Fig. 4.8f Votive Palette of King Narmer, side A.

Fig. 4.8g Votive Palette of King Narmer, side B.

who has been identified with Menes, the first king of the first Egyptian dynasty, appears three times. As the largest figure on side A, he wears the crown of Upper Egypt and brings under his control a figure who probably represents Lower Egypt. At the bottom of side A are two more defeated antagonists and small symbols of a fortified city and a gazelle trap that suggest victories in the city and countryside. The nearby human-headed figure with six papyrus blossoms, being held captive by the god Horus (shown as a falcon), almost certainly refers to the submission of Lower Egypt to Upper Egypt. The use of symbols to represent complex ideas is an innovation that points to the later development of Egyptian hieroglyphs, in which figures or pictures signify words or sounds.

6   At the bottom of side B, Narmer himself appears as a symbol—a horned bull, victorious over an enemy and the enemy's fortified city. Near the top of side B, Narmer, wearing the crown of Lower Egypt and accompanied by a processional retinue, views the decapitated corpses of enemies, their heads between their legs. The central symbol at the top of both sides represents Narmer's name and his palace. It is flanked by horned animals, representing the sky mother Hathor, to whose shrine the palette was probably offered. In addition to Narmer's assumption of the two crowns, the union of Egypt is also suggested by the joining of two fantastic, long-necked lionesses (female lions) on side B, their serpentine necks intertwined to form the shallow indentation that refers to the function of the object as a palette.

7   The *Votive Palette of King Narmer* probably had several functions: as an object to be used in a religious ritual; as a votive offering to the god or goddess (most likely Hathor); and as a commemoration of the military and territorial victories of Narmer. Such a union of political statement with religious ritual is typical of Egyptian art and culture. Narmer is, in every case, represented as unnaturally larger than his subordinates and enemies through the use of hierarchical scale, which is common in Egyptian religious and political art. Narmer's large scale and the lucid design make the meaning of the palette more easily comprehensible. As unrealistic as this representation is, it is easily read and it emphasizes strength. This style of representing the figure would continue in Egyptian art for more than 3,000 years.

Fig. 4.8d King Menkaure and His Wife, Queen Khamerenebty

8   The sculpture *Menkaure and His Wife, Queen Khamerenebty,* carved in ancient Egypt about 2515 B.C., proclaims stability; the poses of the Egyptian king and his queen are confined with a rectangular composition, and there is no suggestion of movement. There is a slight hint of portraiture in their faces, but their bodies are idealized, abstracted to conform to a standard of perfection dictated by Egyptian cultural preferences.

9   Menkaure and his queen ruled in ancient Egypt, and the iconography (meaning) of the sculpture is their representation as royal personages. The portrait is one of several similar sculptures intended to provide a home for the enduring aspect of the individual personality, called the *ka* in the afterlife. This enduring strength is reinforced by the use of greywacke (a dense, hard stone) as a medium.

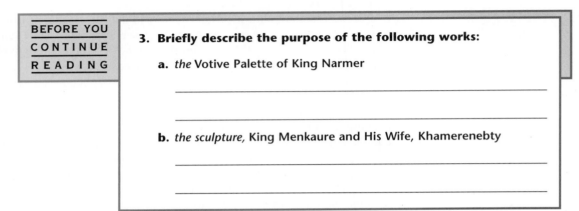

BEFORE YOU CONTINUE READING

3. **Briefly describe the purpose of the following works:**

   a. *the* Votive Palette of King Narmer

   _____

   _____

   b. *the sculpture,* King Menkaure and His Wife, Khamerenebty

   _____

   _____

10   The walls of Egyptian tombs were decorated with painted, low-relief sculptures or with paintings on plaster applied over the walls. The requirement that tomb decoration preserve pleasant everyday life for the delight of the *ka* throughout eternity means that these paintings tell us a great deal about ancient Egyptian life and customs and have a broad human interest and appeal. *Pond in a Garden* [see the illustration below], from a New Kingdom tomb, with its rectangular pool with ducks, fish, and lotus blossoms surrounded on all sides by flowering and fruit-bearing trees,

Fig. 4.8e Pond in a Garden

provides a demonstration of the Egyptian approach to representation. Completeness and clarity were demanded of the Egyptian painter, for anything not clearly included in the tomb painting would not be available to the *ka* in the afterlife. This explains why each object has to be shown in its most easily recognized view—the pond is represented as if seen from above, while everything else is in profile. The relationships among the objects in reality are also made clear in the representation: fish, duck, and lotus are seen as within the pool, while the trees surround it. The trees are seen right side up and sideways, but not upside down—those at the bottom side of the pool are upright. Despite the lack of a consistent viewpoint for the scene and the flatness with which each object is rendered, we can still easily recognize that this is, indeed, a pond in a garden.

Checking Comprehension

A **What did you need to know or understand about ancient Egypt in order to understand the three examples of art described in the Main Reading? Check all that apply.**

1. ___ Egyptian historical events

2. ___ Egyptian religious beliefs

3. ___ the climate of Egypt

4. ___ Egypt's geographical features

5. ___ Egypt's system of government

6. ___ Egypt's dynasties

7. ___ Egyptian marriage customs

8. ___ the Egyptians' beliefs about death

9. ___ Egypt's artistic conventions

10. ___ Egyptian agricultural techniques

11. ___ beliefs about Egyptian rulers

12. ___ Egyptian music

13. ___ Egyptians' perceptions of life and death

14. ___ the significance of the Nile River in Egyptian life

15. ___ the Egyptian social system

16. ___ Egyptian artistic conventions

17. ___ Egyptian family life

How much of this information did you get from pages 202–207?

B Refer to paragraph 10 in the Main Reading on pages 206–207. Identify the referents.

1. In the second sentence, *these paintings* refers to _____.

2. In the third sentence, *its* refers to _____.

3. In the fifth sentence, *this* refers to _____.

4. In the seventh sentence, *those* refers to _____.

C Answer the following questions in complete sentences.

1. In what ways did ancient Egypt's rulers influence Egyptian civilization and art?

_____

_____

2. What were some of the Egyptians' religious beliefs?

_____

_____

3. How did the Egyptians' religious beliefs influence their building and their art?

_____

_____

4. What was the purpose of the *Votive Palette of King Narmer?* What story does it tell?

_____

_____

5. King Menkaure had a sculpture made of himself and his wife. What impression did he wish to make on the people who looked at this statue?

_____

_____

6. Why does the *Pond in a Garden* represent all the plants and animals in a certain way? Why was it so important to draw the plants and animals this way?

_____

_____

D Review your annotations on pages 202–207. Do you have any questions that have not been answered? If so, discuss them with your classmates or your instructor.

Learning Vocabulary

VOCABULARY FROM CONTEXT

Reread the paragraphs indicated from the Main Reading to figure out the meaning of the italicized words. Then circle the correct choice to complete the sentences that follow.

1. Paragraph 1: *vast span of time, alternates,* and *static*

   (1) The *vast span of time* refers to ___.
   a. a few centuries
   b. 500 years
   c. 2,500 years
   d. 3,000 years

   (2) From this context, we can understand that *alternate* means ___.
   a. develop and improve from one to the other
   b. go back and forth from one to the other

   (3) From this context, we can understand that *static* means ___.
   a. unchanging
   b. changing

2. Paragraph 2: *transition, lasted, pharaoh, revered, divine,* and *divinity*

   (1) A *transition* refers to ___.
   a. a change
   b. a dynasty
   c. a history

   (2) *Lasted* means ___.
   a. ended
   b. changed
   c. continued

   (3) A *pharaoh* is ___.
   a. a supreme ruler
   b. a god
   c. a superhuman

   (4) To *revere* means ___.
   a. to obey
   b. to worship
   c. to follow

   (5) From this context, we can understand that *divine* means ___.
   a. like a god
   b. like a superhuman
   c. like a king

3. Paragraph 3: *replica* and *dwell in*

   (1) From this context, we can understand that a *replica* is ___.
   a. a home
   b. a spirit
   c. a copy

   (2) To *dwell in* means ___.
   a. to mummify
   b. to inhabit
   c. to enjoy

USING THE DICTIONARY

Read the following sentences and dictionary entries. Select the best entry for the context. Then circle the correct choice to complete the sentences that follow.

The sculpture *Menkaure and His Wife, Queen Khamerenebty,* carved in ancient Egypt about 2515 B.C., *proclaims stability*; the poses of the Egyptian king and his queen are confined with a rectangular composition, and there is no suggestion of movement.

> **pro·claim** /prouˈkleɪm, prə-/ *v.* [T] FORMAL **1** to say publicly or officially that something important is true or exists: *Phillips has repeatedly proclaimed his innocence.* | [**proclaim sb/sth sth**] *The cave was proclaimed a national monument in 1909.* **2** to show something clearly or be a sign of something: *Nearly everyone there wore a pin proclaiming their support of the union.*

> **sta·bil·i·ty** /stəˈbɪləti/ *n.* [U] **1** the condition of being strong, steady, and not changing: *Our relationship provided the stability and comfort we both needed.* | [**+ of**] *the financial stability of the community* **2** TECHNICAL the ability of a substance to stay in the same state —opposite INSTABILITY

   (1) In this context, the best definition for *proclaim* is number ___.

   (2) In this context, the best definition for *stability* is number ___.

   (3) The sculpture *Menkaure and His Wife, Queen Khamerenebty* ___.
   a. publicly says that the king and queen are strong and steady
   b. is a sign that King Menkaure and his queen are strong and steady

LEARN AND USE WORD FORMS

Complete the sentences below with the correct form of the word in the box. Refer to the word forms chart on page 201. Be sure to use the correct tense of verbs. Use each word only once.

commemorate	preoccupy	unify
establish	submit	

1. Once _____, the Egyptian dynasties lasted for many centuries.

2. Under King Menes, Lower Egypt _____ to the domination of Upper Egypt, and the country was unified under a single ruler.

3. In the past, important historical developments often led to the creation of objects that _____ or interpreted the event.

4. King Menes _____ Upper and Lower Egypt into one kingdom.

5. The ancient Egyptians were very _____ with life after death and spent considerable time and effort preparing for it.

FOLLOW-UP ASSIGNMENTS

Before you begin any of the follow-up assignments, review the content-specific vocabulary and academic vocabulary below, and look over the vocabulary in the word forms lists on pages 191 and 201. If you are still unsure what any words or terms mean, go back through the chapter and review. As you complete the assignments, be sure to incorporate the appropriate vocabulary in your writing.

Content-Specific Vocabulary

aesthetic	innovation	sculpture	visual
carving	*ka*	see	background noise
conservatism	look at	static	
formulaic	pharaoh	transition	visual elements
image	replica	unprecedented	

Academic Vocabulary

alternate between	convey	emerge	repel
analysis	desensitized	foster	revere
confound	divine	to last	stability
context	dwell in	proclaim	trivialize

Writing Activities

1. Examine the cave paintings in Chapter 3. Consider this artwork within its historical context. Write three paragraphs. In the first paragraph, describe what you think the paintings conveyed to the artists and their audience. In the second paragraph, write what they convey to you. In the third paragraph, explain the reasons for the similarities and differences.
2. Examine the Sumerian sculptures and carvings in Chapter 6. Write three paragraphs. In the first paragraph, describe what these artworks conveyed to the artists and their audience. In the second paragraph, write what they convey to you. In the third paragraph, explain the reasons for the similarities and differences.
3. Examine the artworks of one of the cultures you and your classmates researched in the Follow-up Assignments in Chapter 7. Write three paragraphs. In the first paragraph, briefly describe the culture. In the second paragraph, describe the work of art. In the third paragraph, explain the work of art within the context of the culture.

Extension Activities

1. Choose one of the early civilizations that the class researched at the end of Chapter 6. Research the art of that civilization, and get one or more examples. Prepare a brief presentation for the class. Be sure to place the art within its historical context.
2. Choose the art of any time and culture. Research it, and get one or more examples. Prepare a brief presentation for the class. Be sure to place the art within its historical context.
3. Go to a museum, and select a work of art that you particularly like. Research the artist. Prepare a brief presentation for the class. Describe the artist's work within the artist's cultural and historical context.
4. Go to a museum, and select a style of art that you particularly like. Research the style. Prepare a brief presentation for the class. Describe the style within its cultural and historical context.

Internet Research

Go online, and go to one of the websites listed below. Investigate a topic related to the information you read about in Chapter 8. Choose a topic that especially interests you. Use some of the website's search features. Search by keywords such as *Egyptian art, frontalism, brush painting, ancient Roman art,* and *ancient Greek art.*

Bergen County, New Jersey, technical schools website:
http://www.bergen.org/AAST/Projects/Egypt/egyptian_art.html
Celtic Art website:
http://www.celtic-art.net/Symbols/Page44.htm
Asia Art websites:
http://www.asia-art.net/history.html
Select a topic from the menu.
Detroit Institute of Art, Detroit, Michigan website:
http://www.dia.org/collections
Click on "Ancient Art" and select from the choices offered.
The State Hermitage Museum, St. Petersburg, Russia website:
http://www.hermitagemuseum.org
Click on "Collection Highlights" and select from the choices offered.
Metropolitan Museum of Art, New York website:
http://www.metmuseum.org/collections
Select a topic from the menu.

HOW DOES OUR SOCIETY INFLUENCE HOW WE PERCEIVE THE WORLD?

CHAPTER 9

SOCIETY'S INFLUENCE ON OUR BEHAVIOR

Skills Goals

- *Review skills from Chapters 1–8.*
- *Understand graphs.*

Content-Specific Goals

- *Understand the concept of social psychology.*
- *Learn how people are influenced by others.*
- *Learn how people interpret the behavior of others.*

Chapter Readings

Understanding the Influence of Other People in Our Lives

The Power of Social Influence

INTRODUCING THE READING

Activate Your Knowledge

Work alone or in a small group. Do the following activities.

1. *Social psychology* can be defined as "the scientific study of the way in which people's thoughts, feelings, and behaviors are influenced by the real or imagined presence of other people" (Aronson, Wilson, & Akert, 2002, p. 6). Who might these "other people" be? In what ways might people be influenced by the real or imagined presence of these other people? Use the diagram below to help you organize your ideas. When you are finished, work as a class to put all the groups' ideas on the board.

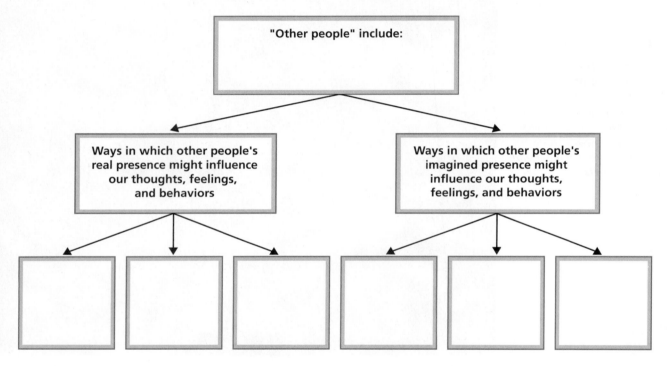

2. Work together in groups consisting of students who are from two or three different cultures or are very familiar with a different culture. Use the chart on the next page to help you organize your answers to this question: In the same situation, are people in different cultures affected by the same people in the same ways? When you are finished, work as a class to put all the groups' answers on the board.

Situations	Culture: _____	Culture: _____	Culture: _____
Your parents want you to study a specific major in college, but you are interested in something else. What do you do?			
All your friends are wearing a certain style of clothes, and they think you should too, but you don't like that style. What do you do?			
A stranger on the street needs your help. No one else is nearby to see you. Do you help the stranger? Why or why not?			

Reading and Study Skill Strategies

PREVIEW KEY VOCABULARY

Read the list of concept-specific vocabulary and check the ones you are familiar with. Leave the other spaces blank. Do not try to learn the unfamiliar items before you begin reading. You will learn them as you work with the chapter.

___ conflict	___ influence	___ phenomenon
___ construal	___ interpretation	___ situational
___ convey	___ overt	___ social norms
___ determinant	___ peers	___ social psychology
___ domain	___ perception	___ tendency
___ inclination	___ persuasion	

USE TITLE AND HEADINGS TO PREDICT CONTENT

A **Work with a partner or in a small group. Before you read the Introductory Reading on pages 219–222, go through it and write down the headings on the lines below. Then try to answer the questions that follow.**

Understanding the Influence of Other People in Our Lives

_____

_____

1. What is the nature of social influence? Put another way, people like our friends, teachers, parents, and other relatives influence us. How do they do so?

   _____

   _____

2. Like social psychology, anthropology and sociology also focus on how people are affected by their social environment. How is social psychology different from anthropology or sociology?

   _____

   _____

B Go to page *vii* in the Table of Contents. Read the brief summary of the Introductory Reading. Then review your answers above, and decide whether to make any changes to your predictions.

LEARN AND USE WORD FORMS

A Study the following chart which contains words from the Introductory Reading. Note the spelling changes. Pay attention to the words as they are used in the Introductory Reading.

VERB	NOUN	ADJECTIVE	ADVERB
clarify	clarification	clear clarified/clarifying	
decide	decision	decisive	decisively
extend	extension	extensive	extensively
inspire	inspiration	inspiring/inspired	
interpret	interpretation	interpretive	
perceive	perception	perceptive	perceptively
persuade	persuasion	persuasive	persuasively
predict	prediction	predictable	predictably
influence	influence	influential influencing/influenced	influentially
view	view		
behave	behavior	behavioral	behaviorally
construe	construal		

B Complete the following paragraph by writing the correct form of the word in parentheses. When you are done, check your answers by reading paragraph 5 on page 221.

We are all _____ by other people. An example
1. (influence)
will _____. Imagine that Jason is a shy college
2. (clarify)
student who admires Debbie from afar. Suppose that as a social
psychologist, you have the job of _____ whether or
3. (predict)
not Jason will ask Debbie for a date. One way you might do this is to observe
Debbie's objective _____ toward Jason. Does she pay
4. (behave)
attention to him and smile a lot? If so, the casual observer might
_____ that Jason will ask her out. As a social
5. (decide)
psychologist, however, you are more interested in _____
6. (view)
Debbie's _____ through Jason's eyes—that is, in
7. (behave)
seeing how Jason _____ Debbie's behavior. If she
8. (interpret)
smiles at him, does Jason _____ her behavior as
9. (construe)
mere politeness, the kind of politeness she would
_____ to any of the dozens of losers in her classes?
10. (extend)
Or does he _____ her smile as an encouraging sign,
11. (view)
one that _____ him to gather the courage to ask her
12. (inspire)
out? If she ignores him, does Jason figure that she's playing "hard to get"?
Or does he take it as a sign that she's not interested in dating him? To
predict Jason's behavior, it is not enough to know the details of Debbie's
behavior; it is imperative to know how Jason _____
13. (interpret)
Debbie's behavior.

INTRODUCTORY READING

The following reading, "Understanding the Influence of Other People in Our Lives," is from Social Psychology. *As you read, highlight the important ideas and vocabulary used to express those ideas. Annotate the text.*

Understanding the Influence of Other People in Our Lives

1   At the very heart of social psychology is the phenomenon of social influence. We are all influenced by other people. When we think of *social influence,* the kinds of examples that readily come to mind are direct attempts at persuasion, whereby one person deliberately tries to change another person's behavior. This is what happens in an advertising campaign, when creative individuals employ sophisticated techniques to persuade us to buy a particular

brand of toothpaste or during an election campaign when similar techniques are used to get us to vote for a particular political candidate. Direct attempts at persuasion also occur when our friends try to get us to do something we don't really want to do ("Come on, have another beer—everyone is doing it") or when the schoolyard bully uses force or threats to get smaller kids to part with their lunch money or homework.

BEFORE YOU
CONTINUE
READING

1. **What is the main idea of the introductory paragraph?**

   a. *Direct attempts at persuasion come mainly from advertisers.*

   b. *Direct attempts at persuasion are rare in our personal lives.*

   c. *Direct attempts at persuasion happen in many areas of our lives.*

THE NATURE OF SOCIAL INFLUENCE

2   To the social psychologist, social influence is broader than attempts by one person to change another person's behavior. For one thing, social influence extends beyond behavior—it includes our thoughts and feelings as well as our overt acts. In addition, social influence takes on many forms other than deliberate attempts at persuasion. We are often influenced merely by the presence of other people. Moreover, even when we are not in the physical presence of other people, we are still influenced by them. Thus in a sense we carry our mothers, fathers, friends, and teachers around with us as we attempt to make decisions that would make them proud of us.

3   On a still subtler level, each of us is immersed in a social and cultural context. Social psychologists are interested in studying how and why our thoughts, feelings, and behaviors are shaped by the entire social environment. Taking all of these factors into account, we can define **social psychology** as the scientific study of the way in which people's thoughts, feelings, and behaviors are influenced by the real or imagined presence of other people. Of particular interest to social psychologists is what happens in the mind of an individual when various influences come into conflict with one another. This is frequently the case when young people (like many of our readers) go off to college and find themselves torn between the beliefs and values they learned at home and the beliefs and values their professors or peers are expressing.

BEFORE YOU
CONTINUE
READING

2. **Social psychologists are interested in studying how ___.**

   a. *other people influence our actions whether we are with them or not*

   b. *our actions, thoughts, and feelings are influenced by other people, whether they are with us or not*

   c. *we think about the way other people influence our thoughts, feelings, and actions, whether we are with them or not*

SOCIAL PSYCHOLOGY AS A DISTINCT DISCIPLINE

4   Other disciplines, like anthropology and sociology, are also interested in how people are influenced by their social environment. Social psychology is distinct, however, primarily because it is concerned not so much with social situations in any objective sense, but rather with how people are influenced by their interpretation, or **construal**, of their social environment. To understand how people are influenced by their social world, social psychologists believe it is more important to understand how people perceive, comprehend, and interpret the social world than it is to understand the objective properties of the social world itself.

5   An example will clarify. Imagine that Jason is a shy college student who admires Debbie from afar. Suppose that as a social psychologist, you have the job of predicting whether or not Jason will ask Debbie for a date. One way you might do this is to observe Debbie's objective behavior toward Jason. Does she pay attention to him and smile a lot? If so, the casual observer might decide that Jason will ask her out. As a social psychologist, however, you are more interested in viewing Debbie's behavior through Jason's eyes—that is, in seeing how Jason interprets Debbie's behavior. If she smiles at him, does Jason construe her behavior as mere politeness, the kind of politeness she would extend to any of the dozens of losers in her classes? Or does he view her smile as an encouraging sign, one that inspires him to gather the courage to ask her out? If she ignores him, does Jason figure that she's playing "hard to get"? Or does he take it as a sign that she's not interested in dating him? To predict Jason's behavior, it is not enough to know the details of Debbie's behavior; it is imperative to know how Jason *interprets* Debbie's behavior.

3. Unlike anthropologists or sociologists, the social psychologist is interested in _____.

    a. *the dating customs of college students*

    b. *society's expectations of college students when they date*

    c. *an individual's interpretation of another's behavior in a dating situation*

6   [1]Given the importance placed on the way people interpret the social world, social psychologists pay special attention to the origins of these interpretations. [2]For example, when construing their environment, are most people concerned with making an interpretation that places them in the most positive light (e.g., Jason believing "Debbie is going on a date with Eric because she is just trying to make me jealous") or with making the most accurate interpretation, even if it is unflattering (e.g., "Painful as it may be, I must admit that Debbie would rather go on a date with a dog than with me")? [3]A great deal of research in social psychology has addressed these and other determinants of people's thoughts and behaviors.

7   Another distinctive feature of social psychology is that it is an experimentally based science. As experimental scientists, we test our assumptions, guesses, and ideas about human social behavior empirically and systematically rather than by relying on folk wisdom, common sense, or the opinions and insights of philosophers, novelists, grandmothers, and others wise in the ways of human beings. As you will see, doing systematic experiments in social psychology presents a great many challenges— primarily because we are attempting to predict the behavior of highly sophisticated organisms in a variety of complex situations. As scientists, our goal is to find objective answers to a wide array of important questions: What are the factors that cause aggression? How might we reduce prejudice? What variables cause two people to like or love each other? Why do certain kinds of political advertisements work better than others? What causes a person to do something harmful to himself or to another?

Checking Comprehension

A **Answer the following questions.**

1. What is the nature of social influence? Put another way, people like our friends, teachers, parents, and other relatives influence us. How do they do so?

    _____

    _____

    _____

2. Like social psychology, anthropology and sociology also focus on how people are affected by their social environment. How is social psychology different from anthropology or sociology?

_____

_____

Compare these answers with your responses on page 218. How accurate were your answers?

_____

B **Refer to paragraph 6 in the Introductory Reading on page 222. Identify the referents.**

1. In the first sentence, *these interpretations* refers to _____.

2. In the second sentence, *their* refers to _____.

3. In the second sentence ("... *it* is unflattering ..."), *it* refers to _____

_____.

4. In the last sentence, *these* refers to _____.

C **Answer the following questions in complete sentences.**

1. In what ways can people influence our thoughts, feelings, or actions even when they are not with us?

_____

_____

2. a. How do social psychologists test their ideas about the social behavior of people?

_____

b. What kinds of methods do they reject?

_____

3. Generally speaking, what is it that social psychologists want to find out?

_____

_____

D **Review your annotations on pages 219–222. Do you have any questions that have not been answered? If so, discuss them now with your classmates or your instructor.**

VOCABULARY FROM CONTEXT

Reread the paragraphs indicated from the Introductory Reading to figure out the meaning of the italicized words. Then circle the correct choice to complete the sentences.

1. Paragraph 1: *persuasion* and *bully*

    (1) In this context, *persuasion* refers to the act of ___.
    a. trying to change another person's actions or feelings
    b. making someone believe you are correct
    c. getting someone to believe you like him/her

    (2) From this context, we can understand that a *bully* is a person who gets other people to do something ___.
    a. willingly
    b. through fear
    c. exciting

2. Paragraph 4: *construal*

    From this context, we can understand that *construal* means ___.
    a. influence
    b. situation
    c. interpretation

3. Paragraph 5: *clarify* and *playing hard to get*

    (1) From this context, we can understand that *clarify* means ___.
    a. give a number of details
    b. make something easier to understand
    c. provide a specific definition

    (2) From this context, we can understand that *playing hard to get* means ___.
    a. pretending you are not interested in another person to make that person more interested in you
    b. ignoring someone who likes you because you do not like the other person
    c. showing your interest in another person so that person will be more interested in you

4. Paragraph 6: *e.g.* (in both sentences)

    From the context, we can understand that the abbreviation *e.g.* means ___.
    a. however
    b. and
    c. for example

USING THE DICTIONARY

Read the following sentences and dictionary entries. Sometimes an entry has only one definition. In such cases, read the definition for that specific meaning. Then circle the best choice to complete the sentences that follow.

1. To the social psychologist, social influence is broader than attempts by one person to change another person's behavior. For one thing, social influence extends beyond behavior—it includes our thoughts and feelings as well as our *overt* acts.

   > **o·vert** /oʊ'vɜt, 'oʊvɜt/ *adj.* FORMAL overt actions or feelings are done or shown publicly, without trying to hide anything: *an overt attempt to force landowners to sell* | *overt racism* —**overtly** *adv.* —opposite COVERT¹

   Which of the following are examples of overt acts?

   a. ___ smiling at another person to show you like him

   b. ___ feeling happy about another person

   c. ___ a mother telling a child to do his homework

   d. ___ a child thinking his mother wants him to do his homework

   e. ___ cooking dinner for a sick friend

   f. ___ feeling sad because a friend is sick

   g. ___ telephoning a sick friend

2. Another distinctive feature of social psychology is that it is an experimentally based science. As experimental scientists, we test our assumptions, guesses, and ideas about human social behavior *empirically* and systematically rather than by relying on folk wisdom, common sense, or the opinions and insights of philosophers, novelists, grandmothers, and others wise in the ways of human beings.

   > **em·pir·i·cal** /ɪm'pɪrɪkəl, ɛm-/ *adj.* [only before noun] based on scientific testing or practical experience, not on ideas: *His theory is inconsistent with the empirical evidence.* —**empirically** /-kli/ *adv.*

   > **em·pir·i·cism** /ɪm'pɪrə,sɪzəm, ɛm-/ *n.* [U] the belief in basing your ideas on practical experience —**empiricist** *n.* [C]

   (1) Empirical research is based on ___.
   a. reading and asking about something
   b. conducting studies to prove or disprove something

   (2) A person who is an empiricist ___.
   a. would take the medicine that a doctor prescribed for curing his illness
   b. would take his grandmother's remedy for an illness because he trusts his grandmother

LEARN AND USE WORD FORMS

Complete the sentences below with the correct form of the word in the box. Refer to the word forms chart on page 218. Be sure to use the correct tense of verbs. Use each word only once.

construe	decide	persuade
behave	perceive	

1. It isn't our _____ toward others that is so important; it's how others interpret our actions that is important.

2. The way in which a person _____ a situation affects how that person will respond to it.

3. We can name many people throughout history who have been extremely _____. Sometimes they were able to make thousands of people believe or do extraordinary things.

4. We all know people who have trouble acting _____. Such people are often easily influenced by others.

5. Some people are extremely _____, and can see when another person is trying to make them do something they might otherwise not do.

INTRODUCING THE MAIN READING

Activate Your Knowledge

Work in pairs or in a small group. Read about the following two incidents. Then answer the questions that follow.

> **INCIDENT ONE**
>
> One afternoon, you stop at a roadside restaurant for a cup of coffee and a piece of pie. The waitress comes over to take your order, but you are having a hard time deciding which kind of pie to order. While you are hesitating, the waitress impatiently taps her pen against her order book, rolls her eyes toward the ceiling, glares at you, and finally snaps, "Hey, I haven't got all day, you know!"

1. How might you explain the waitress's behavior?

_____

_____

INCIDENT TWO

Oscar is a middle-aged executive with a computer software company. As a student, Oscar had attended a large state university in the Midwest, where he was a member of a fraternity[1] we will call Delta Nu. He remembers having gone through a severe and somewhat scary hazing[2] ritual in order to become a member but he believes it was worthwhile. Although he had been terribly frightened by the hazing, he loved his fraternity brothers and was proud to be a member of Delta Nu. A few years ago, his son, Sam, was about to enroll in the same university; naturally, Oscar urged Sam to pledge Delta Nu: "It's a great fraternity—always attracts a wonderful bunch of fellows. You'll really love it." Sam did in fact pledge Delta Nu and was accepted. Oscar was relieved to learn that Sam was not required to undergo a severe initiation in order to become a member; times had changed, and hazing was now forbidden. When Sam came home for Christmas break, Oscar asked him how he liked the fraternity. "It's all right, I guess," he said, "but most of my friends are outside the fraternity." Oscar was astonished.

2. Why were Oscar's and Sam's experiences with the same fraternity so different? How can we explain why Oscar loved his fraternity brothers, whereas Sam had few friends among his fraternity?

_____

_____

Reading and Study Skill Strategies

USE TITLE AND HEADINGS TO PREDICT CONTENT

A **Work with a partner or in a small group. Before you work with the Main Reading, go through it and write the headings on the lines below. Then answer the questions that follow.**

The Power of Social Influence

_____

_____

1. In what ways can social influence positively affect our thoughts, actions, and feelings? In what ways can social influence negatively affect our thoughts, actions, and feelings?

_____

_____

---

[1]A fraternity is a college organization for men. Each fraternity's name consists of Greek letters.
[2]Hazing is an initiation (admission) process, often associated with membership into college fraternities. The process is often unpleasant, humiliating, and even frightening. Passing through the hazing ritual is a prerequisite for membership into the group.

2. What are possible consequences of underestimating the power of social influence on ourselves and other people?

_____

_____

3. What kinds of experimental research do social psychologists conduct in order to learn about the power of social influence?

_____

_____

B Go to page *vii* in the Table of Contents. Read the brief summary of the Main Reading. Then review your answers above, and decide whether to make any changes to your predictions.

LEARN AND USE WORD FORMS

A Study the following chart which contains words from the Main Reading. Note the spelling changes. Pay attention to the words as they are used in the Main Reading.

VERB	NOUN	ADJECTIVE	ADVERB
compete	competition competitiveness	competitive	competitively
cooperate	cooperation	cooperative	cooperatively
describe	description	descriptive	descriptively
(over)estimate (under)estimate	(over)estimation (under)estimation	(over)estimated (under)estimated	
explain	explanation	explanatory	
hesitate	hesitation	hesitant	
incline	inclination	inclined	
(over)simplify	(over)simplification	(over)simplified	
influence	influence	influential	
fail	failure	failed/failing	
tend to	tendency		
trivialize	trivia	trivial	

B Complete the following paragraph by writing the correct form of the word in parentheses. When you are done, check your answers by reading paragraph 1 on page 231.

When trying to convince people that their behavior is greatly
_____ by the social environment, the social
       1. (influence)
psychologist is up against a formidable barrier: the _____,
                              2. (incline)
or tendency, we all have for _____ people's behavior in
                       3. (explain)
terms of their personalities. This barrier is known as the
fundamental attribution error—the _____ to
                               4. (tend)
_____ our own and other people's behavior entirely in
     5. (explain)
terms of personality traits, thereby _____ the power
                      6. (underestimate)
of social _____. If you are like most people, when
        7. (influence)
you first encounter examples of social behavior, your initial tendency will be
to _____ that behavior in terms of the personalities
     8. (explain)
of the people involved and to overlook the power of social influence.

UNDERSTANDING GRAPHS

All disciplines use charts and graphs to illustrate how measurements are related to each other. For example, scientists might study the population changes of a species of animal in a changing environment, and create a graph to see how many more or fewer animals are born or die over a period of time.

    Because social psychology is an experimentally based discipline, social psychologists frequently chart the results of their research in order to better understand them.

A Read the introduction below and on the next page. It explains the concept of *justification of effort* and the research that focuses on this phenomenon. Then examine the bar graph that follows.

JUSTIFICATION OF EFFORT

    Social psychologists have observed that people often put a lot of effort into joining a particular group. Sometimes the group is very worthwhile, and sometimes the group turns out to be boring or worthless. In cases where the group is worthless, people often still try to find positive reasons for belonging.

    In one experiment, college students volunteered to join a group that would be meeting regularly to discuss various aspects of the psychology of sex. To be admitted to the group, they volunteered to go through a screening procedure. For one-third of the participants, the procedure was an extremely

(continued)

---

unpleasant one (Severe Initiation); for one-third, it was only mildly unpleasant (Mild Initiation); one-third of the participants (Control Group) were admitted to the group without undergoing any screening procedure.

Each participant was then allowed to listen in on a discussion being conducted by the members of the group they would be joining. Although they were led to believe that the discussion was a live, ongoing one, what they actually heard was a boring, prerecorded tape. After the discussion was over, each participant was asked to rate it in terms of how much they liked it, how interesting it was, and how intelligent the people were. The results supported the researchers' hypothesis: Participants who underwent little or no effort to get into the group did not enjoy the discussion very much. They were able to see it for what it was—a dull and boring waste of time. They regretted that they had agreed to participate. Participants who went through a severe initiation, however, succeeded in convincing themselves that the same discussion had some interesting moments and was, therefore, mostly worthwhile. In short, they justified their difficult initiation process by interpreting all the negative aspects of the group discussion in the most positive manner possible.

B **Examine the graph below. Then answer the questions that follow.**

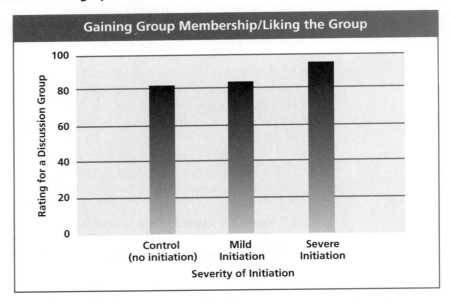

1. What do the numbers on the left side of the graph represent?
   a. the number of people who participated in the group membership study
   b. a measure of how much the study participants in each group liked the discussion
   c. an indication of the proportion of people in each of the three initiation procedures

2. What do the three bars in the graph represent?
  a. the number of people who underwent each of the three initiation procedures
  b. the degree of severity of each of the initiation procedures
  c. the average rating of the people in each of the three initiation procedures

3. Which of the following conclusions appears to be correct?
  a. The more difficult the initiation into a group, the more a person will try to rationalize membership in the group.
  b. The more difficult the initiation into a group, the less a person will try to rationalize membership in the group.
  c. Any person who has not experienced any initiation into a group will not be interested in membership in the group.

MAIN READING

The following reading, "The Power of Social Influence," is from Social Psychology. *As you read, highlight the important ideas and the vocabulary used to express those ideas. Annotate the text.*

The Power of Social Influence

1   When trying to convince people that their behavior is greatly influenced by the social environment, the social psychologist is up against a formidable barrier: the inclination, or tendency, we all have for explaining people's behavior in terms of their personalities. This barrier is known as the **fundamental attribution error**—the tendency to explain our own and other people's behavior entirely in terms of personality traits, thereby underestimating the power of social influence. If you are like most people, when you first encounter examples of social behavior, your initial tendency will be to explain that behavior in terms of the personalities of the people involved and to overlook the power of social influence.

2   Here is an example. Suppose you stop at a roadside restaurant for a cup of coffee and a piece of pie. The waitress comes over to take your order, but you are having a hard time deciding which kind of pie to order. While you are hesitating, the waitress impatiently taps her pen against her order books, rolls her eyes toward the ceiling, glares at you, and finally snaps, "Hey, I haven't got all day, you know!"

3   What do you conclude about this event? When faced with such a situation, most people would conclude that the waitress is a nasty or unpleasant person; consequently they would be reluctant to enter that particular restaurant again—especially when *that* nasty person was on duty. That would certainly be understandable. But suppose we were to tell you that the waitress is a single parent and was kept awake all night by the crying of her youngest child, who has a painful terminal illness; that her car broke down on her way to work and she has no idea where she will find the money to have it repaired; that when she finally arrived at the restaurant, she learned that her co-worker was too drunk to work, requiring her to

cover twice the usual number of tables; and that the short-order cook keeps screaming at her because she is not picking up the orders fast enough to please him. Given all that information, you might want to revise your judgment and conclude that she is not necessarily a nasty person, just an ordinary person under enormous stress.

4   The important fact remains that in the absence of obvious situational information, when trying to account for a person's behavior in a complex situation, the overwhelming majority of people will jump to the conclusion that the behavior was caused by the personality of the individual involved. And this fact—that we often fail to take the situation into account—is important to a social psychologist, for it has a profound impact on how human beings relate to one another.

BEFORE YOU
CONTINUE
READING

1. **What mistake might many people make in interpreting the waitress's behavior? How do social psychologists explain this error?**

_____

_____

UNDERESTIMATING THE POWER OF SOCIAL INFLUENCE

5   When we underestimate the power of social influence, it tends to give us a feeling of false security. For example, when trying to explain why people do repugnant or bizarre things, it is tempting and, in a strange way, comforting to write off the victims as flawed human beings. Doing so gives the rest of us the feeling that it could never happen to us. Ironically, this in turn increases our personal vulnerability to possible destructive social influence by lulling us into lowering our guard. Moreover, by failing to fully appreciate the power of the situation, we tend to oversimplify complex situations; oversimplification decreases our understanding of the causes of a great deal of human behavior. Among other things, this oversimplification can lead us to blame the victim in situations where the individual was overpowered by social forces too difficult for most of us to resist.

6   Here is an example of the kind of oversimplification we are talking about. Imagine a situation in which people are playing a two-person game wherein each player must choose one of two strategies: They can play competitively, where they try to win as much money as possible and make sure their partner loses as much as possible, or they can play cooperatively, where they try to make sure both they and their partner win some money. It is important to note that there are only two basic strategies people can use when playing the game—competitive or cooperative. Now think about some of your friends. How do you think they would play this game?

7   Few people find this question hard to answer; we all have a feeling for the relative competitiveness of our friends. "Well," you might say, "I am certain that my friend Calvin, who is a cutthroat business major, would play this game more competitively than my friend Anna, who is a really caring,

loving person." That is, we think of our friends' personalities and answer accordingly. We usually do not think much about the nature of the social situation when making our predictions.

RESEARCH ON THE POWER OF SOCIAL INFLUENCE

8   But how accurate are such predictions? Should we think about the social situation? To find out, Lee Ross and Steven Samuels conducted the following experiment. First, they chose a group of students at Stanford University who were considered by the resident assistants in their dorm to be either especially cooperative or especially competitive. The researchers did this by describing the game to the resident assistants and asking them to think of students in their dormitories who would be most likely to adopt the competitive or cooperative strategy. As expected, the resident assistants had no trouble thinking of students who fit each category.

9   Next, Ross and Samuels invited these students to play the game in a psychology experiment. There was one added twist. The researchers varied a seemingly minor aspect of the social situation—what the game was called. They told half the participants that the name of the game was the Wall Street Game (a business game) and half that it was the Community Game. Everything else about the game was identical. Thus people who were judged as either competitive or cooperative played a game that was called either the Wall Street or the Community Game, resulting in four conditions.

BEFORE YOU CONTINUE READING

2. **What is the danger in underestimating the power of social influence?**

_____

---

10   Again, most of us go through life assuming that what really counts is an individual's personality, not something so trivial as what a game is called. Some people seem competitive by nature and would thus relish the opportunity to go head to head with a fellow student. Others seem much more cooperative and would thus achieve the most satisfaction by making

sure no one lost too much money and no one's feelings were hurt. Right? Not so fast! As seen in the bar graph below, even so trivial an aspect of the situation as the name of the game made a tremendous difference in how people behaved. When it was called the Wall Street Game, approximately two-thirds of the people responded competitively, whereas when it was called the Community Game, only one-third of the people responded competitively. The name of the game conveyed strong social norms about what kind of behavior was appropriate in this situation. As we can see, social norms can shape people's behaviors in powerful ways.

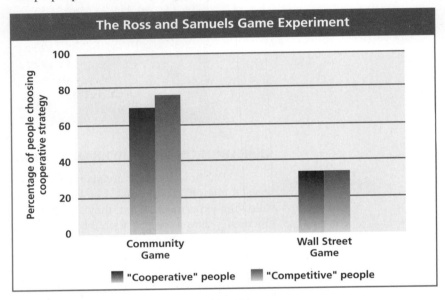

The Ross and Samuels Game Experiment

Percentage of people choosing cooperative strategy

■ "Cooperative" people   ■ "Competitive" people

11   [1]In this situation, a student's personality made no measurable difference in the student's behavior. [2]The students labeled "competitive" were no more likely to adopt the competitive strategy than those who were labeled "cooperative." [3]Clearly, seemingly minor aspects of the social situation can have powerful effects, overwhelming the differences in people's personalities. [4]This is not to say that personality differences do not exist or are unimportant. [5]They do exist and frequently are of great importance. [6]But we have learned that social and environmental situations are so powerful that they have dramatic effects on almost everyone. [7]This is the domain of the social psychologist.

Checking Comprehension

A Answer the following questions in complete sentences.

1. In what ways can social influence positively affect our thoughts, actions, and feelings? In what ways can social influence negatively affect our thoughts, actions, and feelings?

_____

_____

_____

2. What are possible consequences of underestimating the power of social influence on ourselves and other people?

_____

_____

_____

3. What kind of experimental research do social psychologists conduct in order to learn about the power of social influence?

_____

_____

_____

4. Compare these answers with your responses on pages 227–228. How were your answers here different?

_____

_____

B Refer to paragraph 11 in the Main Reading on page 234. Identify the referents.

1. In the second sentence, _those_ refers to _____.

2. In the fifth sentence, _they_ ("They do exist . . .") refers to _____.

3. In the last sentence, _this_ refers to _____.

C Answer the following questions in complete sentences.

1. Review the situation of the impatient waitress described in paragraph 2.
a. Imagine that you concluded that the waitress was a nasty person. Why would you be making a fundamental attribution error?

_____

_____

b. In order for you to interpret the waitress's behavior correctly, what would you need to know?

_____

_____

2. Review the two-person game described in paragraphs 8–11.

    a. In this situation, who underestimated the power of social influence?

    _____

    b. What was the element of the game that actually influenced how the participants chose to play the game, i.e., competitively or cooperatively?

    _____

    c. Which influence was stronger, the students' personalities or their interpretation of the game?

    _____

D Reread paragraph 9 on page 233. What were the four conditions of the study? Use the chart below to help you organize the four conditions.

Condition One	Condition Two
Condition Three	Condition Four

E Review your annotations on pages 231–234. Do you have any questions that have not been answered? If so, discuss them now with your classmates or your instructor.

Learning Vocabulary

VOCABULARY FROM CONTEXT

Reread the paragraphs indicated from the Main Reading to figure out the meaning of the italicized words. Then circle the correct choice to complete the sentences that follow.

    1. Paragraph 1: _inclination, fundamental attribution error,_ and _encounter_

        (1) In this context, a synonym for _inclination_ is ___.
            a. barrier
            b. explanation
            c. tendency

        (2) What is the _fundamental attribution error_?

        _____

        _____

(3) From this context, we can understand that *encounter* means ___.
   a. come across
   b. read about
   c. talk about

2. Paragraph 2: *hesitating* and *glares*

   (1) From this context, we can understand that the word *hesitating* means ___.
      a. not making a decision because you are unsure
      b. not making a decision because you have a lot of time
      c. not making a decision because you want to make someone angry

   (2) From this context, we can understand that someone who *glares* at you ___.
      a. looks at you patiently
      b. looks at you angrily
      c. looks at you romantically

3. Paragraph 3: *nasty*

   From this context, we can understand that a *nasty* person is a(n) ___ person.
   a. mean
   b. tired
   c. overworked

4. Paragraph 5: *ironically*

   From this context, we can understand that something *ironic* is ___.
   a. contradictory
   b. bizarre
   c. destructive

5. Paragraph 11: *domain*

   From this context, we can understand that the social psychologist's *domain* is his/her ___.
   a. environment
   b. situation
   c. field

Read the following sentences and dictionary entries. Select the best entry for the context, and circle the correct choice to complete the sentences that follow.

1. Even so trivial an aspect of the situation as the name of the game made a tremendous difference in how people behaved. When it was called the Wall Street Game, approximately two-thirds of the people responded competitively, whereas when it was called the Community Game, only one-third of the people responded competitively. The name of the game *conveyed* strong social norms about what kind of behavior was appropriate in this situation.

> **con·vey** /kən'veɪ/ *v.* **conveys, conveyed, conveying** [T] **1** to communicate a message or information, with or without using words: *All this information can be conveyed in a simple diagram.* | *Her blond hair and blue eyes convey her Swedish origins.* | **convey a sense/an impression etc.** *Her clothes convey the impression that she's capable and confident.* **2** FORMAL to take or carry something from one place to another: *The guard was charged with conveying drugs to a prison inmate.* **3** LAW to legally change the possession of property from one person to another

   (1) In this context, the best definition for *convey* is number ___.

   (2) The author is saying that the name of the game ___.
   a. communicated a message to the players about whether to be competitive or cooperative
   b. carried something from the game itself to the players
   c. had a legal meaning that the players may or may not have understood

2. The students labeled "competitive" were no more likely to adopt the competitive strategy than those who were labeled "cooperative." Clearly, seemingly minor aspects of the social situation can have powerful effects, *overwhelming* the differences in people's personalities.

> **o·ver·whelm** /ˌoʊvɚ'wɛlm/ *v.* [T] **1** if an emotion, event, or problem overwhelms you, you are very affected by it and you do not know what to do, how to react etc.: *Sometimes a sense of deep frustration almost overwhelms her.* | *Auto theft cases seem to be overwhelming local police.* | *I was **completely overwhelmed** by their generosity.* **2** to defeat an opponent or army completely: *The Lakers overwhelmed the Sonics by the third quarter.* **3** if a color, smell, taste etc. overwhelms another color, taste etc., it is much stronger and more noticeable: *Most preparations overwhelm the flavor of good oysters.* **4** LITERARY if water overwhelms an area of land, it covers it completely and suddenly

(1) In this context, the best definition for *overwhelm* is number ___.

(2) According to the author, what seem like minor aspects of a social situation can ___.

    a. make people's personalities so emotional that they don't know what to do

    b. completely defeat the people involved in the social situation

    c. be much stronger and more noticeable than the differences in people's personalities

LEARN AND USE WORD FORMS

Complete the sentences below with the correct form of the word in the box. Refer to the word forms chart on page 228. Be sure to use the correct tense of verbs. Use each word only once.

compete	hesitate	trivialize
fail	oversimplify	

1. People rarely take dropping one's glasses, losing a pencil, getting stopped by a red light, or other _____ into account when trying to predict or interpret other people's behavior.

2. A person's _____ to interpret another person's behavior accurately can have unfortunate results.

3. Playing a simple board game can influence a person's sense of _____ even when the person is described as being cooperative.

4. The risk we take whenever we _____ a situation is that it decreases our understanding of the causes of a great deal of human behavior.

5. John is very _____ about judging people based on his first impressions. He has often been wrong.

UNDERSTANDING GRAPHS

Reread paragraphs 5–11 in the Main Reading. Study the bar graph below. Then answer the questions that follow.

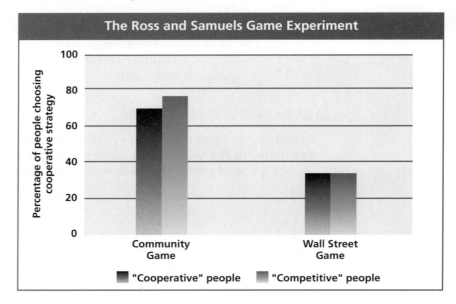

1. When the game was called the Wall Street Game, who played less cooperatively, the people labeled "competitive" or the people labeled "cooperative"?
   a. The people labeled "competitive" played less cooperatively.
   b. The people labeled "cooperative" played less cooperatively.
   c. An equal percentage of both groups played less cooperatively.

2. When the game was called the Community Game, who played more cooperatively, the people labeled "competitive" or the people labeled "cooperative"?
   a. The people labeled "competitive" played more cooperatively.
   b. The people labeled "cooperative" played more cooperatively.
   c. An equal percentage of both groups played more cooperatively.

3. What can we conclude from the information on the bar graph?
   a. People who were identified as cooperative tended to play cooperatively regardless of the name of the game.
   b. People who were identified as competitive tended to play competitively regardless of the name of the game.
   c. People tended to play competitively or cooperatively based on the name of the game, rather than their personality.

4. Who made a fundamental attribution error?
   a. the researchers who designed the study
   b. the resident assistants who knew the participants
   c. the people who participated in the study

5. What, for you, was the most surprising finding of this study?

_____

_____

FOLLOW-UP ASSIGNMENTS

Before you begin any of the follow-up assignments, review the content-specific vocabulary and the academic vocabulary below, and look over the vocabulary in the word form lists on pages 218 and 228. If you are still unsure what any words or terms mean, go back through the chapter and review. As you complete the assignments, be sure to incorporate the appropriate vocabulary in your writing.

Content-Specific Vocabulary

conflict	inclination	perception	social norms
construal	influence	persuasion	social
convey	interpretation	phenomenon	psychology
determinant	overt	situational	tendency
domain	peers		

Academic Vocabulary

behavior	distinctive	hesitate	ironic
clarify	domain	imagined	justification
context	empirical	immersed	overwhelm
deliberate	encounter	inclination	

Writing Activities

1. Think of a time when you made a decision based on the influence of someone who was not present at the time. Write three paragraphs. In the first paragraph, describe the situation. In the second paragraph, write about the person who influenced you. In the third paragraph, describe the decision that you made and how that person influenced your decision, even without being there at the time.
2. Think of a time you were pressured by others to do something you did not want to do. Write three paragraphs. In the first paragraph, describe the situation. In the second paragraph, explain whether you did what others wanted you to do or not, and explain why. In the third paragraph, explain what happened as a social psychologist would explain it.
3. Recall a time someone made an incorrect judgment about you. Write three paragraphs. In the first paragraph, describe the nature of this fundamental attribution error. In the second paragraph, outline the circumstances that the other person was unaware of. In the third paragraph, describe the consequences of this error.

1. Work with one or more partners. Design an experiment to test the fundamental attribution error. Be sure to keep the experiment simple and ethical. Do not ask people to do something that will make them uncomfortable or embarrassed.

2. Work with one or more partners. First, individually write down three personality traits that most people would use to describe you. Then briefly describe a real situation that you were in. For example, "My friends and family say that I am calm, cooperative, and patient. Once I was in a minor car accident." Ask your partners to predict how you behaved in that situation. Then explain how you did behave and what made you behave that way at that time. After you have each taken a turn, discuss how well you were able to predict each other's behavior.

3. Read the following study. Keep in mind that you are interested in how people are influenced by others. After you read the study, you will examine a bar graph of the study findings.

THE PERSEVERANCE EFFECT

Three social psychologists conducted a study to examine whether people's beliefs persevered (persisted) even after the original evidence for them was shown to be false. They randomly divided their study participants into two groups. The social psychologists worked with one participant at a time. They gave the study participants 25 cards. Each card contained a suicide note. The participants' job was to guess whether each note was real or fictitious. In Group One, the experimenter told each of the participants that they had guessed correctly 24 out of 25 times, and that the average was only 16 out of 25. The people in Group Two were told that they had only guessed correctly 10 out of 25 times. The experimenter then explained that the study was finished, and that they were really studying the effects of success and failure on physiological responses. The experimenter said he had not told the truth about the accuracy of each participant's guesses, and that the participants had been randomly placed into one of two groups. Group One had been told that most of their answers were correct whether they were or not, and Group Two had been told that most of their answers were incorrect whether they were or not. What they had been told originally had nothing to do with their actual answers. Then all the participants were given a questionnaire in which they were asked to guess how many of their guesses had really been correct, and how well they thought they would guess correctly on a second test with new cards.

How do you think the participants responded?

1. *The participants who had been told they were "successful"* _____

_____

2. *The participants who had been told they were "unsuccessful"* _____

_____

Even though the participants understood the experimenters' explanation and believed it, the participants who had been told they were "successful" still thought they had done better on the "suicide" test and that they would do better on the second test than did the participants who had been told they had not done well on the first test. This result is called *the perseverance effect* because people's beliefs persevered even after the original reason for their belief had been shown to be false.

How accurate were your predictions of the participants' responses?

_____

1. Examine the bar graph below, which is based on the information in the reading in Extension Activity 3.

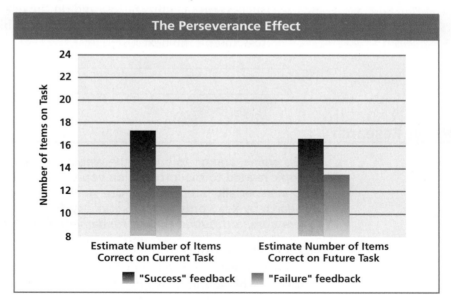

Which group had actually guessed correctly most of the time?
a. Group One
b. Group Two
c. We don't know.

2. After the study had been explained to the participants, they clearly understood that they had been told a lie: The researchers had randomly told the participants that they had been successful (Group One) or unsuccessful (Group Two).

(1) Which group estimated the highest number of correct answers on the guesses they made about the suicide notes?

a. the people who were told they had guessed incorrectly most of the time

b. the people who were told they had guessed correctly most of the time

(2) Which group estimated the highest number of correct answers on the guesses they were going to make on the next test?

a. the people who were told they had guessed correctly most of the time

b. the people who were told they had guessed incorrectly most of the time

(3) Which group estimated the lowest number of correct answers on the guesses they made about the suicide notes?

a. the people who were told they had guessed incorrectly most of the time

b. the people who were told they had guessed correctly most of the time

(4) Which group estimated the lowest number of correct answers on the guesses they were going to make on the next test?

a. the people who were told they had guessed correctly most of the time

b. the people who were told they had guessed incorrectly most of the time

(5) Why did Group One have such a high estimation of their possible success on the current test and on the next test? Why did Group Two have such a low estimation of their possible success on the current test and on the next test?

_____

_____

Internet Research

Go online, and go to one of the websites listed below. Investigate a topic related to the information you read about in Chapter 9. Choose a topic that especially interests you. Use some of the website's search features. Search by keywords such as _social psychology, social environment, peer pressure, attribution theory, fundamental attribution error._

Kids Health website:
http://kidshealth.org/kid/feeling/friend/peer_pressure.html
University of Nebraska at Lincoln website:
http://ianr.unl.edu/pubs/family/nf211.htm
University of Michigan Extension Services website:
http://www.extension.umn.edu/projects/positiveparenting
Allyn and Bacon Mind Matters website:
http://www.ablongman.com/html/mindmatters2/

CHAPTER 10

INTERPRETING HUMAN BEHAVIOR

Skills Goal

- *Review skills from Chapters 1–9.*

Content-Specific Goals

- *Gain insight into human motivation.*
- *Understand human needs.*
- *Learn about human expectations about the social world.*

Chapter Readings

The Subjectivity of Social Situations

Understanding Basic Human Motives

INTRODUCING THE READING

Activate Your Knowledge

Do the following activities.

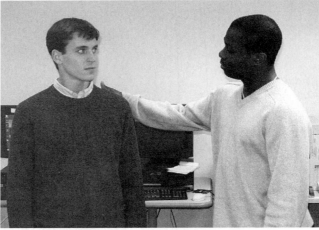

1. Imagine you are in this social situation: A person you know approaches you, slaps you on the back, and asks you how you are feeling.

   a. Answer this question by yourself first: How do you respond?

   _____

   _____

   _____

   b. Now compare your response with your classmates'. Were your responses different? Explain the differences.

   _____

   _____

   _____

2. Now work together. Imagine that Maria and Shawn are your friends. However, they have only recently met each other. Suppose Maria gives Shawn a kiss on the cheek at the end of their first date. How will Shawn respond to the kiss? Explain your reasons for your answer.

   _____

   _____

   _____

PREVIEW KEY VOCABULARY

Read the list of content-specific vocabulary and check the ones you are familiar with. Leave the other spaces blank. Do not try to learn the unfamiliar items before you begin reading.

___ behaviorism	___ hazing	___ self-esteem
___ cognition	___ motivated	___ self-fulfilling prophecy
___ compliance	___ objective	___ self-justification
___ construal	___ outcome	___ social cognition
___ distort	___ perspective	___ subjectivity

USE TITLE AND HEADINGS TO PREDICT CONTENT

Work with a partner or in a small group. Before you work with the Introductory Reading on pages 249–250, go through it and write down the heading on the line below.

The Subjectivity of Social Situations

_____

A Answer the questions that follow.

1. Why are social situations subjective?

_____

_____

2. What are some basic motives for human behavior? *Why* do people do what they do? Make a list.

_____   _____

_____   _____

3. Consider the situation with Shawn and Maria on page 246. Which of the motives you have listed above will help us predict how Shawn will respond to Maria's kiss on the cheek?

_____

_____

B Go to page *vii* in the Table of Contents. Read the brief summary of the Introductory Reading. Then review your responses above, and decide whether to change any of them.

LEARN AND USE WORD FORMS

A Study the following chart which contains words from the Introductory Reading. Note the spelling changes. Pay attention to the words as they are used in the Introductory Reading.

VERB	NOUN	ADJECTIVE	ADVERB
reinforce	reinforcement	reinforced/reinforcing	
require	requirement	required	
interpret	interpretation	interpretive	
intersect	intersection	intersected/intersecting	
motivate	motive motivation	(un)motivated motivating	
perceive	perception	perceptive perceived	perceptively
approach	approach	approachable	
reward	reward	rewarding	
	accuracy	accurate	accurately
behave	behaviorism behaviorist	behavioristic	
comply	compliance	compliant	
construe	construal		

B Complete the following paragraph by writing the correct form of the word in parentheses. When you are done, check your answers by reading paragraph 5 on page 250.

We human beings are complex organisms; at a given moment, myriad (countless) _____ motives underlie our
1. (intersect)

thoughts and _____. Over the years, social
2. (behave)

psychologists have found that two of these _____ are
3. (motivate)

of primary importance: the need to be as accurate as possible and the need

to feel good about ourselves. As we go through life, there are times when

each of these _____ pulls us in the same direction.
4. (motivate)

Often, however, we find ourselves in situations where these two

_____ tug us in opposite directions—where to
5. (motivate)

perceive the world accurately requires us to face up to the fact that we

_____ foolishly or immorally. We will read more
   6. (behave)

about these _____ in the next reading.
                  7. (motivate)

INTRODUCTORY READING

The following reading, "The Subjectivity of Social Situations," is from Social Psychology. *Highlight the important ideas and the vocabulary used to express those ideas. Annotate the text.*

The Subjectivity of Social Situations

1   We have argued that the social situation often has profound effects on human behavior. But what exactly do we mean by the social situation? One strategy for defining it would be to specify the objective properties of the situation, such as how rewarding it is to people, and then document the behaviors that follow from these objective properties.

2   This was the approach taken by **behaviorism**, a school of psychology maintaining that to understand human behavior, one need only consider the reinforcing properties of the environment—that is, how positive and negative events in the environment are associated with specific behaviors. For example, dogs come when they are called because they have learned that compliance is followed by positive reinforcement (e.g., food or fondling); children will memorize their multiplication tables more quickly if you praise them, smile at them, and paste a gold star on their forehead following correct answers. Psychologists in this tradition, such as John Watson and B. F. Skinner, suggested that all behavior could be understood by examining the rewards and punishments in the organism's environment and that there was no need to study such subjective states as thinking and feeling.

3   [1]Behaviorists chose not to deal with issues like cognition, thinking, and feeling because they considered these concepts too vague and mentalistic and not sufficiently anchored to observable behavior. [2]The behavioristic approach can account for a great deal of behavior. [3]But because behaviorism does not deal with cognition, thinking, and feeling— phenomena vital to the human social experience—this approach has proved inadequate for a complete understanding of the social world. [4]We have learned that social behavior cannot be fully understood by confining our observations to the physical properties of a situation. [5]Instead, it is important to look at the situation from the viewpoint of the people in it, to see how they construe the world around them. [6]For example, if a person approaches us, slaps us on the back, and asks us how we are feeling, is that rewarding or not? [7]On the surface, it might seem like a reward. [8]After all, isn't that person's interest in us a desirable thing? [9]But in actuality, it is a complex situation that depends on our thoughts and feelings. [10]We might construe the meaning differently, depending on whether the question is asked by a close friend of ours who is deeply concerned about our health, a casual acquaintance simply passing the time of day, or an automobile

salesperson attempting to ingratiate himself so that he might sell us a used car. [11]This would be the case even if the question were worded the same and asked in the same tone of voice. [12]For example, in responding to the salesperson's question, it is unlikely that we will begin a detailed description of the pain we've been having in our kidney—something we might do in response to our closest friend's inquiry.

BEFORE YOU CONTINUE READING

What is the behaviorist approach to understanding human behavior? What is the drawback of the behaviorist approach?

_____

_____

BASIC HUMAN MOTIVES

4   How will Shawn determine why Maria kissed him? If it is true that subjective and not objective situations influence people, then we need to understand how people arrive at their subjective impressions of the world. What are people trying to accomplish when they interpret the social world? Again, we could address this question from the perspective of people's personalities. What is it about Shawn, including his upbringing, family background, and unique experiences, that makes him view the world the way he does? As we have seen, such a focus on individual differences in people's personalities, though valuable, misses what is usually of far greater importance: the effects of the social situation on people. To understand these effects, we need to understand the fundamental laws of human nature, common to all, that explain why we construe the social world the way we do.

5   We human beings are complex organisms; at a given moment, myriad (countless) intersecting motives underlie our thoughts and behaviors. Over the years, social psychologists have found that two of these motives are of primary importance: the need to be as accurate as possible and the need to feel good about ourselves. As we go through life, there are times when each of these motives pulls us in the same direction. Often, however, we find ourselves in situations where these two motives tug us in opposite directions—where to perceive the world accurately requires us to face up to the fact that we have behaved foolishly or immorally. We will read more about these motives in the next reading.

Checking Comprehension

A Answer the following questions in complete sentences.

1. Why are social situations subjective?

_____

_____

2. What are some basic motives for human behavior? *Why* do people do what they do? Make a list.

_____   _____

_____   _____

_____   _____

3. Consider the situation with Shawn and Maria on page 246. Which of the motives you have listed will help us predict how Shawn will respond to Maria's kiss on the cheek?

_____

_____

4. Compare your responses above with your responses on page 247. How were your answers different?

_____

_____

B Refer to paragraph 3 in the Introductory Reading on pages 249–250. Identify the referents.

1. In the first sentence, *they* refers to _____.

2. In the first sentence, *these concepts* refers to _____.

3. In the third sentence, *this approach* refers to _____.

4. In the fifth sentence, *they* refers to _____.

C Answer the following questions in complete sentences.

1. What is the main difference between behaviorists and social psychologists regarding their approach to understanding human behavior?

_____

_____

_____

2. Why is the behaviorist approach considered inadequate in explaining human behavior?

_____

_____

_____

3. Unlike behaviorists, social psychologists consider the subjective nature of humans' interpretation of social situations. Why is this subjectivity so important? Base your answer on examples from the reading.

_____

_____

_____

D Review your annotations on pages 249–250. Do you have any questions that have not been answered? If so, discuss them now with your classmates or your instructor.

Learning Vocabulary

VOCABULARY FROM CONTEXT

Reread the paragraphs indicated from the Introductory Reading to figure out the meaning of the italicized words. Then circle the correct choice to complete the sentences that follow.

1. Paragraph 2: *compliance*

   From this context, we can understand that *compliance* means ___.
   a. food
   b. obedience
   c. command

2. Paragraph 3: *on the surface*

   From this context, we can understand that the expression *on the surface* means ___.
   a. at the top
   b. at the first meeting
   c. at first glance

3. Paragraph 4: *address* and *fundamental*

   (1) From this context, we can understand that *address* means ___.
   a. examine
   b. interpret
   c. locate

   (2) From this context, we can understand that *fundamental* means
   ___.
   a. clear
   b. basic
   c. correct

4. Paragraph 5: *myriad, tug,* and *to face up to*

   (1) In the paragraph, a synonym for the word *myriad* is
   _____.

   (2) In this paragraph, a synonym for the word *tug* is _____.

(3) From this context, we can understand that *to face up to* means ___.
   a. to see clearly
   b. to be embarrassed about
   c. to admit to

USING THE DICTIONARY

Read the following sentences and dictionary entries. Select the best entry for the context. Then circle the correct choice to complete the sentence that follows.

1. **Behaviorism** [is] a school of psychology *maintaining* that to understand human behavior, one need only consider the reinforcing properties of the environment—that is, how positive and negative events in the environment are associated with specific behaviors.

   > **main·tain** /meɪnˈteɪn/ *v.* **1 make sth continue** [T] to make something continue in the same way or at the same standard as before; KEEP¹: *Our main wish is to help maintain world peace.* | *Volkswagen has maintained close business ties with them for over 20 years.* | *King lives in Chicago but maintains an apartment in New York.* **2 level/rate** [T] to make a level or rate of activity, movement etc. stay the same: *They're finding it difficult to maintain such high interest rates.* | *Dieters should try to reach and maintain a reasonable weight.* **3 take care of sth** [T] to take care of something so that it stays in good condition: *His first job was installing and maintaining computers.* | *It's hard to do this job and still maintain a marriage.* **4 say** [T] to strongly express your belief that something is true: **[maintain (that)]** *Sautter maintains writers do get respect in the film and TV business.* | *During their trial, the brothers* **maintained their innocence** (=continued to say they were not guilty).

   (1) The best definition of *maintain* in this context is number ___.

   (2) Behaviorism is a school of psychology that ___ that to understand human behavior, one need only consider the reinforcing properties of the environment.
   a. continues in the same way to say
   b. makes a movement to say
   c. takes care of psychology to say
   d. expresses the belief

2. What are people trying to accomplish when they interpret the social world? Again, we could address this question from the perspective of people's personalities. What is it about Shawn, including his *upbringing, family background,* and unique experiences, that makes him view the world the way he does?

   > **up·bring·ing** /ˈʌpˌbrɪŋɪŋ/ *n* [singular] the care and training that parents give their children when they are growing up: *a strict upbringing*

back·ground /ˈbækgraʊnd/ *n* **1** the type of education, experiences, and family that someone has: *The kids here have very different religious backgrounds* **2** the sounds, things, movements etc. that are in or happening in a place or picture but that are not the main thing you see or hear: *I could hear cars honking in the background.* **3** [singular, U] ⇨ BACKDROP

(1) The most appropriate definition of *background* in this context is number ___.

(2) Make a list of the factors that make up a person's background.

_____   _____   _____

_____   _____   _____

_____   _____   _____

LEARN AND USE WORD FORMS

Complete the sentences below with the correct form of the word in the box. Refer to the word forms chart on page 248. Be sure to use the correct tense of verbs. Use each word only once.

approach	construe	reward
comply	reinforce	

1. Behaviorists consider the _____ properties—the rewards and punishments—of the environment in order to understand human behavior.

2. The behaviorist _____ has influenced many other disciplines, including language learning.

3. A person's interpretation, or _____, of a situation helps us understand why people behave differently in the same situation.

4. Humans are often motivated to do something by the possibility of receiving _____ for their behavior.

5. Through experience, dogs learn that when they are very _____, they will receive food, be petted, and be spoken to in a pleasant tone of voice.

INTRODUCING THE MAIN READING

Activate Your Knowledge

Work with a partner or in a small group. Reread the portion of the last paragraph in the Introductory Reading given on the following page. Then read the situations and answer the questions that follow, using information from the passage.

> Over the years, social psychologists have found that two human motives are of primary importance: the need to be as accurate as possible and the need to feel good about ourselves. As we go through life, there are times when each of these motives pulls us in the same direction. Often, however, we find ourselves in situations where these two motives tug us in opposite directions—where to perceive the world accurately requires us to face up to the fact that we have behaved foolishly or immorally.

SITUATION ONE

Suppose that a couple gets divorced after ten years of a marriage made difficult by the husband's irrational jealousy. How might the husband explain the fact that his wife divorced him?

_____

_____

_____

SITUATION TWO

Consider Roger; everybody knows someone like Roger. He's the guy whose shoes are almost always untied and who frequently has coffee stains on the front of his shirt. How might Roger explain his own behavior?

_____

_____

_____

USE TITLE AND HEADINGS TO PREDICT CONTENT

Work with a partner or in a small group. Before you work with the Main Reading, go through it and write the headings on the lines below.

Understanding Basic Human Motives

_____

_____

_____

_____

_____

A Reread the following two social situations that were described in Chapter 9:

- Oscar and his son Sam have different feelings about their college fraternity (page 227).
- Study participants guess whether suicide notes are real or fictitious (pages 242–243).

B Consider the basic human motives that will be discussed in the Main Reading. Write the ones that help predict or explain the behavior of the people in these two social situations. Write other human motives that you think of. Use the chart below to help you organize your ideas.

MOTIVES TO EXPLAIN TWO SOCIAL SITUATIONS		
Social Situation	**Basic Human Motives**	**Other Human Motives**
Oscar and his son Sam have different feelings about their college fraternity.		
Study participants guess whether suicide notes are real or fictitious.		

C Go to page *vii* in the Table of Contents. Read the brief summary of the Main Reading. Then review your diagram above, and decide whether to change any of your predictions.

LEARN AND USE WORD FORMS

A Study the following chart which contains words from the Main Reading. Note the spelling changes. Pay attention to the words as they are used in the Main Reading.

VERB	NOUN	ADJECTIVE	ADVERB
adapt	adaptation	adaptive	
admit	admission	admitted	
attend to	attention	attentive	attentively
conclude	conclusion	conclusive	conclusively
distort	distortion	distorted	
interpret	Interpretation	interpretive	
justify	justification	justifiable justified	justifiably
motivate	motivator	motivated/motivating	
	jealousy	jealous	jealously
hypothesize	hypothesis	hypothetical	hypothetically
	competence	competent	competently
respond	response	responsive	responsively

B Complete the following paragraph by writing the correct form of the word in parentheses. When you are done, check your answers by reading paragraph 3 on page 258.

Suppose that a couple gets divorced after ten years of a marriage made difficult by the husband's irrational jealousy. Rather than

_____ the truth—that his jealousy and
1. (admit)

overpossessiveness drove her away—the husband blames the breakup of his marriage on the fact that his ex-wife was not sufficiently

_____ or _____ to his needs.
2. (respond)   3. (attend to)

His _____ serves some purpose in that it makes him
4. (interpret)

feel better about himself—it is very difficult to own up to major deficiencies in ourselves, even when the cost is seeing the world inaccurately. The

consequence of this _____, of course, is that it
5. (distort)

decreases the probability of learning from experience; that is, in his next marriage, the husband is likely to run into the same problems.

MAIN READING

The Main Reading, "Understanding Basic Human Motives," is also from
Social Psychology. *As you read, highlight the important ideas and the*
vocabulary used to express those ideas. Annotate the text.

Understanding Basic Human Motives

1   Earlier in this chapter, we read that social psychologists have discovered two basic human motives: the need to feel good about ourselves (self-esteem), and the need to be as accurate as possible. Let's take a closer look at these motives.

THE SELF-ESTEEM APPROACH: THE DESIRE TO FEEL GOOD ABOUT OURSELVES

2   Most people have a strong need to maintain reasonably high **self-esteem**, that is, to see themselves as good, competent, and decent. The reason people view the world the way they do can often be traced to this underlying need to maintain a favorable image of themselves. Given the choice between distorting the world in order to feel good about themselves and representing the world accurately, people often take the first option.

3   Suppose that a couple gets divorced after ten years of a marriage made difficult by the husband's irrational jealousy. Rather than admitting the truth—that his jealousy and overpossessiveness drove her away—the husband blames the breakup of his marriage on the fact that his ex-wife was not sufficiently responsive or attentive to his needs. His interpretation serves some purpose in that it makes him feel better about himself—it is very difficult to own up to major deficiencies in ourselves, even when the cost is seeing the world inaccurately. The consequence of this distortion, of course, is that it decreases the probability of learning from experience; that is, in his next marriage, the husband is likely to run into the same problems.

4   We do not mean to imply that people totally distort reality, denying the existence of all information that reflects badly on them; such extreme behavior is rare outside of mental institutions. Yet it is often possible for normal people like you and us to put a slightly different spin on the existing facts, one that puts us in the best possible light. Consider Roger; everybody knows someone like Roger. He's the guy whose shoes are almost always untied and who frequently has coffee stains on the front of his shirt. Most observers might consider Roger a slob, but Roger might see himself as casual and noncompulsive.

5   The fact that people distort their interpretation of reality so that they might feel better about themselves is not surprising, even to the most casual observer of human behavior. The ways in which this motive operates, however, are often startling and shed a great deal of light on otherwise mystifying behavior.

1. a. *Which basic human need does the self-esteem approach address?*

_____

b. *How do people often view or interpret reality in order to maintain their self-esteem?*

_____

_____

SUFFERING AND SELF-JUSTIFICATION

6   Let's go back to one of our early scenarios: the case of Oscar and his son, Sam, which you read about in Chapter 9. Why was Sam less enamored of his fraternity brothers than Oscar had been when he was in college? You will recall that Oscar was quick to form the hypothesis that perhaps his fraternity was not attracting the kinds of wonderful people who were there when he was in college. This might be true. But we would assert that a far more compelling possibility involves the hazing itself. Specifically, we would contend that a major factor that increased Oscar's liking for his fraternity brothers was the unpleasant hazing ritual he underwent, a ritual that Sam was able to avoid. That sounds a little strange. Why would something so unpleasant cause Oscar to like his fraternity? Didn't behavioristic psychology teach us that rewards, not punishments, make us like things associated with them? Quite so. But as we indicated earlier, in recent years social psychologists have discovered that this formulation is far too simple to account for human thinking and motivation. Unlike rats and pigeons, human beings have a need to justify their past behavior, and this need leads them to thoughts, feelings, and behaviors that don't always fit into the neat categories of the behaviorist.

7   Here's how it works. If Oscar goes through a severe hazing in order to become a member of the fraternity but later discovers unpleasant things about his fraternity brothers, he will feel like a fool: "Why did I go through all that pain and embarrassment in order to live in a house with a bunch of jerks? Only a moron would do a thing like that." To avoid feeling like a fool, he will try to justify his decision to undergo the hazing by distorting his interpretation of his fraternity experience. In other words, he will try to put a positive spin on his experiences.

8   Suppose that having gone through all that hazing, Oscar moves into the fraternity house and begins to experience things that to an outside observer are not very positive: The fraternity dues make a significant dent in Oscar's budget; the frequent parties are mindless and take a toll on the amount of studying he can do, and consequently his grades begin to suffer; most of the meals served in the house are only a small step up from dog food. Whereas an unmotivated observer—someone who didn't go through the hazing—might consider these experiences extremely negative, Oscar is motivated to see them differently; indeed, he considers them a small price to pay for the sense of brotherhood he feels toward his fraternity mates. He focuses on the good parts of living in the fraternity, and he distorts or dismisses the bad parts as inconsequential. The result of all this self-justification is bound to make Oscar more kindly disposed toward the fraternity than Sam was, because Sam, not having gone through the hazing, had no need to justify his behavior and thus no need to see his fraternity experiences in a positive light. The end result? Oscar loved his fraternity; Sam did not.

SUPPORTING RESEARCH

9   How do we know that the people in the fraternity were not objectively nicer when Oscar was a member than when Sam was a member? In a series of well-controlled laboratory experiments, social psychologists have investigated the phenomenon of hazing, holding constant everything in the situation—including the precise behavior of the fraternity members—except for the severity of the hazing students underwent in order to become members. These experiments demonstrated conclusively that the more unpleasant the procedure the participants underwent to get into a group, the better they liked the group—even though, objectively, the group members were the same people, behaving in the same manner.

10   The important points to remember here are that (1) human beings are motivated to maintain a positive picture of themselves, in part by justifying their past behavior, and (2) under certain specifiable conditions, this leads them to do things that at first glance might seem surprising or paradoxical—for example, to prefer people and things for whom they have suffered to people and things they associate with ease and pleasure.

2. **When people *justify* their behavior, what do they do?**

_____

THE SOCIAL COGNITION APPROACH: THE NEED TO BE ACCURATE

11   As mentioned earlier, even when people are bending the facts to cast themselves in as favorable a light as they can, they do not completely distort reality. It would not be very adaptive to live in a fantasy world, believing that the car speeding toward us as we step off the curb is only imaginary. In fact, human beings are quite skilled at thinking, contemplating, and deducing. One of the major hallmarks of being human is the ability to reason.

12   Given the amazing cognitive abilities of our species, it makes sense that social psychologists, when formulating theories of social behavior, would take into consideration the way in which human beings think about the world. We call this the cognitive approach to social psychology, or **social cognition**. Researchers who attempt to understand social behavior from the perspective of social cognition begin with the assumption that all people try to view the world as accurately as possible.

13   But this is by no means as easy or as straightforward as it may seem. We human beings frequently run into problems because we almost never know all the facts we need to make the most accurate judgment of a given situation. Whether it is a relatively simple decision, such as which breakfast cereal offers the combination of healthfulness and tastiness, or a much more complex decision, such as choosing a marriage partner who will make us happy for the rest of our lives, it is almost never easy to gather all the relevant facts in advance.

14   Sometimes our expectations about the social world get in the way of perceiving it accurately. Our expectations can even change the nature of the social world. Imagine, for example, that you are an elementary school teacher dedicated to improving the lives of your students as best you can. You are aware at the beginning of the academic year how each student performed on standardized intelligence tests. Early in your career, you were pretty sure, but not *entirely* sure, that these tests could gauge each child's true potential. But after several years of teaching, you have gradually become certain that these tests are accurate. Why the change? You have come to see that almost invariably, the kids who got high scores on these tests are the ones who did the best in your classroom, and the kids who got low scores performed poorly in class.

15   This scenario doesn't sound all that surprising, except for one key fact: You might be very wrong about the validity of the intelligence tests. It might be that the tests weren't very accurate but that you unintentionally treated the kids with high scores and the kids with low scores differently, making it look like the tests were accurate. In the 1960s, this is exactly what Robert Rosenthal and Lenore Jacobson found in their investigation of a phenomenon called the *self-fulfilling prophecy*. They entered elementary school classrooms and administered a test. They then informed each teacher that according to the test, a few specific students were "bloomers" who were about to take off and perform extremely well. In actuality, the test showed no such thing; the children labeled as bloomers were chosen by drawing names out of a hat (i.e., randomly) and thus were no different, on average, from any of the other kids. On returning to the classroom at the end of the school year, Rosenthal and Jacobson found that the bloomers were performing extremely well. The mere fact that the teachers were led to expect these students to do well caused a reliable improvement in their performance. This striking phenomenon has been replicated a number of times in a wide variety of schools.

16   How did it come about? Though this outcome seems almost magical, it is imbedded in an important aspect of human nature. If you were one of those teachers and were led to expect two or three specific students to perform well, you would be more likely to treat those students in special ways—paying more attention to them, listening to them with more respect, calling on them more frequently, encouraging them, and trying to teach them more difficult material. This in turn would almost certainly make these students feel happier, more respected, more motivated, and smarter—a self-fulfilling prophecy. Thus even when we are trying to perceive the social world as accurately as we can, there are many ways in which we can go wrong, ending up with the wrong impressions.

BEFORE YOU CONTINUE READING	**3.** *Why is it often difficult for people to interpret the world around them accurately?*
	_____
	_____

OTHER MOTIVES

17   The need to maintain a positive view of ourselves, and the need to be accurate are not the only motives influencing people's thoughts and behaviors. Biological drives such as hunger and thirst, of course, can be powerful motivators. At a more psychological level, we can be motivated by the need for control, by fear or by the promise of love, favors, and other rewards involving social exchange. In fact, we human beings are complex organisms, and under various conditions a variety of motives influence what we think, feel, and do.

Checking Comprehension

1. Write down the basic human motives and other motives that were discussed in the Main Reading. Which ones do you think probably help predict or explain the behavior of the people in the two social situations you read about in Chapter 9 (summarized below)? Use the chart below to help you organize your ideas.

MOTIVES TO EXPLAIN TWO SOCIAL SITUATIONS		
Social Situation	**Basic Human Motives**	**Other Human Motives**
Oscar and his son Sam have different feelings about their college fraternity.		
Study participants guess whether suicide notes are real or fictitious.		

2. a. Can more than one motive explain a person's behavior in a particular social situation? Yes/No

   b. Which of these social situations can be explained by more than one motive?

   _____

3. Compare your chart here with your chart on page 256. How were your ideas similar? How were they different?

   _____

   _____

UNDERSTANDING GRAPHS

A Reread paragraphs 15 and 16 on page 262. Study the bar graph below. Then answer the questions that follow.

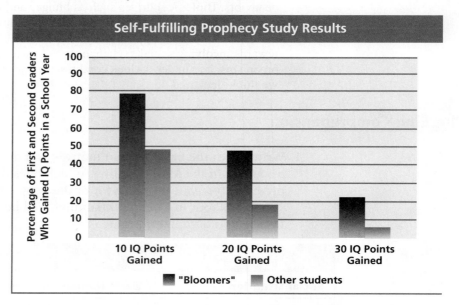

1. Before the start of the experiment, were the "bloomers" more intelligent than the "other students"? Yes/No

2. What was the *only* difference between the "bloomers" and the "other students"?

   _____

3. Did *all* the students in the class gain IQ points? Yes/No/We don't know.

4. As a group, which students gained the most IQ points?

   _____

5. How do the researchers explain the difference in IQ points gained between the two groups?

   _____

6. How does this finding (i.e., the difference in IQ points gained between the two groups) support the *self-fulfilling prophecy?*

   _____

   _____

7. Think about the teachers' behavior toward the students who had been designated "bloomers" and how it affected the students' gain in IQ points. What conclusion might you come to about how the teachers could behave toward *all* the students?

_____

_____

_____

B Review your annotations on page 258–263. Do you have any questions that have not been answered? If so, discuss them now with your classmates or your instructor.

Learning Vocabulary

VOCABULARY FROM CONTEXT

Reread the paragraphs indicated from the Main Reading to figure out the meaning of the italicized words. Then circle the correct choice to complete the sentences that follow.

1. Paragraphs 1 and 2: *self-esteem*

   What does *self-esteem* refer to?

   _____

2. Paragraphs 4 and 7: *put a (positive) spin on*

   What does it mean when someone *puts a spin on* something?
   a. The person turns something around and around very quickly.
   b. The person interprets something in a different way, according to his or her own views and needs.
   c. The person changes the truth in order to persuade everyone else that he or she is right.

3. Paragraph 8: *dismisses* and *inconsequential*

   (1) From this context, we can guess that *dismiss* means ___.
   a. send home
   b. criticize
   c. reject

   (2) From this context, we can understand that *inconsequential* means ___.
   a. irrelevant
   b. negative
   c. inexpensive

4. Paragraph 12: *cognition*

What does *cognition* mean?

_____

5. Paragraph 16: *motivated*

Motivated means ___.
a. able to eat or drink
b. happy at work
c. eager to do something

USING THE DICTIONARY

Read the following sentences and dictionary entries. Select the best entry for the context, and circle the correct choice to complete the sentences that follow.

1. Even when people are bending the facts to cast themselves in as favorable a light as they can, they do not completely *distort* reality. It would not be very adaptive to live in a fantasy world, believing that the car speeding toward us as we step off the curb is only imaginary.

> **dis•tort** /dɪ'stɔrt/ *v.* **1** [T] to explain a fact, statement, idea etc. in a way that makes it seem to mean something different from what it really means: *Some say that the President has distorted facts in order to win the election.* **2** [I,T] if a sound, shape, or character distorts, or someone distorts it, it changes so that it is strange or unclear: *Funhouse mirrors, which are not flat, cause images to be distorted.* —**distorted** *adj.: a badly distorted TV picture* —**distortion** /dɪ'stɔrʃən/ *n.* [U]

(1) The best definition of *distort* in this context is number ___.

(2) People sometimes ___ in order to feel better about themselves.
a. explain a fact or situation to make it seem to mean something different from what it really means
b. change a fact or situation to make it strange or unclear

2. If Oscar goes through a severe hazing in order to become a member of the fraternity but later discovers unpleasant things about his fraternity brothers, he will feel like a fool: "Why did I go through all that pain and embarrassment in order to live in a house with a bunch of jerks? Only a moron would do a thing like that." To avoid feeling like a fool, he will try to *justify* his decision to undergo the hazing by distorting his interpretation of his fraternity experience.

jus·ti·fy /ˈdʒʌstəˌfaɪ/ v. **justified, justifying** [T] **1** to give an acceptable explanation for something that other people think is unreasonable: *Torcuato is a murderer, but his crime can be justified.* | [**justify doing sth**] *How can you justify spending so much money on shoes?* **2** to be a good and acceptable reason for something: *The issue is whether the benefits justify the costs.* **3 justify yourself (to sb)** to prove that what you are doing is reasonable: *I don't have to justify myself to you or anyone.* **4 justify the margins** to type or reprint TEXT so that the words form a straight line on the right and left sides of the page

(1) The best definition of *justify* in this context is number ____.

(2) When people *justify* their actions, they ____.
  a. give proof that what they did was reasonable
  b. give an explanation and have it printed on a page
  c. give acceptable explanations or reasons for what they did

3. The important points to remember here are that human beings are motivated to maintain a positive picture of themselves, in part by justifying their past behavior, and under certain specifiable conditions, this leads them to do things that at first glance might seem surprising or *paradoxical*—for example, to prefer people and things for whom they have suffered to people and things they associate with ease and pleasure.

par·a·dox /ˈpærəˌdɑks/ n. **1** [C] a situation that seems strange because it involves two ideas or qualities that are opposite or very different: *Isn't it a paradox that the airline with the lowest fares is the one with the most customer satisfaction?* **2** [C] a statement that seems impossible because it contains two opposing ideas that are both true **3** [U] the use of such statements in writing or speech —**paradoxical** /ˌpærəˈdɑksɪkəl/ *adj.*

par·a·dox·i·cal·ly /ˈpærəˈdɑksɪkli/ *adv.* [sentence adverb] in a way that is surprising because it is the opposite of what you would expect: *Perhaps paradoxically, the problem of loneliness is most acute in big cities.*

(1) The best definition of *paradox* in this context is number ____.

(2) When a person does something that seems *paradoxical*, ____.
  a. the action seems impossible because another action was better
  b. the action seems strange because the person doesn't usually act that way
  c. the action is the opposite of what you might have expected

LEARN AND USE WORD FORMS

Complete the sentences below with the correct form of the word in the box. Refer to the word forms chart on page 257. Be sure to use the correct tense of verbs. Use each word only once.

conclude	justify	respond
distort	motivate	

1. It is often extremely difficult to predict how a person _____ to a particular situation.

2. Whenever we read about _____ that researchers draw from an experiment, we need to examine the study carefully to be sure that it was well designed.

3. Throughout history, people _____ horrific actions in order to fulfill their need to feel good about themselves.

4. Biological drives such as hunger and thirst can be powerful _____.

5. We sometimes _____ reality in order to maintain our self-esteem.

FOLLOW-UP ASSIGNMENTS

Before you begin any of the follow-up assignments, review the content-specific vocabulary and the academic vocabulary below, and look over the vocabulary in the word forms lists on pages 248 and 257. If you are still unsure what any words or terms mean, go back through the chapter and review. As you complete the assignments, be sure to incorporate the appropriate vocabulary in your writing.

Content-Specific Vocabulary

behaviorism	hazing	perspective	self-justification
cognition	motivated	self-esteem	social cognition
compliance	objective	self-fulfilling prophecy	subjectivity
construal	outcome		
distort			

Academic Vocabulary

account for	consequence	inconsequential	on the surface
accurate	dismiss	justify	paradox
to address	face up to	maintain	put a spin on
background	fundamental	myriad	upbringing

Writing Activities

1. In this chapter you learned that, in order to understand a person's behavior, you need to look at a situation from that person's viewpoint. You need to see how that person construes the world around him or her. Think of a time you observed someone else's behavior and drew a conclusion about it. Later, the person told you why he/she acted that way, and you found that your interpretation was incorrect. Write three paragraphs. In the first paragraph, describe the situation and the person's behavior. In the second paragraph, tell how you interpreted that person's behavior and how the person interpreted his or her own behavior in that situation. In what ways did you interpret the behavior and the situation differently? In the third paragraph, describe the motives that led each of you to interpret the situation differently.

2. Although the behaviorist perspective cannot account for all human behavior, it can explain some human behavior. Write three paragraphs. In the first paragraph, describe the strengths, or advantages, of the behaviorist perspective. In the second paragraph, describe the weaknesses of the behaviorist perspective. In the third paragraph, describe another approach that helps to account for human behavior.

3. Two major motives underlie much of human behavior: the need to be accurate, and the need to feel good about ourselves. Think of a time when you or someone you know was in a situation where you felt one or both of these needs. Write three paragraphs. In the first paragraph, describe the situation. In the second paragraph, tell whether these motives pulled you in opposite directions, and describe what you did. In the third paragraph, explain why you did what you did.

Extension Activities

1. Think about all you have learned in Chapter 10 about basic human motives. Review Chapter 6. Do more research on Sargon and his achievements. What might have been the motive(s) for Sargon the Great to have done what he did? Then, with a partner or in a small group, discuss whether or not what you've studied about basic human motives can provide possible insight into understanding someone from a different time and culture.

2. Review Chapter 7. Research the life of Picasso or Michelangelo. What might have been Picasso's motive(s) for his art? What might have been Michelangelo's motive(s) for not finishing his sculpture of *Saint Matthew?*

3. Research a well-known person you are interested in learning more about. Find out what you can about that person's life. Using what you have learned so far about basic human motives, how might you explain that person's behavior?

4. Read the following hypothetical situation and study. Keep in mind that you are interested in the subjectivity of the social situation. After you read the study, you will examine a bar graph of the study findings.

IMPRESSIONS OF OTHERS' PERSONALITIES

Our impressions of others' personalities are sometimes wrong because of *the fundamental attribution error.* People are too ready to attribute others' actions to their personalities rather than to the situation. For example, suppose you meet Andrea at a party and she is acting in an outgoing, sociable manner. If you are like most people, you will conclude that Andrea is outgoing and sociable. How accurate are you likely to be?

Not too accurate, if it is the social situation that is causing her to act extroverted. Maybe Andrea really isn't, as a rule, outgoing or sociable. In fact, she may be rather shy and reserved, but happens to be in a situation where most people act sociably—a fun party where she knows a lot of people. Our conclusion that she is outgoing will be wrong, due to the fundamental attribution error: overestimating the extent to which Andrea's behavior reflects the way she always acts, rather than something about the situation.

Two researchers, Funder and Calvin, conducted research to test the accuracy of people's impressions of other people's personalities. In the study, strangers watched a videotape of a student and then rated his or her personality. The strangers' impressions corresponded very poorly to the students' impressions of their own personalities. There was more agreement between a close friend's impressions of the student and the student's own impressions.

CORRELATION

A correlation refers to a relationship between two factors. It does not imply a cause/effect relationship, only that two factors appear to be related in some way. However, they may not be related at all. For example, if it rains every time you forget your umbrella, you see a correlation, but you understand that the rain was not caused by the fact that you did not have your umbrella.

Take another situation: You are a heavy sleeper and need a loud alarm to wake you in the morning. Every time you forget to set your alarm clock, you oversleep. There is a one-to-one correlation between your oversleeping and your forgetting to set your alarm clock. This correlation would be expressed as 1.0 because the two factors are associated with each other 100 percent of the time. Now imagine that you toss a coin. Fifty percent of the time the coin shows heads, and 50 percent of the time the coin shows tails. There is a correlation of 0.5, which means that there is an equal chance of either heads or tails on the toss of a coin. The "odds" of getting heads or tails are not greater than chance. The lower the number, the weaker the correlation. Keep this in mind as you circle the correct answers to the following questions based on the bar graph.

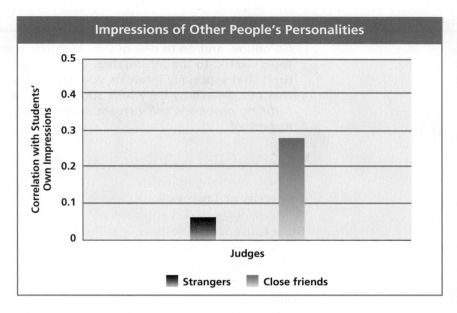

Impressions of Other People's Personalities

Judges

■ Strangers   ■ Close friends

(Y-axis: Correlation with Students' Own Impressions, ranging from 0 to 0.5)

1. In Funder and Calvin's study, what is the correlation between the strangers' impressions of students' personalities and students' impressions of their own personalities?
   a. 0.5
   b. .05
   c. .005

2. What is the correlation between the close friends' impressions of students' personalities and the students' impressions of their own personalities?
   a. .20
   b. .27
   c. .30

3. Are the close friends' impressions of students' personalities correlated with the students' own impressions to a degree that is greater than chance?
   a. Yes
   b. No

4. What can we conclude from this study?
   a. Strangers' impressions of us are very accurate.
   b. Our close friends' impressions of us are very accurate.
   c. Our close friends' impressions of us are not much better than a stranger's.

Internet Research

Go online, and go to one of the websites listed below. Investigate a topic related to the information you read about in Chapter 10. Choose a topic that especially interests you. Use some of the website's search features. Search by keywords such as *B. F. Skinner, behaviorism, self-fulfilling prophecy, self-esteem, human motivation, Jacobson and Rosenthal.*

The B. F. Skinner Foundation website:
   http://www.bfskinner.org/
University of Texas website:
   http://www.utexas.edu/student/cmhc/booklets/selfesteem/selfest.html
State University of California at Fullerton website:
   http://psych.fullerton.edu/swillis/selfjust.htm
Kids Health website:
   http://www.kidshealth.org/parent/emotions/feelings/self_esteem.html/
Companion website for the Main Reading:
   http://wps.prenhall.com/hss_aronson_demo_4/0,1928,10520-,00

INDEX OF KEY WORDS AND PHRASES

justification 259, 260
justify 259, 260
juxtaposition 45

kingdom 65, 203, 204, 206

lack 8, 37, 150, 207
laden with 181
land-dwelling 45
last 36, 150, 152, 203
leap of the imagination 179, 181
liberation 180
likened to 179
Linnaeus 65
logical 19, 37, 64
look at 192
Lystrosaurus 46

macromolecules 20, 22
maintain 249, 258, 260, 263
mammal 87
manipulating 125
membrane 19
Mesosaurus 43, 46
metaphor 179
methane 8, 15, 20, 21
Michelangelo 180
migrate 88, 113, 114, 125
misconception 75, 76
moist 99
molecular oxygen 8, 15, 37
molecules 8, 15, 19–22, 36, 37
molten core 8
motivated 260, 262, 263
multiple 151, 154, 181
multiplication 143, 154, 249
murals 113
mutation 36, 37
myriad 250

narrative 144
nasty 231, 232
natural selection 74–76
Neandertals 88
nitrogen 8, 15, 20
nomadic 124–126
nomenclature 65
nonetheless 114, 127, 151, 169, 181
nucleic acids 19, 20

objective 221, 222, 249, 250
occur 20, 22, 74, 76, 114, 220
on the surface 8, 249
organic 19–22, 36, 37
organism 20, 36, 37, 64, 65, 74–76, 87, 222, 250, 263
organization 127
origin 7, 19, 20, 36, 46, 74, 123, 126, 222
originate 36, 37
outcome 37, 262
oversimplification 232
oversimplify 232
overt 220
overwhelming 203, 232, 234
oxidizing atmosphere 37
oxygen 8, 15, 20, 37

Pangaea 44
paradoxical 260
particle 7, 8, 15, 22
peers 220
perceive 221, 250, 262
perspective 74, 124, 151, 182, 250, 261
persuasion 219, 220
pharaoh 203
phenomenon 178, 219, 249, 260, 262
photosynthesis 37
Picasso 178, 179
pioneered 143
polynomial 65
populated 113
population 65, 74, 76, 96, 124, 125
preceded 152, 179
precedents 154
precursors 95
predict 221, 222
predictions 233
prehensile 96
preoccupation 203
preservation 74, 114
preserve 125, 151, 206
primarily 7, 153, 221, 222
primate 87, 95, 96, 98, 99
proclaims 205
produce 21, 46, 65, 114, 123, 125, 152, 180, 182
production 123–125, 127

profound 143, 169, 232, 249
prognathism 97
prokaryotic 37
proliferated 36
prominent 143
propose 7, 20, 22, 36, 45–47, 74
provoke 127, 169
put a spin on 258, 260

radiate 87
ranking 151
reacted 20, 37
reactions 37
receded 114, 125
recombines 179
record 96, 97, 100, 143, 150, 151, 154, 170, 180
reduce 37, 169, 222
reducing atmosphere 8, 20–22, 37
reduction 37
reinforce 206, 249
reinforcement 249
reliable 124, 262
repelled 192
repertoire 114
replica 204
replicated 262
represent 15, 21, 95, 97, 151, 170, 205, 207, 258
representation 151, 205–207
reproduce 19, 74, 75, 96
reproduction 37, 74, 75, 192
require 75, 99, 182, 231, 250
requirement 206
resided 99, 150
responded 169, 234, 250
response 88, 96, 179, 250
responsive 258
retained 88
retaliation 153
reveal 47, 125, 192
revered 203
revolutions 123, 124
reward 249, 259, 263
role 74, 170
ruled 114, 150, 180, 206
ruler 144, 203

salinization 152
Sargon 150, 152